T0365257

WORD STASH

How Latin, Greek, French and other languages have added words you should know to the mighty hoard of English & how to increase your vocabulary the smart way, ***not*** *by multiple-choice questions but by knowing the origins of words, knowing* ***why*** *words mean what they mean.*

BILL CASSELMAN

Order this book online at www.trafford.com
or email orders@trafford.com

Most Trafford titles are also available at major online book retailers.

Print information available on the last page.

ISBN: 978-1-4907-8492-2 (sc)
ISBN: 978-1-4907-8494-6 (hc)
ISBN: 978-1-4907-8493-9 (e)

Library of Congress Control Number: 2017914954

Trafford rev. 10/12/2017

www.trafford.com

North America & international
toll-free: 1 888 232 4444 (USA & Canada)
fax: 812 355 4082

Dedication

To my friends Dennis Clarke and Wilma Vereyken

"Of all possessions a friend is the most precious"

-Herodotus

Contents

List of My Published Books

Author's Note:

This list of my publications is more extensive than usual in the front matter of a new book, but it is my wish that it be so presented. Please note that, while some of my books are out-of-print, most are still available unused at various online discount booksellers. Several of the later books are available online as e-books.

1.
Casselman's Canadian Words: A Comic Browse through Words & Folk Sayings Invented by Canadians 1995
1st edition 1995 Copp Clark ISBN: 0-7730-5515-0
2nd edition 1997 Little, Brown ISBN: 0-316-13350-7
3rd edition 1999 McArthur & Company, Toronto, Canada
many reprints through 2006
ISBN: 1-55278-034-1

2.
Casselmania: More Wacky Canadian Words & Sayings
1996 Little, Brown Canada Ltd, Toronto, Canada
ISBN: 0-316-13314-0

3.
Canadian Garden Words: The Origin of Flower, Tree, and Plant Names, both wild and domestic, entertainingly derived from their sources in the Ancient Tongues together with Fancy Botanical Names & Why You Shall Never Again Be Afraid To Use Them!

1997 McArthur & Company, Toronto, Canada
ISBN: 0-316-13343-4

4.
A Dictionary of Medical Derivations: The Real Meanings of Medical Words
1998 Parthenon Publishing Group, London and New York
ISBN: 1-85070-771-5

5.
Canadian Food Words: The Juicy Lore & Tasty Origins of Foods That Founded a Nation
1998 McArthur & Company, Toronto, Canada
1999 reprinted with new cover McArthur & Company
ISBN: 1-55278-018-X

6.
Canadian Sayings: 1200 Folk Sayings Used by Canadians, Collected and Annotated by Bill Casselman
1999 McArthur & Company, Toronto, Canada
ISBN: 1-55278-076-7

7.
What's in a Canadian Name? The Origins and Meanings of Canadian Surnames
2000 McArthur & Company, Toronto, Canada
ISBN: 1-55278-141-0

8.
Canadian Sayings 2: 1000 Folk Sayings Used by Canadians Newly Collected and Annotated by Bill Casselman 2002
McArthur & Company, Toronto, Canada
ISBN: 1-55278-272-7

9.
Canadian Sayings 3: 1000 Folk Sayings Used by Canadians Newly Collected and Annotated by Bill Casselman July 2004
McArthur & Company, Toronto, Canada
ISBN: 1-55278-425-8

10.
As The Canoe Tips: Comic Scenes from Canadian Life July 2005
McArthur & Company, Toronto, Canada
This is the first collection of my own original funny pieces, satire and nonsense.
ISBN: 1-55278-493-2

11.
Canadian Words & Sayings July 2006
McArthur & Company, Toronto, Canada
This collection includes new sayings and classic Canadian word stories suitable for the whole family and APPROVED FOR CLASSROOM USE.
ISBN: 1-55278-569-6

12.
Where a Dobdob Meets a Dikdik Mid-October 2010
A Word Lover's Guide to the Weirdest, Wackiest, and Wonkiest Lexical Gems
Publisher: Adams Media
57 Littlefield Street, Avon, Massachusetts 02322 U.S.A.
For the printed paperback -
ISBN 10: 1-4405-0636-1
ISBN 13: 978-1-4405-0636-1
To order the e-book version -
eISBN 10: 1-4405-1004-0
eISBN 13: 978-1-4405-1004-5

13.
At the Wording Desk Summer 2016
Notes Nimble and Spry about the Origin of Words
Publisher: Trafford Publishing
1663 Liberty Drive, Bloomington, Indiana 47403 U.S.A.
ISBN: 978-1-4907-7214-1 (sc)
ISBN: 978-1-4907-7215-8 (hc)

Partial Contributions to other books by Bill Casselman (William Gordon Casselman)

1.
Article on "Canadian Folk Sayings" in
The ITP Nelson Canadian Dictionary of the English Language
ITP Nelson, a division of Thomson Canada Limited, 1997, Scarborough, Ontario, Canada
ISBN: 0-17-606591-1

2.
Essay "See You When the Ice Worms Nest Again" in
Inside Language: A Canadian Language Reader, eds. Jennifer Maclennan and John Moffat
2000
Prentice Hall Allyn and Bacon Canada, Scarborough, Ontario
ISBN: 0-13-011267-4

3.
Essay "*Barrelhouse Kings*: Something Barry Callaghan Left out of his Memoir" in
Barry Callaghan: Essays on his Works
ed. Priscila Uppal
Guernica Writers Series # 24,
Guernica Editions, Toronto, Canada, 2007
ISBN-13: 978-1-55071-253-7

ISBN-10: 1-55071-253-5

4.
Chapter 32 "Digitariat" and Chapter 35 "Bafflegab and Gobbledygook: How Canadians Use English to Rant, to Lie, to Cheat, to Cover up Truth, and to Peddle Bafflegab" in
Readings for Technical Communication, ed. Jennifer MacLennan,
Oxford University Press Canada, 2008
ISBN: 978-0-19-542322-8

5.
Essay "A Blunt History of the C-Word" in
Vocabula Bound: Our Wresting, Writhing Tongue: Essays on the English Language from The Vocabula Review (online magazine about words)
ed. Robert Hartwell Fiske
Vocabula Books, Rockport, Massachusetts, USA, 2008
ISBN: 978-0-9774368-6-6

Magazine & Newspaper Work

I wrote the TV column for *Maclean's magazine* for several years and was a word columnist for *Canadian Geographic Magazine.* My column was entitled "Our Home & Native Tongue." I also wrote book reviews for *The Toronto Star* and articles for a number of smaller Canadian magazines and newspapers.

Preface

Learning new words raises your I.Q.

Is that a mere promo sentence made up by some sleazy author trying to flog his new word book? No. It's a clinical fact of neurology.

Learning long, hard words makes you smarter. Whether you are a student in school, an adult or a grandparent, every scientific study of actively increased vocabulary points to mental benefits, no matter the age of the new-word learner. Acquiring new language skills actually increases the weight of your brain matter. Synapses needed to connect nerve cells together, axons, dendrites, the actual bulk weight of all neurotransmitters, they all increase. Neurologists call this *increment of one's cognitive reserve.*

Students get better marks the more words they know. Grannies stave off the onset of Alzheimer's by learning new terms. Proven in tests! Can getting new vocabulary cure senile dementia? Of course not. But it can stave off the onset of drooling, gibbering senility. Psychologists tested women in homes for the elderly who did one crossword puzzle a day, as opposed to those who sat staring in armchairs. All puzzle-solvers scored higher on awareness, self-possession and intelligence than all chair-sitters.

Are you still in the work force or starting your business career? Top executives have better communication skills than workers at the bottom of the pay scale. To reach the summit in any field, one usually must learn many Englishes. You may retain how you learned to speak at home (called your idiolect or dialect). But, to be of maximum use to your company, you must understand and use easily the private scientific vocabulary used in the sciences that form the basis of your company's manufacturing or business procedures. You must also learn SE, Standard English.

That's three Englishes for most of us. Each one of those Englishes relies on new words, new relevant vocabulary. The more words you know, the higher your potential intelligence. Nincompoops are correctly called dummies, because they can't talk effectively. No vocabulary! Nincompoop probably derives from an old Latin phrase for someone who was insane, who was *non compos mentis* Latin, literally 'not sound of mind.'

No matter what the monosyllabic, illiterate, sneering baboons grunt, no matter that some goofy doofus mocks your superior hoard of words, all those who increase their vocabulary increase their salaries, their status, and their position in life. That's all any word-seeker has to know.

Why so many Latin roots of English words? Because possibly 80% of all English derives from Latin, not just the technical vocabulary of science but ordinary English derived from French for the last thousand years. Most of the French words now thoroughly at home in English, like, say, *poise* came originally from Latin. The French language came from Latin. That's why French is called a Romance language, a Roman's language. So too in a slightly different way, is English a Roman's language.

Start learning elite English. It's fun. My amusing chapters consist of one thousand words each, approximately. Each can be read in several minutes at the rate of one chapter per day.

One of the aspects of our English language I most cherish is unfathomableness, in its prime meaning of 'not being able to reach the bottom.' One can never sound the sea floor of the study of English words. There are millions of them. Nobody, not even multilingual snooty phuds (Ph.Ds.), can plumb the sweet abyss of etymology. Let down into the verbal waters the heaviest lead sinkers you have. Never will they fathom Lake Word. All the merrier reason therefore that I lay out upon the gutting table of the wording room rare and startling forms for your delectation.

Bill Casselman, September 20, 2017

Chapter 1

Spa Words

Moxibustion, effleurage, lomi lomi, pétrissage, tapotement & other massage terms

I had the jittery heebie-jeebies. In a state of tremulous discomfiture did I enter Madame Bijou's Parlour of Flesh Rearrangement. Although the saucy name in neon "FLESH!" promised nubile nymphets (aka jailbait) dancing to "Santeria" while clad in skimpy thongs and carnal indulgence unknown since Belshazzar's Feast, all I sought was surcease from pain between my shoulder blades.

As at the famous Babylonian orgy, ominously there suddenly appeared "the writing on the wall." It was a spa sign that warned: "Persons touching the masseuse in any way deemed inappropriate shall have the offending hand amputated by the scimitar of Abdullah, our staff eunuch." I murmured a compliant eek! and with unmanly haste locked my iron chastity jockstrap.

No, I told a friend, my upper back pain is not due to a Bowie knife embedded in a medioscapular locus by a co-worker — in other words, no shiv in my back. Several other co-workers had sworn up and down, nay averred, that several of Madame Bijou's clientele had risen from her massage table able to walk and — yes! — still capable of extracting one-hundred dollar bills from their wallets.

Forthwith a blizzard of massage terms utterly new to me perplexed my ears. Procedures like effleurage, lomi lomi, moxibustion, pétrissage and tui na entered my habitually paranoid consciousness. It was as if someone had said Tomás de Torquemada, founder of the Spanish Inquisition, is dropping by the house tonight to correct a few minor office errors.

True, most massage terms are in plain English and easily understood: the Swedish Skull-Hammer Cure, the Aztec Brain Cleaner (involves a live condor and nitric acid) and VTIT or Viking Testicular Interchange Therapy. Those did not worry me. After the unfamiliar massage terms were explained, I thought it only kind to share them with any badly kneaded readers. For no more benevolent hermeneut exists than I. Chief of interpreters, that's me.

Tapotement

In Swedish massage, tapotement is quick rhythmic tapping with the edge of the hand, a cupped hand or the tips of the fingers. It is sometimes called finger percussion, but that always sounds to me like a misadventure which might befall one while strapped to the iron bed of that ancient Greek thug blacksmith, Procrustes.

There are several types of tapotement including Beating, Hacking, Tapping (use just fingertips) and Cupping. Tapotement serves to awaken a somnolent nervous system, for example: releasing lymphatic build up in the back by gently tapping the shoulder of the client. Even in traditional medical procedures, tapotement is used on the chest wall of patients with bronchitis to help loosen the mucus in their air passages. In relaxation and maintenance massage, tapotement improves the tissue tone and vasodilates capillaries, thus improving blood flow to remotest cells.

The name of the stroke is taken from the French abstract noun drawn from the common verb *tapoter* 'to drum the fingers rapidly, to tap.'

Effleurage

This is a gliding, stroking movement in massage, mostly over the spine and back, often to warm up muscles before deeper massage techniques are employed, usually at the start and at the end of facial or body massage. Fingertip effleurage of the abdomen is a technique used in the Lamaze method of natural childbirth. Effleurage is also a common mode of spreading oil on bodies to be massaged. Glides are in the direction of the heart which helps push the flow of blood and lymph. Effleurage was developed to affect the skin and superficial muscles.

The French verb *effleurer* in its prime meaning is to 'remove the flower of something,' from French *la fleur* 'the flower.' But, quite early, a developed sense arose, namely 'to skim the surface' hence to stroke the skin lightly, gently.

Pétrissage

This is kneading body muscles as if one were making dough. The masseur or masseuse rolls, squeezes and presses the muscles to improve deep circulation. Pétrissage acts by forcing venous blood onward and bringing freshly oxygenated blood to depleted tissues. Toxins lingering in neural and muscle tissue may be partially eliminated too.

Le pétrissage is the noun from the older French verb *pétrir*. It first appears in thirteenth-century documents as Old French *pestrir* 'to knead dough in baking,' borrowed from Late Latin *pistrire*, itself based on Latin *pinsere* 'to pulverize, to grind grain.' Among cognates of the Latin verb are Greek *ptissein* 'to crush spices or drugs with a pestle in a mortar.' Classical Latin borrowed *ptisana* 'barley with the outer covering pounded off, pearl barley, barley water.' Indo-European cognates include Sanskrit *pinasti* 'he crushes' and Avestan *pixati* 'it bumps into, it bangs.'

Tui Na

(Chinese, literally 'Push-Pull')

This Chinese massage technique follows the theory of qi (chi), life energy flowing through tendons and meridians of the body and able to be redirected therapeutically.

Lomi Lomi

Lomi lomi is an ancient Hawaiian healing massage during which kukui nut, macadamia nut and coconut oils are used as lubricants and nutritional moisturizers. The hands-on manipulations are similar to Japanese shiatsu. Before a procedure begins, the client is allowed one phone call home to a loved one or to a lawyer empowered to draw up a last will and testament.

Like many Polynesian forms, Hawaiian *lomi-lomi* is a noun formed by a doubled verb stem, in this case a reduplication of *lomi* 'to rub with the hand,' so that its prime sense is frequentative, 'a great deal of hand-rubbing.' The ancient Polynesian etymon is *lima* 'hand.' My masseuse of choice would be Uma Thurman and my cry would be "Uma. Uma. Uma. Come to my rooma, rooma, rooma."

Moxibustion

(Chinese pinyin: ji ǔ or Japanese *Moxa*)

In this little skin roast, a glowing moxa stick is used to warm certain acupoints before they are massaged. Moxa is a dried preparation of the herb mugwort, long used in oriental medicine for a variety of menstrual problems. It claims to stimulate blood circulation and speed recovery of many bodily ills.

Now, with that subluxation of my third interior chakra safely returned to my chief spiritual center, namely my kneecap, I feel I can hobble forth to meet anew a brutal world.

A reader emails me to ask if I truly believe in these procedures. Let me put it this way: if you are one who, of a night, leaves out on your bed stand a thimble full of petunia nectar for the tooth fairy, then by all means avail thy cramped musculature of these massage benefits.

Spa: it's Etymology

Spa is a town in Belgium in the province of Liège, famed for centuries because of the curative delights of its mineral springs. European and middle-eastern peoples have known for millennia the benefits of soaking in hot mineral waters. The place name Spa was taken from the Walloon word for fountain or spring, *espa*.

Walloon is a dialect of the language of the people of Wallonia in southern Belgium. Perhaps even the Romans heard the correct Walloon word or an early equivalent, because ancient Rome knew the place as a location to "take the waters." The Latin place name of Spa was

Aquae Spadanae. As for the practice of therapeutic bathing, even the Greek father of medicine, Hippocrates (460 – 370 BCE) wrote about the curative properties of thermal springs and the effects of hot and cold baths on the human body.

Developed Meanings

At first *The Spa* was specific to the Belgian place, then any medicinal spring came to be called a spa. Soon spa named a place or building where balneotherapy was practised (Latin *balneum* 'bath'). Balneotherapy often involves hot and cold water, massage through moving water, relaxation and muscular stimulation. If that sounds like sex, you had a deprived adolescence.

Mineral waters abound at spas with their underground springs rich in such ingredients as silica, sulfur and selenium. In some bubbling thermal springs dense particulates predominate to produce warm clay and mud. Healing through mud baths is known as fangotherapy, from Italian *il fango* 'mud, dirt.'

Spa's Newest Meaning

In the United States, the sense of the word became generalized. A U. S. commercial establishment offering health and beauty treatment through steam baths, exercise equipment and exotic massages may not even have spring waters but still advertises itself as a spa.

Health Note

Scientists now state that having sex twice-a-week improves your immune system's ability to fight infections. As I told my doctor, I have one problem with that. I can't get rid of this runny nose.

Chapter 2

Odd Laughter Words

I spend the summer mostly at the sea. Perhaps a more forthright confession might be: I spend the summer mostly at sea. For it is during the estival season of the rolling year that I read my neglected, confusing or incomprehensible email and am often found giggling in helpless merriment beside a decanter of port placed on my computer desk by Medea, the new maid we've hired to look after the children.

Estival, by the way, is a fancy word meaning 'occurring during the summer.' It rhymes with festival. To hibernate is to pass the winter in a state of torpor. But there are some creatures, including some humans, who pass the entire summer in a state of torpor and they are said to estivate.

But giggling does not seem a manly mode of laughter. Needing to find more bounteous laughing words, nouns and verbs roistering in a guffaw-flung orbit of buoyant exuberance, I set forth among my foxed tomes and leathered volumes in search of synonyms for jollity and mirth. In obedience to my gentle nature, I was not seeking phrases forecasting splanchnic rupture as in "I busted a gut, laughing."

Splanchnic (SPLANK-nick) is a neat medical word referring to the internal organs of the abdomen.

Down through glum eons of word-making, stern coiners of English, the sad, bearded compilers of dictionaries, have had, in general, little use for laughter or its synonyms. Not really British, don't you know?

No jesting Pilate I, to ask Jesus, "What is truth?" I'm just a laugher, not a philosopher. Although the pickings were leaner than bacon bits after a hungry pork-eating convention, I did uncover a few delights and herewith present them in my usual, becoming stoop of modesty.

Chortling I Shall Go

Among the scant but merry verbs and happy nouns, chortling has a pleasing sonic rotundity. It was invented by a famous writer. The Reverend Charles Lutwidge Dodgson (1832-1898) coined the verb *to chortle* as a blend of chuckle and snort. There is no dampening, namby-pamby snigger in a chortle. It's the explosive way a bold stud might laugh.

The Rev. was better known by his pen name, Lewis Carroll, who came up with the happy mixture in one of his greatest nonsense poems "Jabberwocky," found in the sequel to *Alice's Adventures in Wonderland*, namely in *Through the Looking-Glass*. Carroll is notable as a dexterous wizard of word play.

Some early dandy philologists decided to call such terms "portmanteau words," because, like the Victorian suitcase of yore used to transport greatcoats and over-garments, they "ported" several "*manteaux*" of different words. Har-dee-har-har. This overly cute label has mercifully declined in use.

Boffo

Boffo may mean 'a hearty laugh,' although its use in showbiz was first as an adjective. A boffo sight gag in vaudeville was one that brought a good laugh from a live audience. From Italian *buffo* 'comical, burlesque' a boffo is still an unrestrained laugh of boisterous uproar. It is likely the Italian adjective chuckled into English from opera, where one of the modes of operatic composition is still referred to as *opera buffa* 'comic opera.' The word's extension *boffola* may also be used as an adjective and a noun.

Gelastic

"Place one exceedingly rare word in each chapter" is a request of many of my readers. So here it is, this one a medical adjective. A hypothalamic hamartoma is a rare benign tumor located at the base of the brain in an area called the hypothalamus. One of the tumour's symptoms in young people may be various forms of epilepsy. One of these is gelastic seizure, during which inappropriate laughter results. Gelastic 'causing laughter, serving the function of laughter' was borrowed from Greek *gelastikos* 'pertaining to laughter' from Greek *gelan* 'to laugh.' English derivatives are not common but the root was active in classical Greek. Consider the standard ancient Greek word for clown *gelōtopoiós* literally 'laughter-maker' as used by a writer like the Attic historian Xenophon (circa 430–354 BC).

Howls of horselaughs, even volleyed peals of snorts by yockmeisters and yucksters, are macho too. But titters and sniggers are not, teeny chirpings with a hand held over the offending mouth. It must be covered due to its guilty crime of expressing human enjoyment.

The sour-jowled shushers of laughter always remind me of H.L Mencken's excellent definition of a puritan, either religious or secular. The sage of Baltimore wrote that "a puritan is someone with the haunting fear that somebody else, somewhere, might be enjoying themselves."

When a person states, "This is **no** laughing matter," look into their constipated fist of a face and you will determine that very little in their burdensome passage here on earth has brought forth mirth. These doleful, bovine drones have instead endured most of life chewing the bitter cud of rancour. Then let them! May frowns rot their brows; may interior fury consume their innards; may their twisted faces make children scream. May they gag on bile.

Of a summer evening I shall be sitting on the back porch with friends, sipping some pleasant, unpretentious French picnic wine, say a Pouilly-Fuissé, and laughing with the laughers, in the bliss of a mirthquake.

Chapter 3

"Bad Child!" Synonyms and Phrases

English speakers may no longer use negative words to describe the odious spawn of bad parents. Children must never be labelled as *bad*. Politically correct language cops have decreed it shall be so. For all children, angelic vessels of earthly purity and moral innocence, are saintly in speech and manner. There are no ankle-biters, guttersnipes, *enfants terribles*, rascals, scamps or imps. And jackanapes is a long retired insult to unruly rug rats.

But what a lie! Childhood abounds in nasty little whippersnappers.

Yet a fascist onslaught of educational facilitators, child experts and gooey-brained teachers have banished to invisibility's cloakroom any blunt put-down of an unsaintly child. Barbs, slurs, taunts, zings and jibes are now anathema, barred from speech or print. How flabby corrective invective has become, withering away, smothered under the pillow of school-marmish apprehensiveness by "child experts."

To remedy this namby-pamby, tit-suck reluctance to name, indeed to brand bad children, I now and then unearth an apt imprecation, a fitting malediction about wee ones, necessary to be revived in this age of cradled infants telling adults to "screw off." True story! This one exists on a hard disk somewhere: a pleasant woman reporter gently parts the swaddling clothes of one little "Jesus" in his crib, only to be met by the little cherub's lips exploding in a bombardment of f-bombs.

This column is merely to pass on to readers a recent gem which appeared in an article about cursing on the rise among youngsters. I love this sentence about not recognizing little ones who swear and from whom f-bombs burst like moist, glistery mushrooms after a tepid rain: "And if everyone swears, why teach a child that it's forbidden? But you can't exactly **just high-five the sailor-mouthed tot** and send her back to kindergarten, either." The author is Josh Lambert, in a book review he wrote for *The New York Times* September 26, 2016. Josh Lambert is academic director of the Yiddish Book Center and the author of *Unclean Lips: Obscenity, Jews, and American Culture.*

Thus ever to potty-mouths!

Chapter 4

The Inuit "Noise Ghost"

A phrase that may come to haunt you

The Noise Ghost is an Inuit poltergeist (*Poltergeist*, German 'noisy ghost'), an arctic auditory phenomenon of incorporeal guile. This unseen, unbodied noise ghost may announce his haunting visitation by curling around a far-northern house in the quiet of a cold night. Emitting a high-pitched hissing, this spectral wisp seeks to dehouse you. Then, outside, after toxic cold cracks your bones, the noise ghost will jab its snout into your chest cavity, thrusting deep and red to gnaw your ribs and suck the gelid marrow from its osseous encasement.

Now the unhuman hiss whistles through ice chinks and drills into eardrums as the noise ghost hovers, waiting to envelope you in its sonic coil and madden you, long before relieving dawn may come.

The noise ghost circles the igloo and, always the constrictor, wraps the fragile ice in singing folds of death. The hiss susurrates, skitters about the room, swooping on the face of a screaming terrified child. Its high buzz mingles with gasping whispers and low, obscene, anticipatory gurglings as of a meat-lusting animal in full slobber. Sometimes you can see the raw noise itself, curling impudently in the cold air.

Swirling closer and closer to the frightened people inside the house, this evil noisemaker shrieks as if inside your very heart. Should you run jabbering and drooling fear, out, out into snow's numb white ice death? No. Abide a moment and wait out the terror; then wise elders who know the ancient apotropaic words will drive the monster away and silence the noise ghost. This time.

Chapter 5

Cow Words

As well as examining the more than startling origins of the words *cow* and *moo*, here I shout "co, boss!" to some hidden cows of English. Long before coins and paper money, Indo-Europeans used cows to measure wealth. This ancient practice lurks in the history of some English financial words like *fee* and *pecuniary* and in the surprising, original meaning of the word *cattle.*

Cattle

We have only spelled it cattle since the early eighteenth century. It began as Late Latin *capitale* 'principal sum of money,' hence 'property' and 'wealth.' A trip through Provençal and Old French saw the Latin *capitale* shortened and transformed into *captal* and *catel* and then in northern French we first see the Parisian form *chatel.* In the Anglo-French of the legal language this appeared in the familiar phrase "goods and chattels." In the Middle Ages catel was 'movable goods owned' and the feudal system saw catel as 'beast held in possession' that is as '*live* stock,' hence cows and bulls became the chief catels.

Fee

To modern English speakers, a fee is a fixed sum charged and — it is fondly to be hoped — paid. But to King Alfred writing out his laws about 900 CE, *feoh* meant, in its basic sense, 'cattle owned.' Fee has lost that meaning of livestock in English but its modern German cognate *das Vieh* still means livestock and is an active component in word formation, e.g. *der Viehmarkt* 'the cattle market.' To the Vikings who spoke Old Norse, their cognate word *fe* had three common meanings: property, money and cattle.

Even in King Alfred's time, fee came to mean movable goods, and a little later, it signified that which bought movable goods, namely, money. The semantic trajectory of the word *fee* through history is remarkably similar to that of the word *cattle*.

In Fee Simple

In feudal law, a fee was an inherited estate in land and/or that land granted by the lord owner to his vassal for service performed. Often fee referred directly to the land itself. That use survives in real estate law and contracts in Great Britain and North America. If you own your home and the property on which it sits, then you may indeed hold your land 'in fee simple.' In Canadian common law, this form of land tenure is as close as one can get to absolute ownership — thus diminishing any fears of foreclosure or other housing losses. Fee simple permits the tenant to sell or to convey by will or transfer to the tenant's heir upon death without a will. In modern law, almost all land is held in fee simple.

Pecuniary

Pecuniary means 'consisting of or relating to money.' The word *fee* has a cognate in Latin *pecus* which to the

Romans meant 'flock, herd, cattle.' A significant measure of ancient wealth was the number of domesticated animals one owned. In classical Latin the value of one's animal herds was one's *pecunia.* Originally meaning 'cattle wealth' *pecunia* expanded its meanings to include money, the tokens that represented the value of one's cattle herd. *Pecuniarius* was a classical Latin adjective that meant 'of or relating to money.' The word entered English after the Norman Conquest of 1066 CE and soon was written down in the Anglo-Norman form of *pecunier.* But eventually the Latin form and spelling won out. *Pecunier* disappeared from English and *pecuniary* flourished.

But Were Cattle Ever a Roman Sign of Wealth?

There is one small fly in the ointment of this 'cattle as Roman farm wealth' theory. The reader must remember that there was not plenty of good cattle-grazing land near Rome. Well south of ancient Rome lay the fertile green fields of Campania. But the warm climate of southern and central Italy made keeping milk fresh on the way to market a very tricky and often failed procedure. Also, with their stern 'military-peasant' cast-of-mind, the ancient Romans considered milk to be baby food and Roman men generally only drank milk when they were in sick bed.

Yes, the Romans made cheese but most of it was used to feed soldiers. Olive oil was available to replace butter. So where, exactly, in Italy, did all this concept of 'cattle as essential wealth' become embedded in the Latin language? I suggest the Romans inherited the words along with their twin concepts (cow = money) from Indo-European forebears who lived thousands of years earlier somewhere in Asia where green fields made the domestication of cattle a lucrative way to earn a living and feed a family. These words came into Latin from some Indo-European ancestor of Latin, and they came with cow-wealth already embedded in their verbal meanings.

Cow & How!

The Teutonic root for cow whose Old English reflex is *cu* has cognates throughout the Indo-European language family. Consider:

English *kine* (a Southern English plural of the word *cow*)
Dutch *koe*
German *Kuh*
Swedish *ko*
Sanskrit *gau, gaus, gaiy-, go-*
Latin *bos, bovis* (with its Late Latin adjective *bovinus*)
Classical Greek *bous*

A clever commercial use of the Greek word appears in BouMatic, a manufacturer of automatic milking equipment and other dairy-farm systems. Their corporate name began in 1939 when Lawrence Bouma founded Bou-Matic Milkers Inc. in Ontario, California. Someone conversant with Greek soon realized that the company name could also be analyzed as a combination of *bou* Classical Greek *bous* 'cow' + *-matic* from automatic, itself from Greek *automatos* 'self-acting' from *autos* Greek 'self' + *matos* Greek 'ready, willing, able to act.'

Cow from Roots Older than Greece and Rome

My studies convince me that the word *cow* and several other lexemes meaning cow have sources older than Proto-Indo-European and may have been borrowed into PIE from more ancient languages, as I explain below.

The Echoic Cow

Cu demonstrates onomatopoeia, an imitation in letters of the sound made by the animal. The ancient Teutons heard *cu*; we hear *moo*. The ancient Romans and Greeks heard *boo* hence their words for cow or bovine animal: Latin *bos, bovis* and Greek *bous*. The cow call "co-boss" often parsed as English 'come, cow' is still heard in Great Britain and North America but how do you explain its use in several parts of non-English-speaking Europe? My answer is that the call *co-boss* is a kind of doublet from some area of Europe where the Teutonic word for cow *cu* nudged up against the Levantine root as seen in Latin *bos* and Greek *bous*. "Bossy" as a name for a specific cow is widespread throughout Europe.

Cow Words Formed by Imitating a Moo Sound

Below is a sample of world cow words that all seem to be attempts to represent the characteristic lowing of cattle.

Arabic for Cow is *BAH-qa-ra*.

Not too far from Latin *vacca*. Could this be a pre-Proto-Indo-European root, reaching back to a language that preceded the domestication of the cow and the arrival of Indo-European peoples in Europe? I further posit an onomatopoeic ultimate source in which the first syllable of the Semitic cow words is echoic, representing how the hearers heard a cow's moo.

A Common Sanskrit Term for Cow

In Sanskrit, cow is *go,* cognate with the English *cow* and Latin *bos.* The Sanskrit word for cattle is *paśu* obviously cognate with Latin *pecu*, possible PIE root being *peku. Cf. Latin *pecus* 'cattle as wealth.' *Pecus* is a close relative of the Latin word *pecu* 'flock, herd, cattle' and **pec* seems related to the Semitic shoresh for 'cow' *bqr* whose reflex in Biblical Hebrew is *baqar*, in modern Arabic *baqara.* Shoresh is a Hebrew word, the name designating any Semitic verbal root.

Modern Hebrew for cow is *parAH*, the female form corresponding to *par* 'bull' and may be related to the *bqr* root. It was also used in Biblical Hebrew where it is suggested that *parah* is related to an adjective meaning 'fruitful.'

The immediate source of the *bqr* trilitteral verbal root might be a Hebrew verbal root like **bq* 'to pour out, to empty, hence 'to milk a cow.' But it may even predate proto-Semitic forms like *baqr* and hark back to a language that existed thousands of years before Semitic tongues arose. Perhaps then *bqr* is related to the Latin cow word *vacca* whose cognate in Sanskrit is *vaçā 'cow'* from Sanskrit *vaç* 'to moo, to bellow.' And they all stem from some much earlier Mediterranean or Asian language never written down and now utterly eroded from human ken by the sandpaper of abrasive linguistic evolvement and that ultimatum for all languages: time in its merciless, linguicidal mode. Linguicide is my coinage meaning 'the killing of a language.'

Japanese for cow is *oo-shi* imitating the cow's characteristic moo sound. We hear moo; the Japanese hear *oo.*

The Mandarin Chinese word for cow is *niu*. This too is possibly a human imitation of bovine lowing. Does the Chinese character look like the Japanese character? They are identical. Japanese borrowed the character from Chinese. The Cantonese vocalization of this character is *ngau*, also a mimetic moo!

Yakkety-Yak, Do Grunt Back!

The bovine I am fondest of is the yak. There used to be a yak at the zoo near my aunt's house. I loved its zoological name too: *Bos grunnies* or *Bos grunniens*, the domesticated yak, a bovine that makes frequent grunting noises, hence its zoological Latin name *Bos grunniens* 'grunting ox.'

Wild yaks do not vociferate as frequently as domesticated yaks. Presumably they have less to bitch about and are not as bossy as other members of the ox tribe. For a wild yak there may also be a security benefit in not grunting too often, because wandering yetis love to munch down on a fresh yak burger.

So catchy is the zoological label that there was once a Toronto rock band named "Bos Grunnies." One of their members must have been, as I was, a child visitor to Toronto's High Park Zoo.

Vacca & Vache & Vaquero

Another common Indo-European word for cow shows up in Latin *vacca*, cognate with Sanskrit *vaçā* 'cow' root *vaç* 'to bellow, to moo.' As stated above, *vacca* may have been borrowed into PIE from some earlier language. Another sly guess, unproven, suggests that *vacca* is related to Latin words like *vacare* 'to be empty' and ancestors of our English words *vacant* and *vacuum* 'empty,' the metaphor being the emptying of a cow's udder during the act of milking. Thus *vacca* would be the animal that one *empties* by milking. Such an etymology is supposititious, there being no certain evidence of that relationship.

Spanish *vaca* 'cow' is from Latin *vacca* and gives us the American cowboy word *buckaroo,* derived from an early American attempt at the pronunciation of the Mexican Spanish word *vaquero* 'cowboy.'

Bill Casselman's Personal *Vache* Story

I have a good French vocabulary and an accent halfway between Ontario High School French and *joual de Montréal.* So I am not illiterate in French, but I stand out as a foreigner in France trying to speak their language. It has been my experience that, to language beginners or foreign students, the continental French are generally rude, impatient and nasty, quite in contrast to Italians who will smile at your verbal mistakes and cheerfully correct them. The Germans, after you commit a small error in a German sentence, stare at you, *natürlich*, and then scream, *"Aber das is kein Deutsch!"* after which they make furtive attempts to administer a blood test to see if you are an Aryan. Such a test must be firmly refused. It only encourages them.

Anyhow, there I was in southern France, in the pleasant town of Grasse, lolloping through fields of perfumed *fleurs.* Noon came and I entered a small grocery store to buy bread. *"Bon jour. Avez-vous du pain, monsieur?"* I said pleasantly to the owner who had baked bread lovingly ovened and wreathed in warm wheaten aroma sitting in rows along his wooden counter. The grocer/baker pretended he could not understand my French. I tried spelling the word *pain* in French. I pointed dramatically at the loaves and made chomping motions with my parched lips as I brought palsied hands up to my mouth. The grocer had decided never to understand. I unzipped my backpack, took out a set of Parisian sock puppets and performed a modest two-act charade detailing the discovery of bread-baking in ancient Mesopotamia. *Rien!* Nothing availed. I rolled on the floor imitating a French bread stick. He pointed at his head to indicate that I was insane, *tout fou*. I asked him why he refused to understand my simple, clear French. "*Parce que vous parlez français comme une vache espagnole!*" 'Because you speak French like a Spanish cow.'

Mercy buckets to you too, *mon ami*! I said, as I left his shop. The grocer shrugged his shoulders and said in perfect English, "Were you trying to say '*Merci beaucoup*?'

Vacca & Derivative Cow Terms

Vaccine appears first in English as an adjective in 1798, perhaps coined by Doctor Edward Jenner, inventor of vaccination. Jenner seems to have adapted it from the eighteenth-century medical name for cow-pox, *variolae vaccinae* where *vaccinus* is a Late Latin adjective 'pertaining to cows' from Latin *vacca* 'cow.' *Variola* appears in English pathology texts by 1771 as the medical Latin name for smallpox. *Variolae vaccinae* is cow-pox. *Variola* means pustule, that which causes the 'pock' marks of 'pox.' *Variola* is a Late Latin diminutive form of *varius*, a Latin adjective meaning spotted and 'of several colours.'

Soon after its adjectival debut, the word *vaccine* also became a noun (1803) meaning 'the matter used in vaccination' and injected into humans by means of a hypodermic needle (*hypo* Greek 'under' + *derma* Greek 'skin.')

By 1803 the verb *vaccinate* has poked its way into English medical parlance. Its prime and sensuous meaning was "to inoculate a person with a small sample of the virus of cow-pox as a protection against smallpox."

Pecu & Pecus: Latin Cow Words with Modern English Derivatives

We now tiptoe to another stall in the cowshed of words to look at English derivatives of two Latin cow words: *pecu* and *pecus*, both meaning 'flock' (of sheep) or 'herd' (of cattle).

Pecunia is Peculiar

A Latin word for money, *pecunia*, as I wrote above, evolved from *pecus*. An oft-quoted bit of Latin mirth was spoken by the Roman emperor Vespasian when he was told that the treasury of the state was emptying quickly. In order to raise new sources of money, Vespasian ordered a tax on public urinals. Some of the Roman senators were aghast. How vulgar to demean the majesty of Rome by taxing urination! Vespasian listened calmly to the senatorial splutterings of outrage and then said simply, "*Pecuna non olet.*" 'The money doesn't smell.' How widespread was the emperor's little joke? Well, even today, the literary word for 'street urinal' in French is *la vespasienne*. The commoner term is *pissoir*.

What a Servile Herd!

The best known Latin phrase containing the word *pecus* is a tag from a poem (Horace, Epistles 1, xix, 1) in the form of a letter written by the Roman poet Horace:

"*O imitatores, servum pecus!*" the gist of which is—'O (you) imitators (of my poems, what a) slavish herd of cows (you are)!'

Peculiar

Peculiar also harks back to *pecu* Latin 'herd.' Nowadays we possess one extant text of actual Roman etymology, an error-filled but invaluable book entitled *De Lingua Latina* ('Concerning the Latin Language') by Varro. It states that in early Latin *peculium* referred to a person's private wealth as expressed in herds of livestock. By the time of the Roman Empire, *peculium* had developed several special legal senses in Roman law. *Peculium* was your private property. Its adjective, *peculiaris,* meant therefore 'pertaining to a goods and properties, then personal material, personal traits, exceptional talents, in short, anything peculiar to one person. The leap from that meaning of the word to today's English sense where peculiar usually means 'odd' or 'strange' is not great.

Sacred Cow

The phrase 'sacred cow' first appears in English in a book titled *Beast & Man in India* written by John Lockwood Kipling, father of a much more famous son, the English author Rudyard Kipling. It refers to the reverence in which Hindus hold the cow and Muslims don't.

And so, with this bouoctony averted, we shall take our leave. Bouoctony (pronounced boo-**OC**-tuny) is a Greek word referring to the ceremonial slaughter of cows. Seek it not in the staid pages of dictionaries, for I made it up out of two good, solid Greek roots, namely *bou-* Greek 'cow' + *octonia* 'slaughter, killing.'

The moving farmer milks and, having milked, closes the barn door. This extended glance at cow words has been, I trust, as moo-ving an experience for you as for me.

Chapter 6

Haft, Hilt, Handle

Swashbuckling words

Here on this parapet of Milady Gwendolyn's castle, fending off the evil Spanish count, Porco de Swinola, we verbal musketeers swash that buckle with sword words. Do you know the origin of *swashbuckler*? To swash, among other meanings, is to make a loud noise with one's weapons. A buckler is a small shield held by a handle on its back and used to deflect blade slashes of an enemy during a sword fight. A soldier who made a lot of noise with his swords and shields and other weapons, a dick-wagging braggart who banged his blade on his own shield or that of his opponent was a swashbuckling show-off.

As a stock comic type, the boastful soldier is as old as Roman comedy where he appears in the plays of Plautus as *Miles Gloriosus* Latin 'the boastful soldier.' Brought back to strutting life, Miles was a character in the Stephen Sondheim musical comedy "A Funny Thing Happened on the Way to the Forum." Strictly pejorative at first, swashbuckler gained reluctant admiration when applied to, for example, bold pirates who captured ships with swashbuckling derring-do.

Haft

A haft is the handle of a sword or dagger or sickle or large knife. *Hæfte* in Old English meant 'handle,' anything used to grasp an object, directly related to Old English *hæft* 'bond, fetter, captive,' cognate with Old High German *Haft* 'fetter, captivity.'

Once upon a time an untrustworthy man was described as "loose in the haft," unreliable like a knife with a shaky handle.

Hilt

The hilt of a sword is its handle. So hilt is a synonym of haft. Hilt is cognate with Old Norse *hjalt* 'strong' and Old Saxon *hilta*, but its ultimate origin is unclear. The vagaries of war were expressed neatly in this saying in print by 1642 CE: "He that hath the hilt in his hand in the morning, may have the point at his throat ere night." Up to the hilt is still used to mean 'completely' like a sword buried to the hilt in an enemy's chest. I am taxed to the hilt, like you.

Handle

A handle is the part of an object by which it is grasped. Handle descends from hand the same way that thimble descends from thumb, by means of an instrumental suffix, in this case, *-le* or *–el*, a suffix that began in Indo-European -languages as a diminutive and developed an instrumental meaning later. The [vowel] +- /l/ +- [vowel] is still an operative diminutive in German, *Kindl* 'little child> Kind 'child' and *petzel* Yiddish 'little prick' > *Putz* Old German 'penis.' The Proto-Germanic *handuz derives from Proto-Indo-European *kent 'to grasp' with a reflex in ancient Greek *kenteo* 'I poke, I prick.' The Koine Greek of the New Testament displays the related noun in the famous phrase when Jesus speaks to Saul on the road to Damascus, [Acts 9:5, King James

Version] "It is hard for thee to kick against the pricks" (goads, cattle prods, pangs of conscience). In its original Koine Greek, *kentron* is 'a cattle prod, a pointed stick.'

Saint Luke, or whoever wrote *The Acts of the Apostles*, is here quoting a proverbial phrase extremely common in classical Greek literature, the phrase in one form or another being found in the writings of Pindar, Aeschylus and Euripides. Luke suggests that Jesus is telling Saul that Saul's persecution of Christians is against his own conscience and if he would only listen to and obey his inner dictates, he would not have to kick against the moral goads of the Lord that he hears within himself.

Here endeth today's joust with sword words, gentle *sabreurs* and *sabreuses*.

Chapter 7

English *Gym* Words Began As Homoerotic

Today is Nerd Day here at Old Camp Etymology. Today is for all the non-athletic persons who could not dribble a basketball in high school and who were consequently branded "weaklings, lisping sissies, milksops and momma's-boys" by the chest-thumping high-school jocks who rule the corridors and testosterone-damp changing rooms of North American secondary schools.

Today we remember how competitive athletics in the West began in ancient Greece as homosexual obsessional sessions with young nude boys of graceful limb and plump buttock.

Consider first the short-form word *gym* and its ancestor Latin *gymnasium* from Greek *gumnasion* 'place of nudity.' *Gymnos* is the Greek adjective for bare-naked. The literal meaning of gymnast is 'one who exercises in the nude.' *Gymnasion* was the place where muscular young boys and lithe adolescents exercised in the nude while older men stood on the sidelines leering at the boys' genitals, salivating and becoming sexually aroused. But of course, as we know today in 2014, from our knowledge of brisk pedophilic shower activity at the University of Pennsylvania, all those homosexual shenanigans ceased long ago. All the gay underpinning that lurks beneath so much athletic activity has disappeared. Right! Liberace was straight. Rock Hudson was a stud. And many high-school gym teachers are not closeted gays.

Keep all this in mind when modern-day jocks and dick-wagging braggart athletes tell you how masculine and studly organized competitive sports are. Think of all the ball-cupping, grab-ass and towel ass-whips that proliferate in dressing-room showers. As psychiatry states over and over again: all this boy-punching and slap-ass is disguised homoerotic foreplay.

On my inaugural day of high school, six minutes after I entered the school building, gym class began. Boys' gym was first period. A Universal Agility Test was obligatory for All Grade Nine boys that opening day. I failed. I could not dribble a basketball. Never mind that I could accurately conjugate 100 Greek verbs. "Doesn't count, wuss." In my failure the gym teacher branded me "a motor moron." Honest. Out of the class of 30 boys, four of us were motor morons. We were forced to stand at the side during the entire class period, while wholesome, normal lads of sturdy physique enjoyed a game of basketball. There was no effort by the fascist gym teacher to have anyone show us how to dribble a basketball, to have us learn some sports agility. Like all morons who become teachers, he thought learning by humiliation of the pupil was effective. It is not.

Meting out so punitive a vengeance, that class was an accurate forecast of my athletic career in high school. There was only one reason for gym class: to discover and glorify naturally talented athletes: find the winners and screw the stumblebum losers like me and the majority of high-school kids.

Many of us brighter students went on to loathe sports, athletes and exercise. I'm not saying that traumatizing ordinary kids in high school produced obese generations of exercise-haters. But having "motor moron" burnt into one's forehead with a soldering iron (virtually) certainly did not induce an impulse to jog five miles in a sleet storm.

Now the fascist nitwit who was head of physical education (what a misnomer!) in my high school was a failed pro. He was fit but small-boned and short. He had been to the summer try-out camps of two professional football teams and he had been rejected. After all, tackle position cannot always be held by a 110-pound dwarf. So this gym teacher brought to his boy students boiling rage at his pro-football rejection. Like many unaware psychos, he projected his self-hatred, his blaming himself for not being a pro footballer, on those of his students who didn't count, the ones who couldn't play sports. The guys who made up the championship school teams, of course, he worshipped. Hell, he practically went down on them. He did insist on taking nude showers with the teenage football team, but I'll leave that for a later lesson in "sissyology."

Teams that scored many victories were, of course, the dwarf coach's bread and butter. A winning basketball team was exactly what the local school board ordered, especially at their spring hiring meeting, when the board decided whose teaching contracts would be renewed. The coaches of winning teams would surely be invited back, to repeat their victories for another year.

The word *athlete,* officially used at the first Olympic games in 776 BC in Greece, means 'contender' or 'contestant' in ancient Greek from *athlos* 'contest' or *athlon* 'prize.' By the way, a tip to many TV sportscasters and mildly dyslexic jocks: Do NOT say: ath-**uh**-lete. The English word is pronounced ATH-leet. The slovenly infixing of a supernumerary vowel — what I call the dork's "uh" — is quite unnecessary and merely brands the speaker of such vowel excess as an illiterate yutz of the lowest station.

And so, class, what may we take away as today's lesson? Perhaps this truth: high school phys. ed. teachers are among the worst of their so-called profession. They have, by their lazy, shoddy pedagogy, loosed into the world hordes of sports-hating American fatties. Shouldn't high-school phys. ed. class be chiefly conducted to teach the entire class to enjoy athletic activity? Not in North American high schools.

Chapter 8

Rude Words, You Troglodyte!

During this brief spin on the merry-go-round of uncouth and boorish rudeness we shall refer only to the adjective *rude* as applied to persons and offer two rare but apt equivalent attributives.

Scarcely an hour passes when the civilized wayfarer does not encounter manners which reek of low breeding. Instantly one knows the offending lout was the glum spawn of parents who met when both were first out on a day pass.

Because barbarous crowds swarm stadia, arenas and parks and pullulate verminously within towns and inner cities, ever present, ever impudent, ever discourteous, our vocabulary to identify such trash and then label and disparage their uncivil behaviour ought to be manifold and of sufficient variety to keep barbarians aware that we the offended plumb well the untutored abyss of their ignorance.

Step Forward, Odious Neanderthal!

So let us begin with an infrequent adjective that may mean rude and boorish, a stern insulting adjective of ancient Greek provenance, namely: *troglodytic*. Now a troglodyte is a cave dweller, from classical Greek *troglodutes* = *trogle* 'hole, cave' + *duein* 'to enter, to go into, to dwell in, to inhabit.' Borrowed into English from a Latin form, troglodyte first referred to prehistoric cavemen.

One of troglodyte's figurative meanings is a loutish, possibly hairy hermit stooped in a hovel or loping about a cavern on all fours, a low clod who lived in a seclusion unacquainted with modes of civilization. Thus its adjective *troglodytic* fits to perfection the rude and malodorous sales clerk who burps in your face one morning when you are attempting to purchase tooth-gel. Merely report "the troglodytic buffoon" to the management and see him cast into the alleyway where, perhaps, his next meal awaits. Cruel on your part? Not in the least. Stale-breath burpings and gross eructations have no place at a toiletries counter.

Contumely be damned!

Contumely is the language of insolence, insulting and abusive reproach that seeks to inflict upon victims the wounds of humiliation and dishonour. The word entered English through French from the ancient Romans whose Latin possessed the noun *contumelia* 'abuse, insult, reproach.' Contumelious is its adjective, whose sound pleased Shakespeare. Consider his *Henry VI, Part One* "With scoffes and scornes, and contumelious taunts." Among Victorian poets, Alfred, Lord Tennyson, that melodious and syrupy mechanic, has a character in his long, long poem *Maud* "curving a contumelious lip."

Finally, if some insolent peasant behind a shop counter lacks refinement, you may descend to quote famous insults of whose origin the unlettered clerk will be quite ignorant. One of my favorites occurs in Henry

Fielding's novel *The History of Tom Jones*, when Squire Western's well-bred sister must rebuke her churlish bumpkin of a brother: "Your ignorance, as the great Milton says, almost subdues my patience."

Chapter 9

How to Avoid Weather Clichés in English

Humans are social beings. Like many primates, as we approach one another, we make grunting noises to show we are friendly. It has been estimated that 75 per cent of all human speech is semantically void, empty of deep meaning, uttered merely to display non-aggressive proximity. One of the topics we use in such low-key, friendly, audible encounters is the weather. Statements or rhetorical questions about the weather are safe because they are communicated almost entirely in clichés, bits of speech so common as to approach meaninglessness.

"Nice day?"

"Warm for July."

"Heh-heh. Not cold."

"Windy yesterday."

"No breeze this morning though."

"Fair weather ahead. All week."

Yet the fastidious user of English can avoid such platitudinous banality by simply learning new weather words. And Professor Billy is here, as ever, to perform his pedagogue's duty by helping you to aroint from your word hoard every desiccated chestnut of meteorological vapidity.

Sunny

To avoid "Sunny, isn't it?" one may whisper "Sol's lucent realm beams on high" but people might look at you funny. A fig for their looks! Where words are concerned, I am an unrepentant snob. I suggest a much rarer English adjective for sunny, namely *aprique*. It may take penultimate stress as AP-rik or ultimate stress as uh-PREEK. Its origin is Latin *apricus* 'sunny' from the Latin verb *apricare* 'to bask in the sun.' Rarer still is apricity coined and used once by seventeenth-century English dictionary maker Henry Cockeram in 1623 to refer to the warmth of winter sun. *Sol* of course is Latin for 'sun.' Its more familiar derivatives are English words like *solar*, *solarium* and *solstice*, as well as less used terms like *insolate* 'to expose to the sun's rays, to treat a disease by exposure to sunlight.' Do not confuse insolate with insulate.

Fair Weather

The nautical "fair weather" is pleasant and is not heard as frequently as in days of sail. Said even less nowadays is the sentence once spoken when pleasant weather seemed like it might last all day, namely "The day is set fair."

If the temperature is going to be not very hot and not very cold, you might coo "Clemency ensues, *n'est-ce pas*?" But ordinary listeners might judge you a bit snooty. So what? You will have nailed the word *clemency*.

Nonsense Response to Weather Inquiries

Answers to weather questions which are deliberately illogical are not appreciated by most. But devotees of the best English nonsense verse might enjoy a line or two from "The Walrus and The Carpenter" by Lewis Carroll from *Through the Looking-Glass and What Alice Found There*, 1872.

"The sun was shining on the sea,
Shining with all his might:
He did his very best to make
The billows smooth and bright--
And this was odd, because it was
The middle of the night."

Likewise disdained in weather response is understatement. When a small child is blown away down the block towards an operating hay-baling machine, don't say, "Looks like the breeze has freshened." On the contrary, scream and run madly to retrieve the aerial infant.

During weather commentaries, overstatement may also be scorned. At the onset of a thunder-clap which sends a pet dachshund under grandmother's shawl, do not leap on the barbeque canopy and shout, "Action stations!"

Cold

Sudden gales of cold wind are best described by using folk sayings. Some folk sayings are vulgar and may bring a blush to the dewlaps of your maiden aunt. But do consider these gems:

1. So cold this morning, before I could take a piss, I had to kick a hole in the air.
2. It's a tree-snappin' night.
3. Not a fit day for a fence post.
   A very cold and stormy day in Prince Edward Island, Canada

4. We're takin' the mailbox in.
   Meaning, there's going to be a violent ocean storm. from Port Medway, Nova Scotia, Canada.
5. For smaller boys a penile pun may be in order: "It's cold out, especially if you leave it out."

Hot

1. So hot the hens are layin' hard-boiled eggs.
2. Hot enough to fry spit.
3. So hot and dry last week around Virden, frogs were poundin' on the screen door, askin' for a dipper of water.
   Virden is in southern Manitoba on the Saskatchewan border in Canada.

Snow

My own favourite weather expression came into Canadian English from Ukrainian settlers in Manitoba. When I was a child in the 1940s, a snowfall with large flakes used to summon this phrase: "She's comin' down like dinner plates." But years later I heard this description of a fluffy snowfall: "The old woman is sure pluckin' her geese today."

This is a direct translation of a Ukrainian folk saying that also shows up in Manitoba earlier in the 19th century.

Rain

1. Enough rain to choke a toad.
2. It's so wet we're shooting ducks in the pantry.

Wind

1. She's blowin' a gagger.

This is an Ontario expression to describe a north wind blowing south off Georgian Bay.

2. That wind is strong enough to blow the nuts off a gang plough.
   Said of a Saskatchewan storm. Many variants exist, for example, from New Brunswick: Wind strong enough to blow the nuts off the Miramichi Bridge. They are all probably based on: Cold enough to freeze the nuts off a brass monkey. Incidentally, there is not, in all the annals of British naval lexicography, one single printed record or reference of any piece of naval ordnance named a "brass monkey." It was never an object that held cannonballs on a war ship. The expression means just what it says: if a monkey was made of brass, this cold would crack the brass. All the reputed etymologies that claim an origin in the British navy for this expression are to be viewed with suspicion.
3. The wind is blowin' and it's too lazy to go around you.
4. It was so windy, my hen laid the same egg twice.
5. It's a cold wind to calf your ass up against.
6. You can always tell people from Saskatchewan. When the wind stops blowing, they fall over.
7. It's windy enough to blow the horns off a bull.
   Direct translation of Canadian French: *Il vente assez fort pour écorner un boeuf.*

And we'll end our weather watch with one obscure term from Scottish dialect, *dreich* 'wet, dark, unpleasant weather.'

Chapter 10

Proteus, Shape-Shifter of the Gods

Protean things are fluctuant and mutable, as variable in form as brisk, nimble clouds scudding across windy sky. Most uses of the adjective are positive, saluting a pleasing versatility, but protean may be applied to what is erratic and inconsistent too.

Proteus was a mythical Greek sea god, a son of Oceanus, who evaded capture by being able to mutate into many forms and living creatures (see the Homeric passage below). Proteus thus belongs to a very ancient order of supernatural beings whose general descriptive is shape-shifter, a trickster god of polymorphic whim and sportive metamorphosis, found flitting foxlike through many a primordial myth. But when, rarely, humans were able to seize hold of Proteus, the capricious godlet was forced to foretell their future, fishy oracle that he was.

Proteus' name is probably rooted in the Greek word for 'first' *protos*, so common in dozens of English derivatives like protocol, proto-Marxist and proto-punk music. The ancient thought may have been that he's an old divinity of the first order of gods, but he's still a hard worker.

In linguistic terminology, proto- is a prefix that denotes a language's very early stage of development, as in Proto-Germanic or Proto-Indo-European.

Proteus Syndrome

Proteus syndrome, a disorder featuring hypertrophy (morbid overgrowth) of bone and soft tissues, is one useful etiological name for the sundry deformities and macrocephalic anomalies which afflicted Joseph Merrick (1862–90 CE), called the Elephant Man.

Darwin used the word scientifically, as in this sentence from *Origin of Species*: "Genera which have sometimes been called 'protean' or 'polymorphic', in which the species present an inordinate amount of variation."

Protea the Flower

Protea is a flowering shrub of subtropical locales, blessed with wondrously complex blooms, belonging to a genus of more than one hundred species whose individual varieties exhibit diverse and protean forms. Protea as generic name was dubbed so in 1735 by the great pioneer of scientific binomials, Carl Linnaeus, after the Greek god Proteus, who could change his form at will, because proteas have such a wide variety of forms.

Proteus in Homer

In Book 4 of Homer's *Odyssey*, Odysseus visits the house of the warrior king Menelaus, husband of Helen and a leading figure in The Trojan War. At meat-rich banquets, high tales of derring-do are exchanged over food and wine. For his part, Menelaus tells the story of how he himself captured Proteus and forced the seer to reveal Menelaus' own fate.

> ". . . at noon the old man of the sea
> came up too, and when he had found

> his fat seals he went over them and counted them. We were among the first he counted, and he never suspected any guile, but laid himself down to sleep as soon as he had done counting. Then we rushed upon him with a shout and seized him; on which he began at once with his old tricks, and changed himself first into a lion with a great mane; then all of a sudden he became a dragon, a leopard, a wild boar; the next moment he was running water, and then again directly he was a tree, but we stuck to him and never lost hold, till at last the cunning old creature became distressed, and said, "Which of the gods was it, Son of Atreus, that hatched this plot with you for snaring me and seizing me against my will? What do you want?"
>
> *Samuel Butler translation*

In Book 4, lines 561-569, Proteus, in the guise of the wise Old Man of the Sea (*halios geron*, Greek literally 'salty elder' or 'old salt'), is captured and forced to foretell to the voyager Menelaus his ultimate fate, in a vision of heaven that owes very little to native Greek mythology but much more to Egyptian influence. It is a sweet passage in Homer's melodious Greek, but here my own slightly loose translation, following Butler, must suffice:

"You, O Menelaus, nurtured of Zeus, shall not succumb to doomy death in the horse-thick fields of Argos. Rather, those who never die shall carry you to Elysian Fields at the far perimeters of earth, where the golden-yellow god of Underworld reigns amidst an ease of living which all immortals enjoy. For there falls not rain, nor hail, nor snow, but the Ocean God breathes ever in a West wind that sings softly from the sea, and gives fresh life to humans all."

More uplifting, perhaps, than a weekend in Cleveland?

Chapter 11

To Dullen

A verb whose very existence astonished me

Recently I was spooked, not to say *bouleversé*, when reading a right-wing rag of a Canadian newspaper, to observe the reporter, a local Cro-Magnon bigot, use the verb *to dullen*. Dismissively I thought, *oh-oh, another semi-literate bozo reporter unacquainted with the common fact that dull is both an adjective and a verb.*

Yet so venerable a tome as the *Oxford English Dictionary* tells us that *to dullen* has indeed been a verb in our language since 1832 CE when quotation evidence points to its being coined by writer Leigh Hunt, perhaps as a chiming antonym to the long-existing English verb *to brighten*.

Of course the basic adjective *dull*, with variant orthography, appears in Old English before 970 CE, from a Proto-Indo-European root whose reflex in Modern German is *toll* which nowadays has both positive and negative meanings like 'wild, mad, crazy' but in much earlier German could signify 'foolish, like a dullard, stupid, not sharp.'

Now, class, let us employ our new verb in an illustrative sentence: A recent candidate dullened the intellectual level of those running for the office of American president.

Elitist Words a No-No?

To introduce the conclusion of this column we may look to its first sentence and my elitist use of a French past participle *bouleversé* which means 'shocked, knocked on my ass, overwhelmed, upset, overturned.' It's from a French verb with Latin roots: Latin *bulla* 'ball' + Latin *versare* 'to turn,' its prime semantic being 'to turn over and over the way a rolling ball turns.'

Now I beg a picayune space to reply to an email complaint that I use far too many elitist words in my writing. Oh! My most fervid expectancy is that such a wanton indictment may teem with prejudicial surplusage!

The late Australian art critic, Robert Hughes — by my lights one of the best art critics who ever wrote in English — was labelled by fellow Australian journalists as "an elitist" - granted a given that Australian males (all named Bruce) comprise an archaic subspecies of humanity best left to themselves squeezing tits and popping a shrimp on the "barby."

Answering the flimsy charge of the Aussie galoots, Hughes wrote: "I am completely an elitist, in the cultural but emphatically not the social sense. I prefer the good to the bad, the articulate to the mumbling, the aesthetically developed to the merely primitive, and full to partial consciousness. I love the spectacle of skill, whether it's an expert gardener at work, or a good carpenter chopping dovetails, or someone tying a Bimini hitch that won't slip."

Hughes' is a quotable statement because it calls attention to the neglected divide between what is the good and what is the bad, between the artifact worth keeping and disposable schlock, the junk, the kitsch and the garbage choking modern life.

Hughes believed in talent, craft and skill, not welfare, not passing every moron in Grade Seven, not letting some defective brain-stem shoot a cop in the head just because said dunce has been "hard-done-by" or because the retard was deprived of licorice as a child. For those who shoot and kill others, I believe in a brick wall and three rounds in the head . . . after a ten-minute trial, of course.

Hughes did not agree that being able to read a soup can qualified a student to pass Grade 12 English. Hughes loved the thing well made, whether it was a perfect nautical knot, a great painting, or, like me, a superb sentence of English. Culture which endures needs more strict judges like Robert Hughes.

What, you may unwisely ask, was my own aim in writing this collection of short essays about language? In each chapter I tried to select one word not merely rare, but a choice vocable that is in fact *le mot recherché*, a term uncommon to the point of pretentiousness. Email response reveals that my readers, all three of them, seek an expansion of vocabulary. Well then, it is patent that I am here to find, polish and hold up to view verbal shells adorning the sea-beach of verbiage.

Chapter 12

Obscure Verbs of Leaping

The rodeo corral of leaping verbs in English is of modest girth but encloses lively word broncos. To pronk, to stott, to caracole and to saltate have a prancing splendour worth enjoying.

To pronk

Pronk stems from an Afrikaans verb, borrowed from the South African riding vocabulary of Boers. It began leaping into English sentences at the end of the nineteenth century. The Dutch verb *pronken* means 'to show off, to strut one's stuff.' In Dutch a *pronker* is a braggart or stuck-up jerk. Also, in Afrikaans, the Boer plural noun of *pronk* is *pronken.*

Our English noun *prank* 'trick' may have arisen from the same root. The earliest meaning in English of the verb *to prank up* is 'to dress up and strut about.' In Middle Dutch *proncken* meant 'to boast.' In seventeenth-century German *prunken* meant 'to show off.' Germanic variants like *pronken, prangen* and *brangan* are related. English *prank* and *prink* are less certain relatives.

Springbok (Afrikaans 'jumping buck') and other slender ruminant antelope like gazelles and impalas pronk as a form of antic display. They jump up into the air, back arched, springing up on all four legs which are held straight. Is there a happier take-off than a svelte gazelle pronking into a summer sky? In high mountain pastures of the Andes, llamas leap and alpacas pronk. Cavorting vicuñas bound over Andean meadowscapes. All these saltatory shenanigans lead us to our next obscure verb of leaping. Saltatory means 'moving in leaps and bounds.'

To Saltate

To saltate is to leap or jump. *Saltatus* is the Latin root. *Saltatus* is the past participial adjective of the verb *saltare* 'to dance,' which in that verb suggests one early form of Roman dancing was merely rhythmic leaping. *Saltare* in its verbal form is a frequentative, reduced from its original Latin form, **salitare*, from *salire* 'to leap.'

Frequentative verbal suffixes are added to simple Latin verb stems to imply frequency of the action described by the simple verb. In other words, the prime meaning of *saltare* is 'to leap many times.' This quite probably described some hopping dance of early Rome.

Flitting Flies

I'll add one more example of a frequentative Latin verb form, because it shows up in an English medical term. *Volare* in Latin means 'to fly.' It survived into Modern Italian as the name of popular song hit by Domenico Modugno "*Volare*" or "*Nel blu, dipinto di blu.*" *Volitare* is the frequentative of *volare*, meaning 'to repeat a flying action many times,' and so, naturally, the ancient Romans used the verb *volitare* to describe the flight of bats 'to flit' or the flapping of butterfly wings 'to flitter.' In ophthalmology, floating imperfections in the vitreous humour of the human eyeball are formally termed *muscae volitantes* 'flitting houseflies.' Also called eye floaters, consisting of bits of cellular debris that jerk about oddly if you blink or move your eyeball, you've seen them in your own field of vision, even if you could not name them. But now you can, so look them up in an online medical dictionary to find *muscae volitantes.*

Somersault

Saltare was borrowed into all of the Romance languages derived from Latin. From French, English borrowed and did a somersault, an acrobat's head-over-heels leap, a tumbler's pitchpoll. Somersault is close to the Old French form *sombresault* < *sobresault* < *sobresaut* Provençal < *sobresalto* Spanish < *supra* Latin 'above' + *saltus* 'a leap.' The Italian phrase for somersault is much more honest about the dangers of such a jump. Italians call the somersault *salto mortale*!

Sault Ste. Marie, Ontario

In Canada, one of our Ontario cities is Sault Ste. Marie. *Sault* is 17th-century French spelling of *le saut* Modern French 'waterfalls.' In the 18th century *sault* could mean 'rapids.' In both cases, it refers to places where water *leaps.* When Jesuit missionaries founded a mission nearby, they named the leaping rapids after the Virgin Mary. Modern French would probably use *la chute* or *les chutes* to name rapids in a river. *Saut à la corde* is kids skipping rope. To take a leap in the dark in French is *faire un saut dans l'inconnu.* Italian has a lively, hopping and skipping dance called the *saltarello* 'little leap.'

This *saltare* root hides in many common English words and is worth searching out some rainy day when a dictionary and a fireplace beckon you to a window seat.

Check the origins of words like *assault, desultory, result, exultant, sauté* (make that fat leap up!), *salacious, military salient, resile* and the delicious *saltimbocca*, Italian 'jump into your mouth.'

To Stott

In northern England and Scotland this trig little verb means to bounce off, to spring up, to jump, and to rebound. The secondary verbal use of stott describes moving with a jumping or springing step, to bound along. To stott may be related to a Teutonic root that shows up in modern German *stoßen* where the *stoss* root signifies 'punch' or 'kick' and in Dutch where *stuiten* is 'to rebound, to bounce.' Possibly influenced by the Dutch form is a rarer English dialect verb, to stoit 'to bounce' or, said of certain fish like pilchards 'to leap above the surface of the water.' It sounds like the start of a feisty provincial exclamation: *by the stoitin' pilchards!

To Capriole

From Italian *capriola* 'a young goat, a fawn' comes this verb used in horsemanship to name a certain high leap in equitation made without going forward. In form, the word is the diminutive of *capra* 'she-goat.' If you are skimming over the waves to the Isle of Capri you are approaching what was simply in Old Italian the island of "goats." Movie director Frank Capra possibly had a founding ancestor of his family who was a goatherd. A much more common short form of this verb and noun became popular in English. If you caper about, you are leaping and jumping like a goat. A caper is a little trick such as a sneaky goat might play.

To Caracole

This is another verb describing a movement in equestrian skill, a half-turn or wheel to the right or left. This elegant verb takes its name from spiral shells like periwinkles. Its line of descent looks like this: *caracol* French < *caracollo* Italian 'wheeling of a horse' < *caracol* Spanish 'snail, periwinkle.' Beyond Spanish, the derivation is shrouded in the sea-fog of history.

And so, as tendrils of moist mist creep up the steadfast bulwarks and stone battlements of stately Casselman manor on this rainy afternoon, I'm off to mull some wine and sip surcease from a warmed goblet.

Chapter 13

Carnal, Fleshy Words like Excarnation

We've all heard of **incarnation**, when an airy spirit or incorporeal deity assumes fleshly form. Incarnation is the literal embodiment of an entity not customarily provided with a perceptible body. For Christians, the incarnation of Jesus Christ is a moment of supreme religious importance.

But its opposite, **excarnation**, particularly in the sciences of archaeology and anthropology, names a common human burial practice: removing the flesh and organs from a corpse and burying or preserving only the bones. Ancient Egyptian mummification procedures involved partial excarnation. Various world peoples expose a new corpse on a high place and permit birds like buzzards to pick clean or even carry off the bones of the dead.

Excarnation may also be a natural process, for example the flesh of a dead body exposed will rot away by natural putrefaction, from Latin *puter* 'rotten' + *facere* 'to make, to render.' A cadaver or, in the charming euphemism of ambulance drivers, mortal remains that have VSA (vital signs absent), any corpse may find itself outside, subject to natural law, and thus subject to be torn or consumed by plundering predators, vulturine raptors, botfly larvae and the entire hellish circus of saprotrophic fauna and flora evolved to devour our fragile and oh-so-temporary mammal flesh.

Saprotrophic = 'feeding on dead or decaying matter' from *sapros* a Greek adjective meaning 'rotten' + Greek *trophe* 'food, nourishment, feeding.'

Excarnation can bear a less common theological sense too, where it signifies the separation at death of the soul from the fleshly body.

Some Carnal Etymology

Latin *caro, carnis* 'flesh, meat' sprang from a Proto-Indo-European stem *ker- or *sker- whose prime sense was 'to cut.' Hence carnal material was originally whatsoever flesh to be eaten could be cut away from a dead hunted animal or person — should your local cave-dweller favour cannibalism. The form has many interesting Indo-European cognates: English *shear*, Dutch *scheren*, German *scheren*, Norwegian *skjære*, Swedish *skära*; Attic Greek *keirō*, "I cut off," Lithuanian *skìrti* "separate," and Welsh *ysgar* "separate.

Other Carnal Words

Carnival is among the more intriguing derivatives of Latin *caro, carnis*. This festive time just before Lent, often given over to riotous sexual revelry and mutinous imbibements, was once said to stem from the Italian *carnevale*. The term — it was mistakenly supposed — was at first a two-word phrase, an apostrophe (to use its proper syntactic name). This spurious but delightful derivation claimed that it was a person bidding a Lenten goodbye to pleasures of his or her own flesh, the Latin being a playful address to the self, *O Carne, vale!* 'Oh flesh, farewell!'

But, in etymological fact, Italian *carnevale* stems from misspellings and variants of admittedly similar, medieval Latin compound nouns like *carnelevārium*, *carnilevāria*, *carnilevāmen* from a Latin verbal phrase like **carnem levāre* 'to put away, remove or deny the flesh.'

Animals & Plants Carnivorous

Other carnal terms are less exotic in origin. A carnivore devours meat or flesh, as an herbivore eats grass-like food. The zoological order of *Carnivora* encompasses a diverse order of terrestrial and aquatic carnivorous mammals consisting of ten families grouped into suborders.

1. Caniformia including Canidae (dogs, foxes)
2. Ursidae (bears)
3. Otariidae (sealions)
4. Ailuropodidae (giant panda)
5. Procyonidae (racoons)
6. Mustelidae (weasels, otters)
7. Phocidae (hair seals)
8. Feliformia including Felidae (cats)
9. Viverridae (civets)
10. Hyaenidae (hyenas)

Carnage, the savage slaughter of many humans, was borrowed from French into English. The French word appeared first in Italian as *carnaggio* from a Medieval Latin form *carnaticum* 'a heap of meat or flesh.' One modern meaning dwindled slightly to accommodate our popular practice of butchering riders in automotive accidents.

Goosebumps Ahead!

Among the Gauls, the Latin word *caro, carnis* transformed to the French word for flesh, *chair*. English has a colloquial term for a pronounced roughness of the skin during which hair follicles on the neck and arms stand erect through fear or coldness. The condition resembles the skin of a plucked goose, hence our English word *gooseflesh*. The French call it 'chicken-flesh' or *chair de poule*. The arrector pili (anatomical Latin 'thing which makes erect a hair') is a little muscle in mammals, several of which are attached to the base of each hair follicle. When these muscles contract the hairs stand on end. Shakespeare has a vivid passage describing this effect in Act One, Scene 5 of *Hamlet*, when the young Dane sees and hears his father's ghost tell his son of his own murder. It is among the most sweetly-cadenced speeches in all of English drama:

"**Ghost**

I am thy father's spirit,
Doom'd for a certain term to walk the night,
And for the day confined to fast in fires,
Till the foul crimes done in my days of nature
Are burnt and purged away. But that I am forbid
To tell the secrets of my prison-house,
I could a tale unfold whose lightest word
Would harrow up thy soul, freeze thy young blood,
Make thy two eyes, like stars, start from their spheres,
Thy knotted and combined locks to part
And each particular hair to stand on end,
Like quills upon the fretful porpentine."

Porpentine is merely an Elizabethan spelling and probable mishearing of our more modern form *porcupine*.

Into the Dank Flesh-house

An interesting doublet of our Latinate adjective *carnal* entered English through French as *charnel*. Until the dawn of the twentieth century a charnel-house was a mortuary chapel or a house of dead bodies, a vault piled up with the bones of the unburied dead. There is an extant glossary (an early, primitive, pre-dictionary word list) that offers a blunt and sturdy Old English synonym for charnel and that is *flæsc hus* 'flesh-house.' Old French *charnel* evolved from Late Latin *carnale*, possibly influenced by another form meaning 'bone house' and that was *carnarium*.

Hail, O Queen of Health!

Slender, weedy apostles of health food, seen all sallow-skinned and yellowly sepulchral, furtively nibbling bunny food at organic markets, have given us our newest, creepiest term, *carnophobia* 'fear of or aversion to the eating of meat.' A first date with such a female carnophobe is likely to be reported by the male with these words: "I tried to kiss her, but her ear fell off." Geez, a guy'd have more fun attending a Fund-the-Prosthesis Charity Dance at a leper colony.

Chapter 14

On William Blake & Theolalia

A New Year's Day essay

"To see a World in a grain of sand
And a Heaven in a Wild Flower,
Hold Infinity in the Palm of your hand
And Eternity in an Hour."

from *Auguries of Innocence* by William Blake

This is a commentary on William Blake's illustrations for *The Book of Job.* A professional engraver by trade, William Blake (1757 – 1827) was one of Britain's greatest printmakers. I have as well made bold to jot down a few thoughts on life upon waking one New Year's Day and celebrating a crisp winter morning in southern Canada. For me, in the words of *Job 38:7,* it truly was a time:

"When the morning stars sang together,
And all the sons of God shouted for joy."

And that is no small order for a convinced atheist! Poor Job asks why he, a just man, is suffering and God speaks out of the whirlwind to the undeservedly downtrodden Job and has no comfort to give the lowly Job.

If you have access to the internet, find a photo of Blake's painting "The Ancient of Days," a watercolour and relief etching of 1794 now in the British Museum in London. The title is one of the names of God, as mentioned, for example, in the *Old Testament Book of Daniel*. This is a favorite image of architects, as it shows God as the divine architect planning creation with a bronze compass. In Blake's personal mythology, this is Urizen, who began as satanic but later partakes of God power, representing reason and law. For Blake, Urizen's architectural tools, like the compass in his divine hands, are used both to create the world and to constrain it.

Theolalia

God's first speech in Chapter 38 of *The Book of Job* is one of the most powerful theolalias (religious writing in which God speaks) in all of world literature. Unfortunately—or fortunately, depending on your piety—the speech reflects perfectly what a vindictive, senile old sadist Yahweh is, branding man as a puny idiot in the face of God's created earthly wonders. "Hey, Job," brays the Almighty, "were you around when the morning stars sang together? I don't think so, loser!" Thanks, Almighty Dude, for your modesty and thrilling logic. Maybe I'll just smite you on one side of your cloud. That IS what you best understand, isn't it? Smiting those who worship you? Just to keep them crawlin', right, Big Beard?

Etymology of Theolalia

For a technical term still in wide use, a word not too obscure, theolalia is surprisingly absent as a headword from both the current *Oxford English Dictionary* online and *Webster's Third New International Dictionary, Unabridged*. The two components of this compound

Greek noun are *theos* 'god' + *lalia* 'a speaking' from the Hellenistic Greek verb *lalein* 'to talk, to speak; also pejorative: to chatter on, to babble.' Blake's watercolour of God "The Ancient of Days" is, of course, a theography, an image of divinity.

The most common scientific word with the root is probably echolalia, a psychiatric disorder in which the patient repeats robotically every word that is said to him. The religious phenomenon of speaking in tongues has a fancy name too, glossolalia (ancient Greek *glossis* 'tongue, 'Attic dialect form *glotta*) no doubt to make the performance seem authentic. Once upon a time, girls could bear the given name Eulalia 'she who speaks well.' Lalophobia is a fear of public speaking. Dyslalia is a speech impairment due to malformation of the external speech organs. Idiolalia is speech so defectively uttered as to be unintelligible to another human.

Blake's "Job" on *Job*

Among William Blake's later artistic works, the 21 illustrations to the *Book of Job*, completed when Blake was almost 70 years old are also well worth finding on the internet. If you have ever wondered what a masterpiece looks like, here is one. You can wait around dawdling on the corner for the masterpiece-man to drive up in his Lexus SUV and unload a "major work" into your trembling hands. Hey, you can wait for the Boxing Day sale of the eons—but you will not see the like of Blake's vision again any time soon.

Although the biblical story of Job is an account of undeserved suffering by a righteous believer, Job suffered, according to Blake, because Job adhered too closely to the letter of religious, written-in-a-book law, instead of allowing his own spiritual imagination to guide him in understanding his physical plight of bad luck and boils.

Job's suffering was a consequence of his humanity not of his paltry share of divinity.

Blake would have told Job that mystical spirituality must be explained reflexively too, that, as the ancient Greeks put it rather vatically "the way in is the way out."

Confused? Well, that's good! Blake wanted people to employ fully our human capacity for wonderment. Fat chance!

The Credulous Ninnies of Orthodoxy

Blake particularly loathed the credulous ninnies of orthodoxy running to ask mansion-homed priests and corrupt TV-show-hosting reverends, mealy-mouthed robbers and deceivers of the poor all of them, to interpret Holy Writ, when it was, felt Blake, up to each experiencing imagination to supply its own meaning to religious moments and feelings.

Analysing by oneself a portion of life mystery, of course, takes mental effort. It is far more common for the slobs of devotion to loll about the earth like stunned rebel angels, still dizzy from The Fall, too prostrate with spiritual laziness to rise up, cast off the torpor of piety, and cogitate about a specific spiritual occasion.

So troublesome a vice was this to early fathers of the Christian church that theology has its very own technical term to describe it: acedia, from ancient Greek, meaning a metaphysical listlessness, precursor to one of the seven deadly sins, Sloth.

Was your moment a divine visitation or a brain chemistry event? I can promise you this: if you try it, you may just experience a thinking New Year!

My Favourite Quotation from the Life of William Blake

It was not said by Blake but by his wife, Catherine Boucher. Catherine was once asked by an acquaintance what it was like being married to a mystic and a poet. She replied, "I have very little of Mr. Blake's company. He is usually in paradise."

What lengthy desert nights of spousal disparity lurk in that reply! Still, Catherine was a true helpmeet, assisting Blake in the making of his engravings throughout their marriage.

Did my New Year's review of William Blake's masterpiece leave a piquant residuum? I hope so, humble though it be. Even in a spiritual quest begun in atheism, one must press onward forever toward the broad, sunlit uplands of belief. The vista at trail's end is said to stun the traveler.

Chapter 15

Squirrel

The abundantly bushy tail of the squirrel bestows its name upon this agile rodent. The word scampered across to England just after the Norman conquest in 1066 CE as Anglo-Norman *esquirel* < Medieval Latin **scurellius* or possibly **scuriolus*, putative diminutive forms of Latin *scurius/sciurus*, from Greek *skiouros* < *skia* 'shade' + *oura* 'tail,' playfully named from the comic supposition that the squirrel's tail was so big that it provided portable shade for the lively arboreal nut-lover. One zoological genus is *Sciurus* 'shadow-tail.'

Skia 'shadow'

That Greek root for shade, *skia*, is found in several uncommon English terms like the learned adjective *sciurine* which means 'pertaining to squirrels.' Among the immensely silly modes of foretelling the future is divination by chatting up the shades of the dead or sciomancy < Greek *skia* 'shadow' + Greek *manteia* 'prophecy, prediction.'

There are dozens of foolish methods of predicting the future encapsulated in words ending in –mancy. Consider the most familiar word *necromancy* – predicting the future using the arts of witches and sorcerers and other "dead" knowledge. *Nekros* is Greek for 'dead.' Ancient Roman seers poked through chicken guts and rabbit entrails to guess at future events. Other Europeans practiced the messy art of scatomancy, divining the future by examining excrement and feces. Onychophagomancy foretells what is to come by looking at precisely how people chew their fingernails! Hippomancy involves observing the movement of horses in a corral. Chiromancy is another word for reading one's palm or palmistry. What about reading history, knowing current events and thinking as means of guessing the future? Forget it, pal. Too much trouble. I'd rather try to read the smoke from the incense at church.

Anthurium

This Greek word gives us the clue to several botanical binomials which some plant lovers will recognize. That familiar greenhouse import from Hawaii and Central America, the anthurium, is a bit of Botanical Latin made from two Greek words *anthos* 'flower' + *oura* 'tail.' It is a 'tail-flower' because the large, showy spadix of the genus looks like an animal's tail or penis and thrusts up with phallic brio from its flat spathe, a modified bract. In fact, one of the trade names for the plant is Boy Flower. Because so many of the species sold in commerce are pink and red, its most common name is Flamingo Flower.

Eremurus

Another exquisite garden subject is the foxtail lily with its single, densely-flowered raceme of bright florets on a spike. The scientific moniker is Eremurus, Botanical Latin from Greek *eremos* 'solitary' + *oura* 'tail.'

Eremos can also mean 'uninhabited' to give us a very familiar English word. One of the Greek words for lonely desert was *eremia*. A person who chose to live a lonely life alone in the desert was, first, an *eremite* and, eventually in English, a *hermit*! It came to us through Medieval Latin *heremita* and then Old French *hermite*.

O Gilt Uraeus, Symbol of Divine Power

Finally, uraeus, a term ablaze in ancient pomp and Pharoanic splendour. The uraeus is the modern Latin version of an old Greek name for a serpent *ouraios* 'the one with the tail,' that is, the sacred Egyptian asp, the divine snake of power.

The uraeus was the Latin name of the image of the asp worn as a forehead head-dress by Egyptian kings, queens and various Egyptian deities. The uraeus often surmounted and fronted a diadem of burnished gold, a holy snake circlet wrapped round the brow of the gods. The Egyptian asp was and is an extremely venomous cobra, and is usually so shown in uraei.

And now, amidst this slither of uraei, let us depart this den of antiquity.

Chapter 16

Sore & Eke

Two Old English Words in Modern English

And They Were Sore Unschooled

We begin with a misunderstanding common when reading the Christmas story in *The Gospel of Saint Luke*, in the English translation of 1611, the one best steeped in flowing English, namely *The King James Version*. No modern translation approaches the grace, annunciatory charm and verbal music of the KJV's Elizabethan cadences and kindly spoken rhythms.

Luke 2: 8-11
And there were in the same country shepherds abiding in the field, keeping watch over their flock by night.
And, lo, the angel of the Lord came upon them, and the glory of the Lord shone round about them: and they were sore afraid.
And the angel said unto them, Fear not: for, behold, I bring you good tidings of great joy, which shall be to all people.
For unto you is born this day in the city of David a Saviour, which is Christ the Lord.

One "biblical scholar" (who no doubt thought that "Hebrew" was the brand name of a New York City hot dog) explained to my infant self that the shepherds were so afraid that it hurt. They were sore! Nonsense! *Sore* is the old English word meaning 'very' and it was the common word for 'very' before the Norman Invasion of 1066 brought many French words into English, some of which, like Anglo-Norman *verrai*, *verrey*, *verai*, *veray*, Old French *verai*, *varai*, *vrai* (modern French *vrai*, Provençal *verai*), meant adverbially 'truly, really, very' all from the Latin etymon *verus* 'true.' The French word *verrai* utterly displaced *sore* and so *sore* disappeared from modern Standard English. Thus many modern translations of Holy Writ tell us that the shepherds (boringly) "were very afraid."

In Biblical English, there are several meanings of *sore* but a familiar one is the adverb's use as an intensive. Thus *sore* came to mean 'greatly, strongly, severely, to a very great extent.' Sore's Germanic relatives include the modern German *sehr* 'very.'

In Martin Luther's Bible of 1522, in sixteenth century German, the passage "and they were sore afraid" was "*vnnd sie furchten sich seer.*" In a modern German bible (Shlachter 1951) the passage is "*und sie fürchteten sich sehr.*

Eke! Not Eek!

Yet another Germanic husk clinging to life in modern English is the adverb *eke.* Its modern German equivalent is *auch* 'also.' This meaning of eke can still be seen in older passages of English poetry. Among the last users was Longfellow: "Answered the young men Yes! and Yes! with lips softly breathing answered the maidens eke," that from *Children Lord's Supper* of 1856. In the 1760 prose of Laurence Sterne's *Life of Tristram Shandy* we read "Supposing the wax good, and eke the thimble."

Eke is from Old English *ēac*, akin to Latin *aut* or Greek *au* again, both from a Proto-Indo-European root.

A verb in English permits us *to eke out* a bare living, a mere subsistence, from another form of the same PIE root seem in Old English *éaca* and Old Norse *auke.* To eke means 'to grow, to add on, and to prolong by making do.' This is an example of what one of my old English teachers called "the sticky 'n' words." Once, in English, an additional name was called an eke-name. Then people misheard "an eke-name" as 'a nickname' and a new word was born.

I shall be sore sore if you don't bear in mind both *sore* and *eke.*

Chapter 17

Louis: Fascinating Origin of a Common Name

Why so many French names are German! Mon Dieu!

Many, many French given names like Édouard, Gérard, Guillaume, Louis and Richard are pure German in origin. Equally Germanic are thousands of French surnames like Baudin, Géroux, Lambert and Roget.

Uneducated French citizens explode in chauvinist rage when told that indisputable historical certainty and solid linguistic fact. *Mais non! Ce n'est pas possible!* One must remind these persons that the Franks were German. *Ohé*, you know, the people after whom your country is named. Get it? Franks. *Les francs. La France. Français.*

Here's how Wikipedia explains the Frankish diaspora: "The Franks (Latin: *Franci* or *gens Francorum*) were a confederation of Germanic tribes first attested in the third century AD as occupying land on the Lower and Middle Rhine. In the 3rd century some Franks raided Roman territory, while others joined the Roman troops in Gaul. The Salian Franks formed a kingdom on Roman-held soil that was acknowledged by the Romans after 357. After the collapse of imperial authority in the West, the Frankish tribes were united under the Merovingians. During the 6th century they succeeded in conquering most of Gaul. They were active in spreading

Christianity over Western Europe and had created one of the strongest and most stable post-roman kingdoms."

The name *Frank* itself probably stems from a Germanic word for javelin. Compare Old English *franca* and the Vikings' word, Old Norse *frakka*.

Before we reveal the origin of Louis, it is worthwhile explaining compound warrior names in the history of Europe and India.

Compound Warrior Names of the West

The two-part nature of Proto-Indo-European male warrior names is widespread in languages from Sanskrit to the earliest German and includes some Greek given names for males like Thrasyboulos 'he who is bold in planning.' Many Greek given male names did make sense, like Astuanax 'prince of the town.' Sometimes the two morphemes which made up the word created a compound name compelling to reason, as with Nicolas 'victory of the people.' But, more often, compound PIE warrior names were simply macho braggadocio, being simply boastful glory words strung together to provide a studly sound. Remember that the two roots in each Germanic binomial name never HAD to make clear sense; they merely had to be taken from an agreed-upon list of manly "name" roots.

One thinks of the literal meaning of Teutonic trumpet-blast names like Gerhart (Germanic *gar* 'spear' + Germanic *hardt* 'hard' or my given name William from Wilhelm 'helmet of strong will.'

In the given male name Oscar, the root is hidden. Its Old English original was Osgar made up of OE *os* 'any god' + OE *gar* 'spear.' Before the Norman conquest of England in 1066 CE, even the Viking version of the name was in use, that is, the Old Norse form *Asgeirr.*

There are a number of Portuguese, Spanish and Italian surnames like Berengár and Beranger derived from the Teutonic name *Beringar* 'bear-spear.'

King Hrothgar is a character in the poem "Beowulf." His name is composed of the Anglo-Saxon elements *hroth* 'fame' + *gar* 'spear. By means of a French form introduced into England after the Norman Conquest in 1066, this evolved into our familiar modern given name, Roger and its derived surname, Rogers.

The Germanic adjective *–hart* or *–hard* was an extremely frequent component of two-part Teutonic warrior names like Richard. Remember that the two name-making roots merely had to be taken from an agreed-upon list of "name" roots:

Everett or Everard = *Ebur* Germanic 'wild boar' + *-hardt.*

Leonard means 'brave as a lion' from German Leonhard = *leo, leonis* Latin 'lion' + *-hard.*

Nicholas is one of the most popular male given names in the West. Nicholas began as an ancient Greek warrior name compounded of two parts. Nikolas = Greek *nike* 'victory' + *laos* 'people,' hence 'victory of the people.' The *lao- root is found in our English words laity, layman, and lay person. Lay, meaning 'of the people and not of the clergy,' comes from older French *lai* < ecclesiastical Latin *lāicus* < Greek adjective *laikos* 'civilian, common, unofficial,' but literally *laikos* meant 'of the men, of the soldiers, of the people ruled by a prince.' Cognate words appear in Dutch *leek* and modern German *Laie* 'layman.'

Randolph, from Anglo-Saxon *rand* 'shield' + Anglo-Saxon *wulf* 'wolf.'

Reinhart may be construed as *rein* + *-hart,* the German word for pure *rein* + the German word for hard or tough *hart.*' Sometimes the two roots in the name made a kind of sense; for example, it isn't too odd to dub a boy child whom you wish to grow into a warrior with a moniker that means 'pure and tough.'

Richard = *Reich* Germanic 'kingdom' + *-hardt* Germanic 'enduring, tough, hardy.' Some modern English and French surnames began as Germanic binomials, for example, Richard has ancestors like Ricohard and Reichart, comprised of *Ric, Reich* 'power' + *-hard,- hart* 'strong.' Another male warrior name with different roots stems from Old English and became the name Randolph from Anglo-Saxon *rand* 'shield' + Anglo-Saxon *wulf* 'wolf.'

Wolfgang originally meant swift-of-foot or literally 'ran like a wolf,' *Gang* being part of the German verb *gehen* 'to go.' Another way to interpret *Wolfgang* is 'wolf path,' habitual track through the woods taken by wolves.

Louis as Name

Whether pronounced loo-EE in French or LOO-is in English, Louis is what's left after longer Germanic names like Ludwig and its Latinized form Ludovicus have been put through the laundromat of Old French and Norman French, in which process consonants get dropped and vowels get spin-dried. Louis began then as *Hlut-wig* (Ludwig) = Old High German *hlut* 'fame, renown' but literally 'heard' or in its modern descendant English form 'loud.'

The second part of the compound is Germanic *wig* 'warrior,' so renowned warrior is its import, but remember these old warrior names did not have to make literal sense; they just had to sound ferocious or pompous. I would not want some gnarly dude named Hlutwig following me in a dank alleyway. A Normanized form, Lewis, became a popular spelling in Wales and England. Louisa is feminine and a German diminutive Lulu became quite popular in North America among nineteenth-century, German-speaking immigrants.

The first French king Clovis' name is also a form of Louis, and eighteen subsequent French kings bore the name and a few saints as well. King Louis IX was canonized as Saint Louis for all his good work slaying heathens in two crusades.

Famous Louises have included Louis Pasteur, French scientist, Louis Riel, Métis leader who led a rebellion against Canada, Robert Louis Stevenson, Louis Armstrong, Louis B. Mayer of MGM movie fame who began life as Eliezer Mayer and Lou Costello film comedian. Louis-forms sprout in non-Indo-European languages too; in Hungarian Louis is Lajos; in Italian Luigi, in Portuguese Luis, in Swedish Ludde, in Polish Ludwik, in Provençal Aloysius.

Not everyone likes the names glued on at birth. Canadian media guru Marshall McLuhan disliked his own names intensely and said, in his 1964 book *Understanding Media*, "The name of a man is a numbing blow from which he never recovers."

Fervently do I hope you have recovered from your baptismal moniker --- should it have discountenanced in any way your onomastic composure.

Anthroponomastics is the study of personal (human) names from the Greek word for human being, *anthropos*. Onomastics is the study of the origin and history of proper names, from the Greek word for name, *onoma* and its combining form showing the full stem, a Greek genitive case, *onomatos*. That's why etymological citations of Greek nouns often appear as *onoma, onomatos*.

Chapter 18

Turquoise

A mellow word of dulcet resonance

As turquoise shone bluely like a robin's egg, greenly like tropical shallows, through centuries, through millennia, this ornamental gemstone whose finest grades are still treasured, had many English spellings. But one French form won out, *la pierre turquoise* "the Turkish stone." Yes, *turquois* is just the French adjective meaning Turkish.

On his TV travel show, Rick Steves, true to his indolent, mispronounced, sloppy and linguistically ignorant research, tells viewers that *turquoise* meaning "Turkish" arose when French visitors first saw the deep blues of interior tiles at The Blue Mosque in Istanbul. No, little Ricky, believer of folktales, you are wrong, Backpack Breath. Turquoise the color entered European languages well before your gullible burblings attest its onset.

Sold in Turkey, yes; first brought back to Europe by medieval Venetian gem merchants shopping in Byzantine bazaars, yes. But the traditional and chief point of supply of turquoise were mines in the Nishapur district of Iran, once called Persia, where the gem has been mined for more than 2,000 years. Thus one will see it as "the Persian gem" offered by legitimate jewellers. An alleyway peddler of dubious probity may whisper from his shadowed burnoose, "Effendi, look, gaze, Persian blue turquoise. Sooo beautiful. This particular gem is known to the connoisseur as "The Blessed Eye of Allah." But I can let you have it for a mere thirty-five thousand dollars. American, of course, Effendi."

In a non-poetic, physical description, turquoise is, of course, a mere chemical, a hydrous phosphate of copper and aluminum whose formula is CuAl6(PO4)4(OH)8·5H2). Turquoise's only important use is in the manufacture of jewelry and ornamental objects. Copper gives the mineral a blue coloring; iron a greenish turquoise, and zinc a yellow hue. Website color pickers know turquoise as a color command for fonts.

There is an Arabic proverb too: "A turquoise given by a loving hand carries with it happiness and good fortune."

Turquoise is one of several gem words that sound well on the pronouncing tongue, especially accompanied by a rich scroll of other precious stones. With all due lack of humility I confess that I once wrote "of amethyst and turquoise, chalcedony and jasper, of amber and of opal, all met in the jewel-box of Earth."

Chapter 19

Galilee

A Hebrew place name and a pagan god partake in "the end of the ancient world."

Galilee is a large region in northern Israel, mountainous and reasonably fertile. Galilee was the setting for the ministry of Jesus Christ. The Sea of Galilee, the countryside, and the towns — Cana, Capernaum, Tiberias, Nazareth — are mentioned frequently in the Gospels. Jesus himself was called the Galilean, and his disciples were chosen from local fishermen.

The conventional etymology of Galilee suggests that it is derived from the Hebrew and Aramaic *galil* 'ring, circle' hence 'region' or 'surrounding district' or 'province.' The fellow Semitic Arabic name is *al-Jaleel.* But it may, in fact, hark back to a much older West Semitic place name known to the ancient Egyptians as Galulu, with a possibly locative meaning that signified 'North Canaan.'

Other derivations of Galilee suggest it could have sprung from the triliteral Semitic shoresh or verb root, G-L-L 'to roll' so that a Hebrew noun like *Galil* (Galilee) derived from such a verb might mean 'rolling land' or 'hill country' or 'undulant terrain.'

Noted Use of the Word in English

The Victorian poet Algernon Charles Swinburne was perhaps the most eloquent atheist ever to write in English. From Swinburne's "Hymn to Proserpine" comes the most familiar of his atheist apostrophes, one of many that rendered Victorian Christians aghast. "Thou hast conquered, O pale Galilean; the world has grown grey from Thy breath." Swinburne was remembering the apocryphal last words of the Roman emperor, Julian the Apostate, "*Vicisti, Galilaee*" Latin 'You won, Galilean.' Dying during the Battle of Ctesiphon in 363 CE, Julian, avowed pagan, was distressed to know, but nonetheless did know, that Christianity would conquer paganism and become the new state religion of the crumbling Roman Empire. By some later historians, Julian's sentence was taken to mark the final breath of classical civilisation.

The God Pan Dead!

An eloquent quotation embodying this sad knowledge of the end of the ancient world is: "The great god Pan is dead!" In his *Moralia*, Plutarch, Greek biographer and essayist (46-120 CE), tells of a sailor passing by the island of Paxi who heard an otherworldly voice call across the waters, three times, this divine command: "When you reach Palodes, proclaim that the great god Pan is dead." When the sailor obeyed and shouted his message to the islands, from shore he heard lamenting and moaning.

Although this mythic messaging was said to have happened during the reign of the Roman emperor Tiberius, many writers of later antiquity took Pan's death to signal the onset of the end of ancient times.

Enlightenment scribes considered it the first tentative breath of an oncoming and obliterating modernity, after a brief time-out for the "Dark Ages."

Plutarch said, memorably, that Pan was the only Greek god who ever died. His name *Pan, Panos* stems from a Greek verb *paein* 'to pasture.' Among other godly duties, Pan was an old fertility spirit of sown fields, a god of groves and orchards and deer-haunted glens of Arcady. Each year on goaty hooves, Pan piped spring into greening Hellenic valleys. But he never really died. One hundred years after Plutarch wrote, the writer of the one of the first travel guides, the Greek Pausanias, toured all of Greece and found country shrines to Pan beside many a swatch of new-scythed hay, at the mouth of many a holy cave, and Pan altars on the banks of many a rural stream.

For centuries afterward, Pan lived on in Europe where he became The Green Man whose wooden face, set up at the margin of crop fields, was kissed by virgins to bring fertile luck to their father's crops.

Never one to intrude on a virgin's kiss, I shall reverently take my leave, tiptoeing offstage to await the Pan-prompted surge of spring.

Chapter 20

In Praise of Modest Breasts

Real men go ape for big breasts! Many an internet porn site depicts women with freakishly large knockers and delirious male faces with drooling mouths buried in blubbery gazongas. This sexist falsehood is repeated ad nauseam: *Guys want women with hypermammalian hooters and that's the stud truth.*

But is that obsession true of all real men? It is not.

Yet nobody speaks for the male who appreciates modest breasts. Well, this essay does. That is the only reason for this informal mastological jotting, my humble contribution to current boobology. Toxic feminist response-jibes shall be therefore briskly deleted.

First, let us deal candidly with male psychology. The "big stud" who wants to bury his face in voluminous bazooms is actually seeking a return to his nourishing mother's milk. He wants Mommy's titty once more in his widdle mouth. He's an infantile tit-suck, not Paul Bunyan.

Breast Droop

When plastic surgeons meet on a golf course they rub their hands together and hunch over to emit conspiratorial cackles. These happy doctors know that almost every operation of a cosmetic nature which they perform will have to be performed soon again. "Every plasty is a replasty!" they chuckle. No matter how many face jobs and boob jobs they suture upward, gravity wins. Silicone gel migrates downward. The tautest of tucked flesh sags. Hence the number of women who, after a few years of dragging around giant watermelons, want breast reductions.

There is even a weekly television "medical" show in which distraught droopers trudge into plastic surgeons' offices and demand reductive mammoplasty. Some of the preposterously bad breast implants would cause Sir Galahad to lose his breakfast. One observes nipples touching ankles, women pushing their breasts to the doctor's office in wheelbarrows and chrome steel brassieres devised by persons ordinarily charged with the design of suspension bridges. Okay, perhaps I exaggerate? But it is solely for rhetorical purposes.

Ptosis?

Mammary ptosis or breast sagging is a natural consequence of getting old. The rate at which a woman's breasts droop and the ptotic degree depends on many factors, including smoking, number of pregnancies, gravity, higher body mass index, larger bra cup size and significant weight loss or gain.

The other point to cogitate whilst viewing these television "help" shows is your own estimation of the intelligence and moral rectitude of the women who sign up for breast reduction. Very few of those clad in see-through, glow-in-the-dark panties follow the tenets of Mother Teresa. Most look like Las Vegas floozies who do quickies in old phone booths and don't mind if a household pet accompanies Dad. One shady lady I watched on TV, as she whimpered and whined to her plastic surgeon as she bumped into a solid black door, appeared to have the I.Q. of a shucked oyster.

Are "Breast Men" Sick?

Is breast fetishism a disease? Probably not. But note that abnormal psychology has given it a name consistent with other scientific maladies, namely, mastophilia. In several modern manuals of mental disease, breast worship is footnoted as a paraphilia (sexual disorder), in which male eroticism depends on the female partner's breast size to the abnormal exclusion of all other female secondary sex characteristics. To which I would add a few cautionary questions. For example, can Miss Twin Sixty-Fives of East St. Louis actually walk upright and breathe at the same time?

Be honest. Would you want to marry a woman with gargantuan grapefruits and spend your entire life defending your wives' tits from obscene whistles and vulgar hoots by low-browed Blutos and scummy hunks passing by? You would not.

Advice

Therefore the next time some bimbo waggles her casabas in your face, give her a pass. Tell her if you need such udders, you'll visit a cow shed.

Relevant Word Origins

English word *breast* stems from a Germanic root like Old High German *Brust,* probably related to the Germanic verb *burst*, signifying a "burst" of flesh that comprises female mammary glands.

The word for breast in many other Indo-European languages is related to mother words like *mamma* and *mammary*.

English *mother* and Latin *mater* and many similar maternal words contain the worldwide etymon *ma* 'breast' + *ter* an Indo-European agent suffix, so that the etymological meaning of the word *mother* is 'breast-feeder.' For other words ending in the Indo-European *-ter* suffix, look at: brother, sister, daughter, *pater*, *frater*, German *Schwester* 'sister.' The dental *t* sound often alters slightly to become a dental *d* sound, as in the German word for brother, *Bruder*.

Mamma is the formal English medical word for breast. Mamma is a reduplication of the much older Proto-Indo-European root **ma*, breast or mother. This is not only the first sound uttered by many human infants, it may also be the most widespread word root in the world. **Ma* forms the basis of the word for mother in many different and possibly unrelated language families around the world:

- Latin *mater*
- Greek *meter*
- French *mère*
- German *Mutter*
- Russian *mate*
- Icelandic *modher*
- Sanskrit *mata*
- Irish *mathair*
- Welsh *mam*
- Arabic *oum*
- Hebrew *em*
- Swahili *mama*
- Chinese *ma*

- Hawaiian *makuahine* (maka first, beloved < *ma-k Proto-Polynesian, the mother (?) + wahine female, woman)

Why so widespread a word? The sounds of *m* and *a* are among the easiest to make and are often the first sounds acquired by a human infant. The first noise in life associated with deep pleasure may be the sound made by the infant's mouth sucking milk from the mother's breast. This sound is frequently some variant of *ma-ma*. The slight smacking movement of the lips made in uttering an m-sound is similar to the lip movement required to suck a nipple.

But that is merely what the word *mother* means. There is no one way to express all an individual mother signifies. The sum of our sentiment is not contained in or exhausted by a mother's day card. Irish playwright Sean O'Casey, laying on his deathbed, was asked by an attendant what he thought of life. Said the dying man, "I should have kissed her more." So too with our mothers.

Chapter 21

Latin for 'Outdoors' *Foras* Gives English Words Familiar & Unfamiliar, like Forum and Circumforaneous

> "To me the outdoors is what you must pass through in order to get from your apartment into a taxicab."
>
> — Fran Lebowitz

A majority would not agree with Ms. Lebowitz, one of America's funnier agoraphobes. In youth, as we became socialized, many of us found who we were only when we encountered, mingled and conversed with other citizens. The place to do that in ancient Rome was at the Forum.

In Latin, the prime meaning of *forum* was 'what is out-of-doors, an outside space or defined place' derived as the noun is from the adverbs *foras* or *foris* Latin 'outside, out of doors.' Indeed *foris* is cognate with English *door* and its many reflexes like Swedish *dörr,* Dutch *deur,* the common modern German word for door, *Tür* and the ancient Greek *thura* 'door.'

Foras is outside the door of any hut, hovel, abode or habitation however low. Early in Roman history, the Latin word *forum* came to mean a space outside, set aside for people to meet, to market goods, to perform money transactions like loans and to talk politics and perhaps appoint or elect their next king.

Later, during the early years of the Roman Republic, public buildings were erected facing the forum and structures like pleasantly walkable colonnades helped *fora* (Latin and formal English plural of *forum*) become the centers of judicial and public business in most of the great Roman cities. Still later, when emperors ruled Rome, imperial poobahs often vied with one another in the building of sumptuous marbled forums encircled by opulent temples dedicated to one or another of the Roman gods and godlets who thronged a tatty Roman Olympus. One of the most elaborate was the Forum of Trajan which boasted richly patterned vaults over colonnades whose ornate coffering hid the wedged voussoirs that comprised and upheld the arch.

From these sundry uses descend the other meanings of forum in current English: a court or tribunal and an internet site for users to share information or opinions, often on one particular topic.

Forensic

From the Latin noun *forum* proceeds their adjective *forensis* 'public, of a law court' and later our own English adjective *forensic* and its many uses in the technical language of the professions. A forensic autopsy is one conducted at the behest of the police, perhaps to obtain bodily evidence of a murder. Samples from a corpse may be sent to a forensic pathologist. Forensic medicine involves the relations of medicine with the law. A criminal may be convicted on forensic evidence.

Farouche

Now, as always to word-thirsty readers, I offer the cooling chalice of peculiarity, the cold spring water of rarer, obscurer terms. *Farouche,* a borrowed French adjective, enjoyed a brief lifespan in English prose and then waxed obsolescent in the middle of the twentieth century. Novelist D.H. Lawrence used the word and liked its sound. It means sullen in a shy manner which may repel some people.

The farouche peasant lacked all the social graces.

She was a farouche bit of a tart, with not an inkling of polish.

Rarely *farouche* can mean wild, ferocious, untamed.

The disorderly household he entered was a nightmare of farouche child raising, with half-naked, dirty-faced infants crawling across the broken linoleum of the unclean kitchen. How I dislike persons of no means who use poverty as an excuse to give up personal hygiene. I'm trying to plumb this toxic aquifer from which loathing bubbles up and quite overfoams the calm cistern of my tolerance. To date, the probe has been of scant avail.

Farouche stems from a Late Latin adjective *forasticus* 'like a bumpkin, unmannered, having come from somewhere else, exhibiting "outdoor" behaviour not fit for civilized life.' The ultimate root is *foras* 'out of doors,' akin to *foris* or *fores* Latin 'door.'

A Pet Obscurity

Since this is my own word column, I permit myself to include the most obscure verbal delight which questing diligence may discover. Here it is: the wonderfully bloated adjective, circumforaneous (sir-come-for-ANEE-ous). Its literal import is 'sauntering from market to market,' admittedly of limited use in customary English. Circumforaneous is compounded of Latin *circum* 'around' + *forum* market + a common adjectivizing suffix.

But the word's developed meanings, though equally recondite, make it worthy of revival. On the stroll from market to market was an activity thought eventually to indicate criminal behaviour: the wicked thievishness of a varlet or the pert ruses of a quack. This dodgy meaning allows the word to be paired well with others descriptive of villainy and iniquity. For example, I have coined phrases like "the circumforaneous skullduggery of an aluminum siding salesman."

Latin *Foras* Derivatives in Other Languages

Fuori is an Italian adverb and preposition that means 'out, outside.' One thinks immediately of an Italian fire: *"Tutti, fuori!"* 'Everybody out!'

Fuori i Barbari" ("Out with the Barbarians!") was the title of a little anti-German propaganda sheet that appeared in Rome during the Second World War. Every Italian was **not** like Mussolini, kissing kraut ass whenever a Nazi bent over.

An Italian elevator may be *fuori servizio* 'out of service.' A distraught person may be *fuori di sé* 'beside himself.'

Some Outside Spanish

Fuera de in Spanish means 'outside, outside of.'
fuera de límites = "off limits"
fuera de lugar = "out of place"
¡fuera! = get out!
fuera de línea = (computer term) off-line

But now, gentle toe-dippers in the fathomless pool of verbiage, we too are *fuori tempo e fuori dallo spazio* 'out of time and out of space.'

Chapter 22

Down by the Old Mill Stream of Words

Mill in many languages: grinding words like meal, emollient and remoulade

Throughout all the languages that sprang up from our Proto-Indo-European mother tongue, there is a vocabulary item, a reflex of the PIE root *me, like English *meal* or *mill* that first meant 'thing ground up' or, as in *mill* 'place to grind (grain).' Ablauts of the prime root *me are common.

An ablaut is a change of vowels in related words or forms that stem from the same simple root word. Observe some of these ablauts. Modern German has *mahlen* 'to grind.' The occupation name and its common German surname display ablaut: Müller. Dutch *windmollen* was translated directly into English as windmill. Russian has *molot'* 'to grind' and the common Slavic occupational surname Melnik 'miller, owner of a mill.' Classical Latin has *mola* 'a mill to grind grain' and we English have in our mouths *molars* 'teeth whose function is to grind up food.' Italian has the common surname Molinari 'descendant of the miller.' Spanish has *molino* as its mill word and Molina as a surname, both from post-classical Latin *Molina* '*millhouse.*'

America had the deeply regretted president Richard Milhous Nixon, in whose surname his Quaker ancestors tried to disguise the fact of their descent from a common miller by removing some letters from millhouse. It is a familiar ploy among persons ashamed of their ancestral name. One of the most famous alterations in English surname history are those medieval Brits whose last name was Pygge for pig. But that was too stark a reminder of the mucky pen, so their surname became Swine, Swyne, Swoin, and Swehen. That too was infra dig. So by the middle 19th century, the Pygge family had become the Swain family.

The Creole of Haiti has *moulen.*

French has the name of a world-famous Parisian cabaret, *Le Moulin Rouge* 'The Red Mill' shared with the title of Victor Herbert's 1906 mawkish operetta with its Euro-Kitsch plot.

Common French for 'miller' is *meunier* and may appear to be unrelated to our PIE root. But it is. Modern French *meunier* had much earlier forms like *molnier* from street Latin *molinarius* 'operator of a grain mill.'

Classical Greek had *myle, mylos* 'mill, millstone.'

Meal is the edible part of grain ground up in a mill. Note that the word *meal* as 'eating of food' is not from the PIE etymon given above, but from another PIE root, *mel 'measure of time,' so that a meal was in its prime sense 'time to eat.' The word *meal* did **not** originally refer to eating something that was *ground* or *milled* like an edible grain.

Mill

This little word has reductive ablauts (vowel shortenings and changes) from its Germanic cousin *Mühle* which itself appears to be a very early borrowing from classical Latin *mola* 'mill.' The map of Great Britain is mealy with places named after a local mill. Milton has several meanings but one of them is 'farmstead (Anglo-Saxon *tun*) with a mill.' Milford names a place with a mill on a stream or waterway narrow enough for domestic animals to cross the stream or ford it. A pure blast of Old English is found at Millom which is the Old English locative dative meaning "at the mills." Milnrow is 'mill with a row of houses.' There's a British private school named Mylnhurst. *Hurst* means 'wooded hill' and *miln* is the Old English nominative for mill. A bourn is a stream or brook, so Milborne and Milbourne mean 'mill stream.' I remember it as the first name of a wonderful character actor, Milburn Stone, who played the crusty town "Doc'" on the CBS television western "Gunsmoke." Actually his true name was Hugh Milburn Stone but he thought Hugh was too precious a moniker for a surly actor.

Other English Relatives of *Mill*

An **emollient** is something that softens or relaxes animal textures like your skin. Its Latin root is the verb *emollire* 'to soften thoroughly as if it had been ground in a mill to a fine flour.'

An **emolument** nowadays is a monetary reward based on your job or some public office you hold. But in classical Latin *emolumentum* literally was the money you paid the miller for grinding up your grain at the mill.

Multure is a rarer bit of Scottish English referring to the fee charged by the miller for grinding your grain at his mill. It's a contraction of the post-classical Latin *molitura* 'a grinding' based on the Roman verb *molere* 'to grind.'

Rémoulade is my favorite 'mill' word in French but borrowed in English cookery too. It's a cold sauce like mayonnaise often used as a salad dressing and usually made by beginning with the yolks of hard-boiled eggs. Its verbal source may be *remoudre* 'to grind again' referring to how finely chopped are some of the ingredients in this sauce.

Well, Zeke, that's all the grist in my mill for this chapter. Sling that burlap bag of learnin' over that there mule. We gots to skedaddle.

Chapter 23

Tomb & Death Words

Cemetery terms and their origins: barrow, vault, crypt, ossuary, coffin, sepulcher, boneyard, Boot Hill, charnel house, necropolis, polyandrion and grave

Are you **ever** going to hear the word *polyandrion* from an English speaker's lips? Of course not! Then why learn these obscure rarities of English's burial vocabulary? Because, if you are to proceed beyond the monosyllabic simplicities of mere introductory conversation in English, then you must read English of an historical nature, where you shall encounter a vast word hoard and manifold synonyms whose abundant array blesses our language.

I maintain, for example, that you cannot become adept at the construction of magisterial English sentences of power and authority without reading some of Gibbon's *Decline and Fall of the Roman Empire* (where you will encounter the Latin term *tumulus*, a word for the mound of earth heaped over a burial site.) Perusal of several chapters of Lord Macaulay's *The History of England from the Accession of James the Second* (1848) will let you observe sonorous prose bricked in periodical sentence structures by a master builder of words. Likewise, great writers of fiction show the English student how rich, flexuous and diverse an instrument our Anglo-Saxon tongue may be. Reading the novels of James Joyce, Virginia Woolf, Charles Dickens, Jane Austen, George Eliot and Evelyn Waugh will improve your own perhaps dowdy, simple expository prose, even if written and destined to adorn the label of a soup can.

About the succinct expression of crisp wit, a student will learn more by reading the novel *Pictures from an Institution* (1954) by American poet Randall Jarrell than by weeks spent in soporific stupor bent over a how-to-write-and-be-funny text by some vulgar television schlockmeister.

But let us now, reverend noggins humbly bowed, return to the sanctified loam of sundry churchyards.

Cemetery's first meaning was bedroom. In classical Greek *koimeterion* signified 'place to rest, place to sleep, dormitory.' Only in later Christian writers looking for a euphemistic word to describe the grisly underground slots of the catacombs did the Latin borrowing *coemeterium* come to name a sort of 'burial-ground.'

The Greek *koimeterion* and the word *coma* share the same ancient Greek etymon. The Attic word *koma* referred to deep sleep or lethargy. Its full stem *koma, komatos* explains the adjective form *comatose.* Coma is related to Greek *keîmai* "I lie down" and Greek *koimao* "I lay down, lull, put to sleep a child, calm another." Only in much later British pathology did coma mean an unnatural unconsciousness often terminating in death.

Barrow

Naming a mound or hill, barrow is the modern English reflex of the same Germanic root that gives *Berg*, modern German for mountain. By 1000 CE *beorg* also developed a secondary sense of earth mounded over a grave or a pile of stones heaped on a gravesite, a *tumulus* as the ancient Romans would have termed it.

Boot Hill

Beloved last resting place seen in many classic American western movies, Boot Hill was the name of many cemeteries in the Old West. Late in the nineteenth century, Boot Hill became the title of choice for boneyards where gunslingers were buried, pistol-packing poltroons who died with their boots on, that is, died violently, pumped full of hot lead (bullets). The demise of these ornery cowpokes was not a peaceful exitus, abed in bare feet, tenderly tended by loved ones. The very first Boot Hill was at Hays, Kansas about 1870 CE. Wild Bill Hickok was sheriff in Hays in 1869.

Catacomb

This is not a classical Latin or classical Greek term. Naming a long underground vaulted tunnel with side slots for storing the bones of the dead, catacomb did not appear until late in the fifth century and was a specific place name first. For more than a thousand years, catacomb regularly named only one Roman cemetery. The everyday Late Latin name for these subterranean vaults was *cœmeteria* 'cemeteries.'

Cœmeterium Catacumbas was the name of the cemetery of Saint Sebastian just beyond Roman city limits, out along the Appian Way. The other cemeteries were also named for their locations. Modern etymologists think Catacumbas was a local place name, perhaps so old that it predated the Romans and was not even Latin. Various guesses down through the ages have suggested that catacomb might have been street Latin *cata cumbas* 'near the tombs.' Why then would uneducated Romans need to use a Greek preposition in an area that never saw true Greek invasion? Highly unlikely. Another problem: no inscriptional or textual proof of "cata cumbas" is extant. *Cumbas*, of course, would have to be an illiterate misspelling of *tumbas*, formally an accusative plural of the Latin word *tumba* 'tomb.' Funny. No other similar mistaken spelling appears in 1,500 years of Latin epigraphy.

Charnel House

This one creeps into English through French from a Latin word for flesh *caro, carnis*. Think of English derivatives like carnal. Thus it was a house of dead flesh, a corpse room, a mortuary, a cemetery, any burial place. Its unpleasant sound came to taint the very word and speakers of Victorian English shunned it.

Coffin

The corpse box began in fourteenth-century English as a mere transliteration of Greek *kophinos* 'wicker basket, container woven of bulrushes' and its borrowed-from-Greek Latin forms like *cophinus* and *cofinus*. Over the next two hundred years, coffin's developed meaning in English came more and more to refer to the box in which a deceased person was buried.

Crypt

Ancient Romans borrowed *crypta* or *crupta* from Hellenistic Greek where *krupte* meant 'underground vault for burials' from Greek *kruptos* 'hidden, buried, concealed,' part of the Greek verb *kruptein* 'to hide.' Think of related words like cryptic, cryptanalysis 'breaking up hidden codes' and the crypto-Fascist who hides his true Fascist beliefs. Nowadays crypt often refers to an extensive burial place beneath a church or cathedral.

Grave

Its basic etymological sense is 'hole dug' from an Old English verb *grafan* 'to dig.' Compare that with its Germanic reflex *graben* 'to dig' and with German *das Grab* 'grave' and German *der Graben* 'ditch.'

Graveyard

English has the stark, blunt term *graveyard* but, perhaps surprisingly, German becomes evasive and euphemistic by calling its graveyard *der Friedhof,* not, as many Germans think, 'yard of peace' (German *der Frieden* 'peace') but actually a shortening of the phrase *eingefriedetes Grundstück* 'enclosed plot of land.' Although German does have more gruesome, more Teutonic but lesser used synonyms like *Leichenacker* 'corpse field' and *Totenacker* 'field for dead bodies.'

Lych-Rest

This is our most obscure and obsolete graveyard word where *lych* is an older English word for a dead body. Compare its modern German cognate *die Leiche* 'corpse.' Also sometimes heard among rural speakers in Britain is lyke-wake, in which relatives of the deceased keep a watch over the dead body by night, lest the deceased feel too alone. A lyke-wake is usually performed at home, but may take place at a funeral parlour or church.

Necropolis

This is just Hellenistic Greek for 'city of the dead,' applied first as a name for part of the ancient city of Alexandria. Think of other 'polis' words in English: Acropolis, cosmopolitan, metropolitan, police, polity and political.

Ossuary

The operative root is Latin *os, ossis* 'bone.' Classical Latin *ossuārium* was a stone urn or terra-cotta receptacle for dead bones, later expanded in scope to mean a charnel house or cemetery.

Polyandrion

This rarity is used chiefly in texts about ancient Greek history and was borrowed into English from post-classical Latin *polyandrium*, itself snitched from Hellenistic Greek *poluandrion*, literally 'many-people place' from Greek *polus* 'many' + Greek *aner, andros* 'man, male, person.' It referred to a place of burial for many people, as opposed to a solitary tomb.

Sepulcher

Latin *sepulcrum* arises out of *sepultus* 'buried,' a past participle of *sepelire* 'to bury,' cognate with Greek *hepein* 'to care for' and with Sanskrit *saparyati* 'he honors.' A sepulcher (more common spelling sepulchre) is a more-ornate-than-usual tomb or building designated for the interment of an important human or divine body.

The Latin etymon appears in several English words now mostly sunk into the swamp of desuetude near the bog of obsolescence. How many now know that a *gentleman sepult* is one buried? Occasionally some sniffish author will seek a synonym for burial and find sepulture. But his editor will red-pencil the rarity as obscure and therefore offensive to readers. Said editor would never have met Alexander Pope's delicious Englishing of *The Iliad* (1720) "The common Rites of Sepulture bestow, / To sooth a Father's and a Mother's Woe."

Now, fast falls the eventide and our musings may darken as the shroud of twilight brings mortal thoughts. Abide, I say to you, with thine own stern and sceptical counsel concerning tall tales from the ancient Near East concerning life after death or inklings about little angels with tufted winglets, plump-bummed putti in abbreviated white nighties, elevatoring dear Dada up, up, up, into the cerulean ethers of a highly dubious paradise.

Chapter 24

International Words from *Culus*, Latin for 'ass, bum, arse, fanny, fundament, bottom'

Warning: This column contains vivid language as people actually speak it.

The most common English derivative of Latin *culus* 'ass' is from its French version, in the phrase *cul-de-sac* meaning 'dead-end street' or 'blind alley.' When first borrowed into English, cul-de-sac was a term in anatomy 'termination or end of any sack-like bodily part.'

In modern French *cul* is still the word for 'ass.' A note to new French speakers, the l of *cul* is NEVER pronounced. "Kiss my ass!" in French is *baise mon cul!* But French learners, be precise, because: *baise moi le cul* may mean 'screw my ass.' To avoid the slightest anal embarrassment in Paris, polite language best becomes the foreign visitor, always. The least common English derivative is cules, a now obsolete term for the derrière, human buttocks and rump." A cule is one buttock. Though obsolete, the word is worthy of revival. Why, the names of several current politicians who need a kick in the cules spring immediately to mind!

Italian

The Romance languages, that is, all European tongues evolved principally from soldiers' Latin, make use of the Roman word for ass. Its modern Italian form, *culo* 'ass' is one of the most used of Italian vulgarisms. It is part of *vaffanculo,* a contracted form of *va' a fare in culo* (literally 'go do (it) in the ass' meaning 'fuck you!' or 'fuck off! Like all vulgar words, it behooves foreigners to use it carefully. Shouted aloud, *culo* alone can mean 'faggot!' or 'cocksucker!' Very careful use by foreigners is advised.

Culo is frequent in Italian insults too. *Avere una faccia da culo* 'to have an ass-like face' indicates a cheeky braggart. Sometimes it is not an insult but indicates that the speaker considers the person's brazen nature a positive trait. Latin for asshole is, of course, *anus,* also used in English anatomy along with its common adjective *anal.* In modern French, anus is *trou du cul,* also a prominent spoken insult.

Spanish

In Spanish, *culo* also means 'ass' and 'twat' and is popular in many vulgar sayings. While traveling, a certain destination once arrived at may not meet your most fastidious touristic requirements. You may say, quietly, "*Está en el culo del mundo*" 'This place is not merely out in the boonies; this is the asshole of the earth.'

More Spanish

"*Si me sigues molestando, te voy a patear el culo.*" 'If you keep bugging me, I'm going to kick your ass.'

¡Si no cierras la boca te voy a dar una patada en el culo!
'If you don't shut up, I'll give you a kick in the butt!'

"*¡vete a tomar pol culo!*" 'Go screw yourself!'

Lame el culo a su jefe para ascender en el trabajo.
'To get ahead at work, kiss boss ass.'

That's our brief look at *culus* derivatives. Ass me no questions, I'll tell you no lies.

Chapter 25

Platitudes & Clichés: How to Avoid These Stale Words

Constant use of clichés and platitudes indicates a lazy speaker or a stupid writer. My least favorite old chestnut is now rife. I was in a 40-seat restaurant and three seats were occupied. So I attempted to engage the more alert-looking waitress in conversation. The other beldam was slouched in a dark corner of the back kitchen with several needles sticking out of one arm while the other upper limb was attempting to insert a vacuum-cleaner tube into a private portion of what was left of her anatomy. I mentioned the growing difference between the rich and the poor among earthly citizens. "It is what it is," sighed the waitress. Of course, it was eight in the morning and Gloria had been on the job for two long, arduous minutes.

What a graceless, somnolent slug! Customers could see through Gloria's blouse. But they didn't want to.

If I had said, "Your mother was just skewered on a spit over a slow fire and then eaten by several mail carriers," then Gloria would have replied, "It is what it is." That sentence, as a response, is meaningless, semantically void. What such a platitude says to the hearer is, "I'm too tired or too stupid to respond to you." Now, when I encounter that particular hackneyed sentence, I am wise enough to end the conversation, for

I perceive that my interlocutor was either born dead or attained that state quite recently. And if not quite dead, I, casting myself in a rare subsidiary status, shall be most happy to hone his scythe for the Grim Reaper as he prepares his ghastly harvest.

The unending din of broadcast news delivered by moronic writers and announcers who could not wipe their asses if such advice were not on the Teleprompter now condemns radio listeners and TV news-viewers to a trite stew of shopworn thought throughout the day and night. Therefore synonyms for the terms *platitude* and *cliché* ought to be known and be to hand for anyone describing contemporary utterance.

Lack of original expression is the central semantic weight of nouns like banality, maxim, boiler-plate, stale slogan and truism, as well as adjectives like cobwebby, moth-eaten, cookie-cutter, barren, arid and humdrum.

But now and then less known vocabulary items should be used too. Jejune and vapid are apt. *Ieiunus* in Latin meant 'hungry, fasting' and such was the prime sense when the word entered the English vocabulary as jejune in the seventeenth century. But the chief current meaning of jejune is 'not satisfying as thought or speech, insipid (having no taste), scanty, meagre.'

Latin *vapidus* is the adjective of the Latin noun *vapor* whose basic meaning was steam, but in Latin *vapor* was also the essential, inner, animating spirit of a being or thing or process. When this life-stirring vapor had escaped an entity, had skittered out like fetid air from a balloon, then that entity was *vapidus* 'flat, unfresh, stale.' So too are clichés of thought, speech and writing. When met, they are to be vilipended. The chief reason to avoid platitudes is: they are usually dead wrong. Let's examine a few old chestnuts and witheringly stupid bromides. My comment comes afterward **in boldface type**.

- Good things come to those who wait. **So does death, you moron!**
- Time heals all wounds. **I like the switcheroo: Time wounds all heels.**
- Forgive and forget. **Why? When vengeance is such fun!**
- Everything happens for a reason. **If that were true, where would poor illogic rest its tiny microcephalic head?**
- Winners never quit. **Balderdash! Thoughtful winners quit all the time. Observe the wise and graceful retirement of champion sports figures who quit while they are at the top of their game.**
- What doesn't kill me will only make me stronger. **Really? So the car accident did not kill you. It only left you a drooling quadriplegic with the I.Q. of a peach pit. Most would rather be dead.**
- Hard work always pays off. **Yeah. Ask Bernie Sanders.**
- God has a plan for you. **Yeah! You're born, you live, and you go the boneyard. Hallelujah!**
- God never gives us more than we can bear. **So leprosy, dick cancer, crotch rot and bad breath are A-Okay?**

Chapter 26

International Words from Latin *pupa* 'a child's doll'

Words like puppet, pupil of the eye, pupate, poppet, pup, puppy, German verbs einpuppen and entpuppen, French poupée, Vietnamese búp bê and Hungarian báb

Considering how vast English vocabulary is, our language is not manifold in expressions of secondary emergence, as when some inceptive form, some nascent rudimentary entity bursts forth in a stronger, post-primal form. A weak metaphor drawn from insect life is often the best figure of speech we can summon. In entomology a pupa is a life stage between larva and adult, typically a quiescent resting phase during which interior transformation takes place. So we may read: "His life in the provinces was pupal, but when he moved to the city the brittle chrysalis of his talents seemed to burst asunder and explode in boy-like, multifarious joy."

To Pupate versus *Entpuppen*

English has the glum verb *to pupate* 'to change into a still pupal form and lie quiescent and possibly dormant.' But we have no opposite verb to describe breaking forth from the cocoon, a verb like *expupate. German has such a useful verb, *entpuppen* literally 'to de-pupate, to turn out, to emerge from a cocoon and transform into.'

Sich als Betrüger entpuppen 'to turn out to be a cheat'

Leider entpuppen sich nicht alle Maden zu Schmetterlingen. 'Unfortunately not all maggots turn into butterflies.'

Etymology of Pupa

In 1758, Linnaeus, the Swedish father of uniform scientific nomenclature, borrowed the Latin word for chrysalis, which was *pupa*, and began to use it in non-Latin texts of insect study. That's essentially how it found its way into English. Among the Romans, it is likely that Latin *pupa* was what we call a loan translation from classical Greek where one of the meanings of *nymphe* was this stage of an insect's development. For as Latin *pupa* meant 'little girl, little form, doll' so too did the Greek word *nymphe* mean 'doll, sexy young girl, small form.'

But, as a Proto-Indo-European root, the word has many reflexes throughout history. We may speculate (there is no proof) that the PIE etymon is, in its starkest form PIE *pau- 'small, little. The Latin form *pupa* would be a reduplication of the root *paupau which became *pupa*. Now reduplicating a root usually intensifies the meaning of the basic root. So that a pupa was 'a very small thing.' Quite an apt name! Some of the other reflexes of this PIE root appear in words like *few, pauper, pony, pullet, foal,* Latvian *pups* 'teat,' Latin *paucus* 'few' and its Italian and Spanish derivative *poco*. The Latin word for small *parvus* and the Romans' term for child or boy *puer* 'little one' also contain the root, as does the ancient Greek word for boy: *pais, paidos*.

The root may even predate Indo-European. For there it is in ancient Semitic languages! Hebrew *buba* 'doll' gives a common modern Yiddish expression of endearment *bubele* literally 'little doll' but frequently used by parents when speaking with their children.

Even the PIE root has been widely borrowed by languages all around the world. Consider Vietnamese *búp bê* and Hungarian *báb.*

How about the American colloquial "Hey, Bub!" a still familiar form of address for men and boys.

The French word *poupée* 'puppet' is from Latin *pupa* and is also the origin of our English *poppet* 'little child'

Pupil from *Pupilla*

Pupil came into English through French from Latin *pupilla,* literally 'little girl,' but also meaning 'doll, puppet, pupil of the eye.' The proto-Latin root **pu* carried the meaning of young child. *Pupilla* was the diminutive of *pupa* 'girl.' Consider the dozens of other Latin words we know with the same root: *puer* 'boy,' *puellus* 'little boy,' *puella* 'little girl' and *pullus* 'young of an animal, in particular of a chicken' giving us the term *pullet* in English. Puberty and pubic hair are related words. *Pupa* and later Latin *puppa* give many English words, as we have shown above, like pup, puppy, poppet, puppet and to pupate.

The ancient Romans named the pupil of the eye *pupilla* 'little doll face' because, in good light, when you look closely into another person's eyeball, you see a tiny doll-like reflected image of your own face. As they did with so many social and linguistic matters, the Romans may have copied the notion from the Greeks. In classical Greek *kore* meant first 'young girl or maiden,' then the sense was transferred so that *kore* also meant 'pupil of the eye.' Although it seems to be black, the pupil is the opening in the iris by which means light passes into the eye to be processed. Both the Latin and the Greek roots, *pupilla* and *kore,* show up in the technical vocabulary of eye surgery and other areas of ophthalmology (*ophthalmos* Greek 'eye').

This is a Real Eye-Opener

In closing, I offer, in low humblement like the abject toady I am, my own modest but original etymology of that Greek word for eye. *Ophthalmos* is related to the verb *horan* 'to see, to look', one of whose passive infinitive forms is *ophthenai*. But *horan* as a Greek verb of seeing is a complex linguistic artefact, its many tenses and moods and conjugations made up, in stark linguistic fact, of parts of three or four earlier separate verbs of seeing and looking. I believe the form *ophthalmos* may have been influenced by a folk compound like **ope-thalamos,* later contracted and lightly altered into *ophthalmos. Thalamos* was the common ancient Greek word for inner chamber or room inside the house. I think the word for eye and eyeball may have begun as a compound meaning 'the chamber of seeing.' Greek *opsis* meant 'vision, seeing.' The optics of this little etymology seem clear, at least to me.

Well, that's been quite an arduous outing on the word trail. Of course the vista at trail's end brought a lump to my throat, if not to my spine. Therefore I find it fitting to unzip my larval sleeping bag and pupate ever so briefly.

Chapter 27

Alas, Poor Dight!

Once one of the most widely used words in English, *dight* is nowadays obsolete, smothered under the moss of discontinuance. Protracted desuetude has consigned dight to bygone wordbooks brown-spotted with foxing, making the term a timeworn fossil — except for dight's one current poetic use.

As a verb it was first borrowed into Old English as *dihtan* from a Latin verb of many meanings *dictare* 'assert, compose, dictate (for writing/speaking), draw up (a will), fix, order, prescribe, pronounce.' From the principal parts of the verb, as commonly given in the study of Latin, namely *dicto, dictare, dictavi, dictatus*, one may see the Roman verb's many derivatives in English, among them words like (drug) *addict, benediction, contradict, diction, dictate, dictator, dictamen* (a pronouncement), even *ditty!, edict, valedictory, verdict* and *vindictive.*

The modern German verb *dichten* means "to write poetry" with its related agent noun *Dichter* 'poet' and its non-relatives like the common German adjective *dicht* cognate and synonymous with English *thick* meaning 'dense, water-tight, air-tight, closed' etc. Note well that dight is NOT cognate with the common German adjective *dicht* 'thick, close,' a Teutonic husk akin to our English adjective *tight.*

To dight had a similar semantic plethora when it was a common verb in Middle English, from just after the Norman Conquest to the 15th century, from, say, 1067 CE to 1500 CE. Middle English meanings of *to dight* included to appoint, to ordain, to manage, to rule, to deal with, to handle, to inflict, to adorn or equip as for battle, to compose or set down in words. Most important for its final modern use is 'to dight' meaning 'to clothe, to dress, to adorn." *The Oxford English Dictionary* adds this note: "In this sense the past participle dight is used by Sir Walter Scott, and in later poetic and Romantic language it appears to be often taken as an archaic form of decked."

Modern Examples of Use

Instances of *dight* in Modern English, roughly from 1500 CE to the present, include mostly poetic and pseudo-poetic use. Milton wrote of "clouds in thousand liveries dight," by which he meant "dressed." He also waxed rapturous over "storied windows richly dight, / Casting a dim religious light." Here the adjective *dight* means 'decorated.'

Sir Walter Scott, who loved the archaizing use of older English words burbled "But, O! What maskers richly dight," that is, costumed visitors pretty well dressed.

Wordsworth, in a customary paroxysm of his predisposition for verdancy said that "All the fields with freshest green were dight." The fields, we lesser mortals may surmise, were "decked" with green.

Lesser poetasters wrote "There stand the village maids… dight in white" and spoke of "Orion, in golden panoply dight." All dressed! As they say of potato chips.

"She had plenty of time to dight her wardrobe in readiness for the coming winter." To dight = to make ready, to prepare

"I'll just dight the table before I bring you your dinner." Dight = make neat, make ready

William Morris in *The Water of the Wondrous Isles* wrote "She nodded yeasay, and began by seeming to dight the craft for return." That is, prepare the boat for return.

How may modern writers best employ this word? My example takes advantage of its monosyllabic starkness when I write that a recent American election teemed with trailer trash dight in bigotry.

Chapter 28

Meed

An archaic English noun worth reviving

Just how long has *meed*, a noun meaning 'wages, salary, just reward' been obsolete in English prose and conversation? Well, consider this quotation from a personal letter written by Thomas Gray (poet who composed the often quoted "Elegy Written in a Country Churchyard"). Gray was advising a fellow writer: "I think we should wholly adopt the language of Spenser's time, or wholly renounce it. You say, you have done the latter; but, in effect, you retain *fared forth, meed, wight, ween, gaude, shene, in sooth, aye, eschew*, etc.; obsolete words, at least in these parts of the island, and only known to those that read our ancient authors, or such as imitate them." Gray wrote that the word *meed* was obsolete in 1771. Yikes!

Yes, meed was common in bad poetry of the early Victorian period:

"O Wealth! To Misery's claims awake;
Thy meed bestow for Pity's sake!"

Still, I deem *meed* to warrant a revival. It is a sturdy monosyllable of the earliest English (Old Saxon *mede*, akin to Old English *meord* 'recompense, reward'). Its etymology harks back to our mother tongue, Proto-Indo-European, with noble cognates in modern German *Miete* 'rent,' Sanskrit *midha* 'prize,' Avestan *mizda* 'reward,' Old Church Slavonic (archaic Russian) *mzda* 'payment, bribe' and in ancient Greek, from Homer right down to the New Testament, *misthos* 'wages, proper payment for a duty performed, a deed either good or bad.'

Meed has what I may term sonic appropriateness; meed sounds like a just reward for labour, for talent, for service, for prized achievement. Meed may also signify just punishment for bad behaviour, especially if one chooses a biblical mode for the rebuke: "Ignominy be thy meed, for thou hast sinned." True, I don't hear that sentence as a useful modern criticism of some brain-stem who has just mainlined with Comet so he can get "clean." I can hear the offender yelling at you to "go keep watch over your flocks by night, asshole!"

Meed is useful in cheap jokes and puns: "I feel like I meed all the help I can get." Yes, you may deserve it.

"They chose lovely Chryseis as the meed of Agamemnon." And what a bride she was!

"If only she could get her small meed of happiness first!"

"His research had already received its meed of praise from world scholars."

"Had they written for the meed of careful readers' approval, their work would not be so full of careless error."

Yes, nowadays meed in print is usually a mere synonym for 'reward.' But do look the word *meed* up in a comprehensive dictionary. Manifold are its other shades of meaning.

To end on a brief note of disambiguation, do not confuse meed with Mede 'an ancient Persian.' Media was an empire established in the 7th century BCE that included most of present-day Iran. One of my favorite American humorists, S.J. Perelman, punned splendidly upon it: "One man's Mede is another man's Persian."

Chapter 29

Harvest & Autumn: Two Fall Words

Autumn we borrowed from Latin *autumnus* 'the harvest time of plenty.' The ancient Romans deemed autumn related to the verb *augere* 'to increase,' because the crops increase and bestow their yield at harvest time. Some modern etymologists dismiss this explanation as quaint folk etymology. Some think it correct. Yet the newish and authoritative *Oxford Latin Dictionary* marks a relationship to the Latin verb *augeo, augere, auxi, auctus* as "doubtful." The chief problem is the unusual disappearance of that first hard consonant. It is not customary for *auct to dwindle into *aut-*. So autumn may even be pre-Roman, perhaps a time-tweaked husk of Etruscan, a language that preceded the Romans into Latium.

"The Sere and Yellow Leaf"

Others say Romans originally named the fall season *vertumnus* from *vertere* 'to turn,' since it is the season when weather turns from warm to cold and leaves turn or change colour. But the Romans kept getting their seasonal name *vertumnus* mixed up with an old Etruscan god of the seasons named *Vertumnus* (similar in form but stemming from quite different Etruscan roots — we think).

Thus some etymologists claim that the Romans altered the first syllable and made the word *autumnus.* Such a transformation would be unique to Latin word formation. Events that appear to be unique in linguistic history, that lie far beyond the common rules of phonological evolution and deduced derivation, are to be treated with initial caution. It is perhaps best to settle for etymologist Eric Partridge's shrug on the subject of the word *autumn*: 'o.o.o.' — of obscure origin. Fall, now chiefly North American for the season when leaves fall, did begin in England as a synonym for autumn, but in the middle of the sixteenth century.

Sowing Season

A season in Old French, *seson,* was a time of sowing, from the Latin noun *satio, sationis* 'seed-time.' The labels of our seasons like summer and winter are among the oldest words in English, except for autumn.

Harvest is Pickin' Time

Harvest is a modern English reflex of an ancient Proto-Indo-European stem widespread in Germanic and Scandinavian languages. In Old English it was *hærfest* or *hęrfest,* in modern Dutch *herfst,* modern German *Herbst,* Old Scandinavian *haust,* modern Swedish and Danish *host.* The Germanic etymon may have been something like *harbisto-z, perhaps from a root *harb- and that would make it cognate with the familiar Latin verb *carpere* 'to pluck, to pick fruit, to crop' comparable with ancient Greek *karpos* 'fruit, literally 'thing picked, plucked off, cut off' with its many derivatives in modern botanical English like endocarp, pericarpium and that pretty houseplant of the African violet family, streptocarpus.

The Roman verb appears in one of the most commonly quoted scraps of Latin poetry by Horace, *carpe diem* 'pluck the flower of the day's opportunities.' Carpe diem does NOT mean "seize the day!" But see Chapter 27 in my last book, *At the Wording Desk* (Trafford Publishing, 2016).

The Greek word for human wrist is a similar word *karpos* but from an entirely different PIE root, namely *k^{w}erp- 'to turn' akin to Proto-Germanic *hwerbaną 'to turn' and to English *wharf*. That different Greek root gives us English anatomical terms like carpal, metacarpals and carpal tunnel syndrome.

Cognates Ahoy!

The PIE reflexes of the *harvest* root also include ancient India's Sanskrit *kṛpāṇa* 'sword, literally 'cutting implement,' Sanskrit *kartati* 'he cuts' and Sanskrit *krpani* 'shears,' literally 'cutting tool.'

Also cognate is ancient Greek *keirein* 'to cut, to shear, to bind harvested crops into sheaves,' which are crops sheared. This etymology renders all the more apt that splendid old harvest hymn "Bringing in the Sheaves." Since it is one of my favorite hymns, I share the lyrics with you.

"Sowing in the morning, sowing seeds of kindness,
Sowing in the noontide and the dewy eve;
Waiting for the harvest, and the time of reaping,
We shall come rejoicing, bringing in the sheaves.

Refrain:
Bringing in the sheaves, bringing in the sheaves,

We shall come rejoicing, bringing in the sheaves;
Bringing in the sheaves, bringing in the sheaves,
We shall come rejoicing, bringing in the sheaves.

Sowing in the sunshine, sowing in the shadows,
Fearing neither clouds nor winter's chilling breeze;
By and by the harvest, and the labor ended,
We shall come rejoicing, bringing in the sheaves.

Going forth with weeping, sowing for the Master,
Though the loss sustained our spirit often grieves;
When our weeping's over, He will bid us welcome,
We shall come rejoicing, bringing in the sheaves."

That fine old harvest anthem was written in 1874 by Ohio preacher Knowles Shaw, noted composer of gospel hymns and a member of the Disciples of Christ. Shaw got the song idea from his comprehensive knowledge of the *King James Bible*, namely from Psalm 126, verse six: "He that goeth forth and weepeth, bearing precious seed, shall doubtless come again with rejoicing, bringing his sheaves with him."

Our English verb *shear* is akin to Latin *cernere* 'to sift, to separate' and Latin *curtus* 'short, cut short' as in our English adjective for someone too "short" in speech, that is, too curt.

Harvest around the World

Many are the choice words for harvest in world languages. I will give only one especial delight, the Catalan word for harvest is *Tardor*, literally 'the late time of the year' from soldiers' Latin *tardus* 'late,' which through French gives us the English adjective *tardy*. Harvest Home is no new fall celebration. It's been around since the 1570s CE. A harvest moon is a lunar plenitude, a moon that is full within a fortnight of the autumnal equinox.

I save the glowingest jewel in my quote-box for the last, John Keats' "Ode to Autumn." I deem it one of the most perfect short poems in the English language. The English Romantic poet composed the three stanzas on September 19, 1819, after a late afternoon walk through English fields of early autumn. One year later Keats died in Rome. The poem was published in 1820. Keats' personification of Autumn as a deity of the fall season, benign and prone to bestowal of harvest gifts, but at a cost, is superb. Keats' thought and metaphorical dexterity are robed in the richest brocade English offers.

"Season of mists and mellow fruitfulness
Close bosom-friend of the maturing sun
Conspiring with him how to load and bless
With fruit the vines that round the thatch-eves run;
To bend with apples the moss'd cottage-trees,
And fill all fruit with ripeness to the core;
To swell the gourd, and plump the hazel shells
With a sweet kernel; to set budding more,
And still more, later flowers for the bees,
Until they think warm days will never cease,
For Summer has o'er-brimm'd their clammy cells.

Who hath not seen thee oft amid thy store?
Sometimes whoever seeks abroad may find
Thee sitting careless on a granary floor,
Thy hair soft-lifted by the winnowing wind;
Or on a half-reap'd furrow sound asleep,
Drows'd with the fume of poppies, while thy hook
Spares the next swath and all its twined flowers:
And sometimes like a gleaner thou dost keep

Steady thy laden head across a brook;
Or by a cider-press, with patient look,
Thou watchest the last oozings hours by hours.

Where are the songs of Spring? Ay, where are they?
Think not of them, thou hast thy music too,–
While barred clouds bloom the soft-dying day,
And touch the stubble-plains with rosy hue;
Then in a wailful choir the small gnats mourn
Among the river sallows, borne aloft
Or sinking as the light wind lives or dies;
And full-grown lambs loud bleat from hilly bourn;
Hedge-crickets sing; and now with treble soft
The red-breast whistles from a garden-croft;
And gathering swallows twitter in the skies."
After such deft and lyric joy, what insensitive varlet could ever wish for winter?

Chapter 30

Latin & Greek Words & Phrases worth Knowing

Archimime

Here's a suggestion to brighten up burial rites that just might work even nowadays. In ancient Rome, an archimime was an actor, sometimes a court jester, invited to attend funerals of wealthy persons specifically to perform impressions and impersonations of the deceased notable, not usually satiric but rather in praise of the dead person's character. This rare Latin word is mentioned in Suetonius' life of the emperor Vespasian. The Latin term *archimimus* is a direct borrowing from a classical Greek agent noun *archimimos* 'chief actor, leading pantomime artist.'

I see "archimimicry" as an excellent addition to those funerals which contain obituary lines like "Mr. Stenson's demise was a great loss to the hardware industry." To which burbles of bloated praise, I always want to add, "Before or after he stopped selling his daughters into white slavery." My point and firm belief is that 95% of obituary tributes and fulsome approbations are lies, plain and simple. In the same way that most of grief is self-pity, so obituaries do not laud the dead; they praise us, the survivors, who had the good taste and good fortune to have known the deceased. In no way is such mere acquaintance praiseworthy.

Album Græcum

This Late Latin phrase, literally 'Greek white' denoted any distasteful medication, but it referred specifically to dried dog shit, once used to soothe inflammation of the throat.

Ridentem dicere verum

One famous characterization written by the Roman poet Horace comes from his first Satire. The first typifies his facetious manner: "*ridentem dicere verum / quid vetat*" 'What's wrong with someone laughing as they tell the truth?' (Sat. 1.1.24-25)

Apaideusia?

Know-nothing dropouts who disparage all education might pay heed to this little adage by the ancient Greek philosopher and mathematician Pythagoras: *apaideusia ton pathon meter* 'A lack of education is the mother of all suffering.'

Astra castra, numen lumen

This Christian praise of self-denial means "the stars are my camp and God is my lamp." It means that true faith does not require even a roof over one's head "for the Lord will provide all you need." Such a proposition may be dubious to a true believer recently forced to set up household in a culvert.

Pindar calling!

Many consider doubt about who and what we humans are to be strictly a modern malaise. But check out an ancient Greek poet's existential fretfulness: 'What is a person? What is not a person? Man is but a dream of a shadow,' wrote Pindar somewhere around 500 BCE.

In his *Pythian Victory Ode # 8*, Pindar nevertheless held out hope for a moment's splendour, but only if you were a prize-winning jock. Athletic achievers rejoice. All others join the loser's line.

"Creatures for a day! What is a man?
What is he not? A dream of a shadow
Is our mortal being. But when there comes to men
A gleam of splendour given of heaven,
Then rests on them a light of glory
And blessed are their days."

On guard!

Qui omnes insidias timet in nullas incidit.
'He who fears every ambush falls into none.'

In other words, in the long run of reasonable security surveillance, keeping one's guard up is always worth it.

Roman Reading is Good for You

Ubi vivit latinitas, ibi viget humanitas
My translation: Where the study of Latin lives, there too thrives civilized learning.

Chapter 31

Meta-, Metaphysical & Their Manifold Meanings

What's in this chapter? A brief discussion of how the prefix meta- is used in inherited Greek words in English science and everyday linguistic use, emphasizing the use and changing meaning in English of the adjective metaphysical. What does metaphysical really mean? Find out here.

A number of my readers claim interpretive confusion concerning the common prefix *meta-*, as it appears in many English words borrowed through French and Latin from Greek, words like *metamorphosis, metaphysics and metaphor*, plus modern uses of the prefix in 20th-century coinages like *metalanguage.*

American students in first-year college or university courses score very poorly on words like *metaphysical.* They vaguely know that cancer can metastasize but they can't clearly define metastasis. So let's make clear the precise meaning of some *meta-* words right now.

Metaphysics

Metaphysics is the philosophical study of basic principles of reality or things, e.g. first causes of time and being.

The Greek roots are *meta* Greek preposition 'after' + *physika* 'physical things' from Greek *physis* 'nature, what is natural.' The Greek verbal source is *phyein* 'to make, to do, to produce. The Greek verb is cognate with the same Proto-Indo-European base that produced our English verb, to be.

Metaphysics, as a word, has the simplest of origins. *The Metaphysics* was a medieval title of a work by Aristotle. It was named *Meta ta physika* "AFTER the physics" because Aristotle stated that physics should be taught first in philosophy classes and then *after physics*, the instructor should move on to teach ontology, the study of how and which things have being and existence. Again, that study ought to come "after physics,' thus the next part of philosophy was referred to as metaphysics.

The basic sense of *meta-* in Greek is 'after, together with, across,' a match for some of the meanings of the Latin prefix and preposition *trans* 'across.' The earliest English use of *meta* is in borrowed Greek words with a meaning of 'change' like metamorphosis, whose literal sense is 'the act of changing in form,' very like the Latin-based borrowing *transformation*. Latin *forma* = Greek *morphe* 'form,' and the two words may be cognate, this is, sprung from the same Proto-Indo-European root.

Metaphor

Another early borrowing was the word *metaphor*, a figure of speech that compares two things without using 'like' or 'as,' for example, metaphorically, "In battle, the general was a lion." The comparison becomes a simile if *like* or *as* is used: "The general in battle was like a lion." The idea occurs in the ancient Greek word itself *metaphora* = *meta-* 'across' + *phora* 'carrying' (o- grade of the verb *pherein* 'to bear, carry'). The sense of courage and forcefulness in the word 'lion' is 'carried across' to the behaviour of the general.

Latest Use of *Meta-* in New English Words

College students frequently encounter and are flummoxed by technical terms like metalanguage. No need for such confusion exists, once you understand the most modern use of the prefix. In such freshly created words, *meta-* may mean 'with a subsequent development of the original condition suggested by the unprefixed word.' Thus there is *language* and, in the vocabulary of modern logic and linguistics, the term *metalanguage*. Metalanguage, coined in 1936, is a language or set of rules used to express data about or discuss or study another language.

Metastasis

The medical word *metastasis* (pronounced muh-TAS-tuh-sis) perhaps began this use of *meta-*. In ancient Greek *metastasis* first meant 'removal, change.' Its primary use in 16th-century English was as a term in rhetoric signifying the change from one figure of speech to another. It is still used in this way, though rarely.

In modern oncology (the scientific study and treatment of cancer) metastasis names the spreading of cancer from a primary bodily site to a new or secondary site. So a metastatic lesion would be a new cancerous growth at a site different from the original. Nodal lymphatic cancer in an armpit might spread to the chest. It might metastasize, to use the verb. Such malignancies may spread via membranes or blood.

Metaphysical

Return now to the adjective *metaphysical*, which has a long history in English of developed senses. At first it meant 'concerning philosophical speculation, of an intellectual endeavour.' Then it developed a pejorative sense of 'too high-falutin', too airy-fairy, too philosophical by half.' In the twentieth-century philosophical pursuit named logical positivism we can discern another meaning, best done by quoting from one of its great tomes modestly entitled by its author, A.J. Ayer, *Language, Truth & Logic*: "We may accordingly define a metaphysical sentence as a sentence which purports to express a genuine proposition, but does, in fact, express neither a tautology nor an empirical hypothesis." Oh.

In literary studies of 17th-century English, we encounter the **Metaphysical Poets** like John Donne and Andrew Marvell who used complex English and tricky imagery to express abstract ideas.

The **Metaphysical Painters of Italy** named a group of early-twentieth century Italian artists like De Chirico and Morandi who used strange alterations of normal perspective and odd images to impart a dreamy unreality to their works.

The word *metaphysical* may have a general sense in which it is synonymous with adjectives like 'supernatural, imaginary, incorporeal, immaterial, lying beyond the present laws of science.'

We conclude with a few pithy quotations containing our word for today.

"In some mysterious way woods have never seemed to me to be static things. In physical terms, I move through them; yet in metaphysical ones, they seem to move through me."

John Fowles

"(Emily) Dickinson is my hero because she was a joker, because she would never explain, because as a poet she confronted pain, dread and death, and because she was capable of speaking of those matters with both levity and seriousness. She's my hero because she was a metaphysical adventurer."

Helen Oyeyemi

"For me, Moby-Dick is more than the greatest American novel ever written; it is a metaphysical survival manual–the best guidebook there is for a literate man or woman facing an impenetrable unknown: the future of civilization in this storm-tossed 21st century."

Nathaniel Philbrick

"All good children's books, I think, address metaphysical issues in some kind of way."

Duane Michals

"I think that when a film does its job, it poses questions rather than gives answers. It should act as a frustrating counselor who, at your bidding for advice, says, "What do you think?" I think that's some of what the culture critic Greg Tate meant by art leaving a "metaphysical stain."

Aunjanue Ellis

Chapter 32

Foison, Stook, Shock, Haycock and Stover

A bounty of autumn words

A second harvest of autumn words so soon after the initial gathering-in. Yes! For English possesses a surplus of fall terms. Autumn's mellow advent arrays her wares: fair fall weather of a fall fair, crisp polychrome of maple leafage, rusting fern fronds, bristling blades of grass, chrome-yellow bracts encircling vanished flowers. These come to the eye.

But some autumnals come to the lips: ripe pears, plum juice on chin, malic flesh of apples, haws and hips, grains and seeds, pomes and drupes: plump flauntings of October fruitage.

Other fall gifts come to **mind**, namely, ingathering of the words of early autumn; and chief among these for me is *foison* which still means 'plentiful harvest.'

Foison

Pronounced FOYZ-un, this word of autumn bounty is now, unfortunately, marked archaic or old-fashioned in most dictionaries. Foison came into English after the Norman Conquest of 1066 CE and means 'plentiful harvest.' Its root is Old French *foison* 'pouring forth (of crops)' ultimately from Latin *fusio, fusionis* 'a pouring' from the Latin verb base *fundere* 'to pour,' which gives us many derivatives in English like *confound, confute, to fuse together, nuclear fusion, futile, perfuse, profound, refund* and *transfusion.*

Foison's earliest meanings in English made it a simple synonym for abundance. In Scotland, until well into the 19th century, foison signified strength and vigour: "He's a **wee** man, wi' nae foison in him."

I like the word *foison* and feel it ought to be revived and be available for use, as in these three exemplary sentences from my pen:

"That year, lucky weather, hard work and the generous foison of the apple crop saved the orchard from financial distress."

"A foison of mutual happiness swept their marriage through a thirty-year voyage."

In ancient Roman religion, one of the earth goddesses of fertility was *Ops* (Latin *ops, opis* 'abundance, goods, riches') whose annual foison included late harvest and whose sceptre was often one fat stalk of cobbed corn.

Stook

This word naming a style of drying grain like wheat in the field is chiefly British. *The Merriam-Webster Unabridged Dictionary* provides a good, clear definition "a pile or assemblage of usually 8 to 16 sheaves of grain (such as wheat) set up in a field with the butt ends down and one or two of the sheaves often broken to serve as a cap to protect the tops from weather." But that definition is in M-W under the American term for the same harvest technique, *shock.* Yes, this shock = stook. Teutonic *stook* stems directly from a Middle Low German form like *Stuke* 'pile, tree stump, sleeve.' To stook is the verb. It was widely used in Canada. I've never heard it from an American wheat farmer.

A Shock of Wheat

The American term is British in origin and appears to have been first an actual counting of the number of small wheat shafts or even small sheaves combined into a shock. This shock was borrowed into English from Middle Dutch where *schoc* and *schocke* mean 'group of sixty,' hence any 'big pile' or 'heap.'

Haycock

This obsolete British term names a cone-shaped pile of wheat in the field but is apparently stacked differently than a stook is formed.

Stover

This plucky word is now confined chiefly to British dialects but once it named any fodder for cattle collected from a field after harvest. Sometimes stover was stubble from such fields mixed with hay splinters from a threshing-floor, clover-hay and straw or dried cornstalks. I have heard it in England also said aloud by a mother to answer a small child's question: "What's for tea, Moom?" "For the likes of you? Stover!" Tea in southern England is our supper.

Etymology of Stover

First we need to define a term in linguistics that names how a short, unaccented vowel at the start of a word is, in many languages including English, often lost. This is called aphesis. Stover is an aphetic result of *estovers*, an English word borrowed from Anglo-French. Its English pronunciation is es-STOV-ers. So you can see how that initial, short, unstressed 'e', called a schwa, might go unspoken. In Old French *estover, estovoir* meant 'to be necessary' so that English *estovers* were 'necessary things,' just as fodder for livestock was a necessary commodity. The Old French form issued from a Late Latin phrase *est opus* 'there is need' or 'it is necessary.'

Chapter 33

Disfluency

You too commit disfluency. It's a newish technical term in phonology used when analyzing speech. Disfluency names a spoken ploy most of us utter every day. Disfluency is inserting short spacer or filler sounds into a sentence when you can't immediately come up with the next word. For example, *He is the…uh… um…head of the group. His proper corporate title is…you know …darn…use it very day…mmmm…oh…yes! Vice-President in Charge of Public Excuses for Our Continuing Poisoning of the Planet Earth So That Our Executives May Purchase That Third Summer Home on Tahiti.*

Saying um or uh is disfluent. Your fluency in uttering an unimpeded English sentence is very temporarily compromised. For once, I approve of the definition given in a Wikipedia article: "Speech disfluencies are any of various breaks, irregularities, or non-lexical vocables that occur within the flow of otherwise fluent speech." Under that definition, would Homer Simpson's moronic "Duuhhh" qualify as a non-lexical vocable?

My favourite quotation about disfluency is a pun: "to uh is human but unforgivable!" The punster, whose name is unknown to me, is playing with the famous line by English poet and satirist Alexander Pope (1688-1744 CE) "To err is human, to forgive, divine" from

Pope's "An Essay on Criticism." Popey himself was recalling the famous Latin tag *errare humanum est,* 'it is only human to make a mistake' first enunciated using slightly different phrasing in *The Sermons of St. Augustine of Hippo* who lived from 354 to 430 BCE, in *Sermones* 164, 14.

A disfluency or filler can be used as a pause for thought. But more often disfluency is the vocal clue that tells the listener no mental activity worthy of the name *thought* has ever occurred north of this particular jabbering mouth.

For the first several centuries of studying human sounds, this wee morsel of phonology lay neglected and forgotten in the cabinet of vocal curiosities. But recent advances in neurolinguistic brain-mapping have shown disfluency's importance as a marker in cerebrovascular accidents (strokes) and as evidence in elderly patients of memory decline and other verbal symptoms of senility.

Disfluency as Euphemism

Disfluency is used by some doctors and lay persons as a coy cover-up to mean 'stuttering.' It is always a bad idea to coat a clear word like *stutter* with the gummy veneer of periphrastic weasel terms designed to rob words of their factual meaning by hiding behind creepy substitutions that soften the hurtful meaning.

When any part of language devolves into suckababy goo-goo talk, all language and meaning are in danger. People who stutter, stutter. They don't undergo "disfluence;" they are not articulation-challenged, they are not "subdued by unwanted laryngospasmic hesitancies." Bull! Stutterers and (in Britain) stammerers gulp and swallow their tongues when trying to say "Get Gilbert a grape." So let's obtain help for them from speech pathologists and science, not becloud the name of their symptoms in a glutinous fog of pseudo-clinical euphemism.

Here is another cogent reason to not use the term *disfluency* as a synonym for stuttering. All speakers are disfluent at times, especially under brief time spans when they are nervous, stressed, tired out or pissed to the gills. Sometimes too the words they seek to enunciate are too tricky or complex for them. However, stutterers pause more often and display interruptions and hesitations of quite different kinds than non-stutterers do. Medical terminology has enough clarity problems without tossing into its churning waters terms which arrive compromised with dual or triple meanings from fields outside medicine.

But Note: There IS a Medical Term for Stuttering

In the English language, for about one hundred years, there was a now obsolete medical term for stuttering, the modern Latin *balbuties*, along with its learned adjective *balbutiant* 'stuttering' and its rare verb *balbutiate*. But, as a witty phonologist friend of mine said, "It's too hard to say."

Although the Latin word *balbuties* died a lonely death in English from non-use, the root is still alive in modern French, where *balbutier* means 'to stutter' and is the second most common verb used for that meaning, the most used French verb being *bégayer*. The ancient Roman adjective was *balbus* formed, apparently long before Rome in Proto-Indo-European, in onomatopoeic imitation of someone stumbling over a word containing several b-sounds.

Etymology of dis + fluency

Dis is a common Latin-derived prefix which several related senses, but used here in a strictly privative sense that negates the meaning of the noun or verb to which it is attached, as in nouns like *discontent* and *discontinuance*, and in verbs like *displease, dissuade, disconnect* and *disown*.

Fluency is from Latin *fluentia*, one of a large number of Latin abstract nouns of process or action, formed on the present-participial stem of a Latin verb, in this case, the verb *fluere* 'to flow,' so the evolution of the word looks like this: Latin *fluere* 'to flow' > Latin *fluentem* an accusative singular form of the present participle 'flowing' to show the word-forming full stem > Old French *fluencie, fluency* > Modern French *fluence* > English *fluency.*

Oddly, the Latin verb *fluere* 'to flow' is NOT related to the Germanic root in our English verb *to flow* (Germ. root *flô), but to flow, of course, is the usual translation into English of the Latin verb. Another common English word from the Germanic root is *flood.*

Fluere is a Latin reflex of a Proto-Indo-European root *ple which gives Greek *ploein* 'to swim, to float' and *plotos* 'floating, navigable.' Or the PIE root may be *plou/pleu/plu 'get wet, be in water' giving words like Sanskrit *plu* 'to swim,' Greek *plein* 'to sail,' Greek *plunein* 'to wash,' Latin *pluit* it rains, and Modern French *la pluie* 'the rain.'

On that pluvial droplet of knowledge, we shall — ever so briefly — continue drawing refreshment from the wellspring of words.

An email from the department of Philosophy, Psychology and Language Sciences, University of Edinburgh

"Hi,

. . . Disfluency is one of my research interests. Intrigued to see whether you have any etymological insights on disfluency vs. dysfluency -- the field tends (not very consistently) to use the former as you describe, and the latter to signify pathological speech problems (stuttering, aphasia, etc.). I believe the dis/dys distinction is also made in other areas (dispraxia/dyspraxia, for example).

Bill Casselman responds:

I don't have any insights except temporal. The *dis-* suffix is Latin and the *dys-* is Greek. Suffixal *dis-* predominated in the earliest scholarly borrowings into English scientific vocabulary from Classical, Late and Medieval Latin. The Greek *dys-* borrowings and neologies come much later, occurring sparsely during the Age of Enlightenment and burgeoning in the late nineteenth century and positively pullulating throughout the twentieth century.

Chapter 34

Caveat Emptor, Pre-Empt, Emption & Related Words

One of the Latin phrases commonly known by literate English speakers and writers is: *caveat emptor* 'let the buyer beware.' Less known are some of the other English derivatives of the Latin verb *emo, emere, emi, emptus* 'to purchase, to buy.'

For example, to pre-empt (either with or without the hyphen as preempt) 'to take action to prevent something from happening.' The governor's mollifying speech pre-empted a riot by the prisoners. But the most common current meaning of pre-empt is 'to replace one television show by another': News of the landing on Mars pre-empted all the regularly scheduled programs.

The original sense of pre-empt was 'to buy something before anyone else has a chance to buy it,' from classical Latin prepositional prefix *prae-* or *pre-* 'before, in front of' + *emere* 'to buy, to purchase.' Pre-empt was not known to ancient Romans but was made up out of Latin roots by English speakers in the middle of the 19th century. There is, of course, an agent noun *pre-emptor* 'one who or that which pre-empts.'

Not Empty

Disambiguation: Our English adjective *empty* is NOT derived from Latin. Empty is an adjectival form, much altered, derived from an Old English noun *ǣmetta* 'leisure, freedom,' and empty's first sense belonged solely to a person and meant 'at leisure, free, not occupied.' The excrescent *p* after *m* further obscures the true root but was a not uncommon infix used to ease and speed up the pronunciation of certain English words. If such an insertion removed the need for a time-consuming, enunciation-pausing glottal stop in the midst of a word, then it was all the more readily added.

Later in the history of our language the word *empty* broadened its semantic scope and came to be applied to objects, giving the term its current modern use "The cows were in the field and so the barn was empty."

Emption

This word is still active in English law, in a contractual phrase like 'right of sole emption' which assigns the unique privilege of selling something to a specific person or entity. The word's root is classical Latin *emptio, emptionis* 'act of buying, deed of purchase.'

Redeem & Redemption

Redemption too began with a legal sense which it maintains. Redemption was the right at law to buy back something you had sold. Its roots are Latin *redemptiō redemptiōnis* = prefix *re-* 'again, yet, still' + euphonic *d* + *emere* 'to buy.' Euphonic *d* is inserted to prevent two vowels from having to be pronounced together and thus making necessary a glottal stop, an opening and closing of the glottis to expel breath for the second vowel sound. Putting a hard consonant between the vowels eliminates the need to use a glottal stop and makes the word quicker to utter. To the ancient Romans a redemption might be 'purchase of a contract' or 'a ransom' or 'a bribe to a Roman official to change a guilty verdict.' Later, in the virtuous and holy times of the Roman Catholic Church, *redemptio* was the act of forking over some sesterces (money) to a priest or bishop to receive paid forgiveness of your sins.

To redeem had a prime meaning in Late Latin (*redimere*), Old French (*redemer*) and early English of: to be delivered by God or Christ from the stain of sin --- should the sinner have the scratch to pay off the priest.

To conclude, I'll return to *caveat emptor* 'let the buyer beware.' The Latin verb is: *caveo, cavere, cavi, cautus* 'to take heed, to be careful, to beware.' As you can see clearly, its past participle *cautus* bequeaths to English words like *precaution* and *caution.*

Barking & Biting

Even the ancient Romans owned yappy mutts. Thus archaeologists have found carved into the sides of stone walls facing old Roman streets the warning: *cave canem* 'beware the dog.'

Caveat Predator!

Finally here are two useable variations on *caveat emptor.* You might headline a review of a very bad book: *caveat lector* 'let the reader beware!' There are in English more than 1,000 agent nouns ending in –tor, words borrowed from Latin. How about an anti-bully sign for civilized people *caveat apex predator* 'let he who ruthlessly preys on all others beware!'

Chapter 35

LOBBY ROBOTS

What bad parents want

Attention, middle-class parents! Could your kids grow up to be Lobby Robots? I've had to coin that new phrase: Lobby Robot.

Many well-to-do parents are engaged not in child nurture or helping their children enter a complex world by making sure their kids are analytical, compassionate yet critical of the world's dense deception. No, trendy parents seek to raise what I call LOBBY ROBOTS.

These are well-behaved, fashionably dressed little automata of serenely unblemished complexion, sufficiently athletic to make the high school basketball team, attending church several times a year but not out-of-control Christians with an excess of sympathy for the poor or unlucky. Eek!

If a stern parent catches their offspring in an unguarded moment of self-knowledge, even looking in a mirror, or writing a simple exploratory paragraph in Grade Seven entitled "Who Am I?" two punishments occur. Quickly the commissioning teacher is fired. Secondly the child is slapped hard, so that he or she may repent of their obscene need for any sort of attentive perception of who morally and spiritually they are.

Later, in their maturity, unless they have memorized the "compendium of acceptable corporate thought," lobby robots are devoid of the slightest personal opinion and never wear loud neckties or too-high skirts. They vote for the conservative politicians whom "everyone ought to vote for."

They clank to work each day, perfectly at home greeting clients in the lobby, where they never burp or fart or commit the atrocity of an independent thought. Is the company gouging sick people with obscenely steep drug prices? "Well, after all, Tiffany, it **is** business." "Sure, Fred, but think of all the R&D years in our ophthalmology lab testing that drug. Our sand-based eye salve, for example, was tested for more than three minutes on blind gerbils! The cages! The lab fees! Just catching those little rascals! I mean, come on!"

Early in their "junior executive learning module" (translation: childhood), lobby robots learn to distrust the suggestion that humans may have evolved to practice mutual support. The very idea that humans ought to help one another is "communism!"

Likewise early demonized are unions and any significant profit-sharing. Letting manual laborers and factory workers participate in corporate financial gains is socialist nonsense. Yes, executives should have four homes, but workers? None. What do you think DynoSlime Consolidated is running here? A damn welfare paradise?

Did you know that large companies blackmail news media into running anti-union stories? Corporations do this by threatening to cancel media advertising unless the news outlets flood their pages and broadcasts with insights into how evil unions are. Imagine entities believing that everybody should share in profits! Will these commie bastards never stop?

When mating time finally dampens their expensive undies and leaves tell-tale spatterings on the boy's duvet, the lobby robot seeks a mate. Sought spouses must arise from strictly similar economic backgrounds. Your true lobby robot does not want a link-up, carnal or otherwise, with some low-class climber who was scrambling up the splinter-runged ladder of success from a family where the father may have worked as a janitor in a hammer factory. Ye gods! How *infra dig*! As for choosing mates from among the pullulant hordes of "our tinted brethren," no thank you! Puh-leese, white only at a white altar!

The parents of potential lobby robots keep an alert eye on their sullen progeny. If, at the play-park teeter-totter, their spawn display early signs of an easy corruption, parental eyes sparkle. Let's say Dad sees his young Lloyd spritz bug-spray in the eyes of the little pitcher on the other baseball team. Says a proud-as-punch Dad, "My Lloyd could be a rich lawyer. There's nothing low-class about standing in hospital corridors outside the operating room and handing out business cards as what's left of your Mom after the accident is wheeled past on a gurney in three separate HRPs (human remains pouches). It's no sin! After all, most of us will see the inside of a body bag for at least a few post-mortem moments. Is such behaviour sleazy, scummy, and steeped in a squalid greed papered over by a law degree? No, indeed. There is, in fact, a certain nobility of defined purpose in chasing ambulances, and my Lloyd is just the little lobby robot for the job."

Every lobby-robot parent knows the meek will not inherit the earth. They will eat it. Dirt, that is.

The evidence from early psychometric testing is clear: human children are not born with inherent compassion. Parents must teach their kids to have a conscience about others, to display compassion. What police and psychiatric workers often find is that, for the lobby-robot psychopath, other peoples' feelings are not real. One of the truest, most loyal types of employee is the lobby-robot psychopath. He's real. His company is real. His boss is real. But persons external to the company are not real. Most of his coworkers don't have real feelings either. So when Lobby Robot uses the company snitch phone and rats on "those other people", well, that's okay, because his coworkers don't really, really exist. They're phonies. They don't have a real soul or deep feelings like Lobby Robot. As for the young children poisoned by the company's new drugs which were rushed to market before proper testing, that's okay too. They weren't real children, like the psychopath's. Why, some of them don't even live in our neighbourhood. Their parents were not able to buy Lexus SUVs, so we don't talk to them.

Lobby robots have thin skin. Under their sullenly pulsing epidermis (for your true lobby robot resents heartbeats as a possible waste of corporal-corporate energy) one may glimpse the zomboid Gollum within, its etiolated fingers clutching "the precious."

I don't want to conclude here by waxing fascist. But what I'd like to see in front of each entranceway to a company HQ are plywood recanting booths in which lobby robots would undergo obligatory retraining and could not enter the workplace until they'd aced Compassion 101.

Chapter 36

Hope as a Word & as a Mode of Mind

Galileo the great astronomer wrote: "I've loved the stars too fondly to be fearful of the night."

This brief essay is about the English word *hope* and a short note about this Albert Camus quotation: *«Au milieu de l'hiver, j'apprenais enfin qu'il y avait en moi un été invincible.»* 'In the midst of winter, I finally learned there was in me an invincible summer.'

Thesaurus and dictionaries often list many synonyms for the noun *hope*, but, in light of the strict meanings which the word *hope* must have, it enjoys few precise synonyms.

Longing isn't hope. Anticipation isn't hope. Dreaming isn't hope. Aspiration isn't hope. Promising isn't hope.

Hope that does not encompass despair (non-hope) is usually mere drooling nostalgia for the numbness of childhood's "feeling safe with Mommy and a large lactating breast nearby." But that's not hope; that's infantile dependence. Still, it is all many people ever experience of life's horse race of expectation.

Instead of my usual listing of obscure — sometimes delightful — synonyms, I deem hope best presented here by means of a highly personal definition. Hope is a term to be leery of. Consider some of the skeptical but apt quotations, including the old proverb: "Hope makes a good breakfast but a poor supper."

What is hope? Nothing but the paint on the face of existence; the least touch of truth rubs it off, and then we see what a hollow-cheeked harlot we have got hold of.
Lord Byron

Hope springs eternal in the human breast;
Man never Is, but always To be blest
Alexander Pope – An Essay on Man

He that lives upon hope will die fasting.
Benjamin Franklin – Poor Richard's Almanack

He that lives in hope danceth without music.
George Herbert – Outlandish Proverbs

In *The Divine Comedy* what did Dante see written above the portals of Hellmouth? *Lasciate ogni speranza, voi ch'entrate.* 'Abandon hope, all ye who enter here.' Some think a better positioning of that statement might be above the human birth canal.

Let's say that hope expects. It awaits some stated or thought *desideratum* 'thing desired.' But hope is not wholly apprehended as a mere mixture of expectation and desire. Hope nudges in a pushy manner and whispers into the ear of Fate, "I'll get what I want, right? Right?" Hope is bumptious. Hope is a bold, dick-wagging braggart, often a liar. Hope says, "Sure, pal, you'll get what you want." Then, when it's time to deliver the goods, Hope leans in close and confides, "Uh, the transport truck with all that stuff you wanted? Never arrived at the depot! It was hijacked." Thanks, Hope.

Typically Teutonic, this Saxon and Low German etymon seems to have begun in the fetid mass of the earliest Germanic dialects and to have spread into later Scandinavian languages from there.

Camus Quotation

My personal motto of hope was written by Albert Camus in his 1952 book of essays entitled *Retour à Tipasa*. Tipasa was a place beside the sea in his native country of North Africa, Libya. Tipasa was old Roman ruins on a sea cliff beside the Mediterranean, where a youthful Camus once found a reflective solitude. Camus revisited this site of his boyhood imaginings after living in Europe for decades. He went hoping to relive childhood dreams and feelings. The ruins of ancient Tipasa had not changed, yet the thoughts and hopes of boyhood would not return. **Camus learned to analyze hope.** Camus had changed and had to work hard to recover an optimism. That's when he wrote "In the midst of winter, I finally learned there was in me an invincible summer."

A later essay by writer Anthony Lyon explains it well: "The sentence, like much of Camus's most evocative writing, is double. It moves between the natural world and his inner ethical life. He's in Algeria in winter, but he's also been struggling with a moral winter. He'd lost the passion that animated his speaking out on behalf of the suffering. This moral winter, like the rainy December in Algiers, gives way to a day of sunshine, a reminder of the summer to come. For Camus, the summer is a constantly renewing source of strength, and now he has found that "invincible summer" inside of himself. The transcendent moment related in *Return to Tipasa* is not a transference; Camus does not actually take anything from nature, nothing is added to Camus. Rather, he discovers what was always inside of himself."

That is the kind of hope that appeals to me, Bill Casselman. Call it thought-through hope. As Galileo put it in a different but related mode, "I've loved the stars too fondly to be fearful of the night."

What happened to Camus on that long-ago winter afternoon beside the cold sea is hinted at by American poet T.S. Eliot in *Four Quartets*:

"What we call the beginning is often the end
And to make an end is to make a beginning.
The end is where we start from.
. . .
We shall not cease from exploration
And the end of all our exploring
Will be to arrive where we started
And know the place for the first time."

Consider this from yet another explanatory essay by a writer named Darran Anderson: "To fully appreciate Camus' humanism you must set it in the sense of godless post-Nietzsche post-Holocaust futility which he, and the Existentialists, wrestled with and following the very real and often grim experiences of his poverty-stricken childhood in Algeria and his time risking his life in the French Resistance during the Occupation."

If I, Bill Casselman, were to inscribe a tombstone for Albert Camus (1913-1960) it would not read R.I.P. (Latin *Requiescat in pac*e 'May he rest in peace'). My epitaph for Camus would read: *Requiescat in Pace Quaerendo* 'May he rest in a peace that keeps asking questions.'

Chapter 37

Refoulement & Repêchage

Two English words borrowed from French

Refoulement

A lazy reader may pass over, but can never then conquer and possess, an unfamiliar word. I have kept my vocabulary green and luxuriant by NEVER letting a word go by, which I cannot define. Does this make me a bit of a bore at festivities? Certainly. I have brought many a party to a standstill by merely asking, "Does anyone here know what a Sunda Colugo is?" As partygoers edge furtively toward the exits, I perceive that I may have transgressed their IIL (Intrinsic Interest Limit).

Recently, the obscene genocides in Syria fomented by the loathsome Russian dwarf Putin and his Syrian fellow ogre Assad have caused history-altering surges of refugees to flee to Europe. A word used in reports of these mass migrations is refoulement, now an English word but, by its nounal form, a term clearly borrowed from French.

Refoulement is the forced return of refugees or asylum seekers to a country where they are liable to be subjected to persecution. It is an international crime, illegal and prohibited in most agreements between countries — not of course in iniquitous fens of dictatorship like Russia and Syria.

The immediate source is the French verb *refouler* 'to force back, to cause to flow back,' a verb first used in

12th-century Old French to refer to the sea and to water. The French verb *fouler* means 'to tread, to trample, to press.' It is the same root as the English verb in cloth manufacture *to full* meaning 'to tread cloth in order to clean and thicken it.' This gives its agent noun *fuller* and one of the most common occupational surnames in English.

A key facet of refugee law is non-refoulement, the generic repatriation of people, sending refugees back into war zones and other disastrous locales, a horror advocated only by selfish persons who have never fled for their lives.

Repêchage

I heard this term during an Olympic sports report and in the T*our de France* bike races this past summer. Its literal meaning is "being allowed to fish again" from the French verb *pêcher* 'to fish.' In its earliest use, *repêchage* meant 'a second chance,' for example, allowing a student candidate who had failed an examination to take the test a second time. In sports that feature serial competition, repêchage allows athletes who don't meet qualifying standards by a tiny margin to nevertheless compete in the next round.

Readers, be bold enough to use such newly met words. Take heart from one of my favorite little versicles. It is a translation of a Horatian ode originally in Latin, rendered into English by the seventeenth-century British poet John Dryden and then slightly revised by Henry Fielding in his novel *Tom Jones.*

"Happy the man, and happy he alone,
He who can call today his own:
He who, secure within himself, can say,

Tomorrow be damned! For I have lived today."

To which I add this bit: And used the words I chose to use, not words approved by stale custom, by illiterate yahoos or by fascist schoolmarms of both sexes.

Chapter 38

Short Latin Tags to Impress Illiterate Friends

The writer, whether of letters home or of weighty theses, who now and then blithely tosses a Latin tag into his otherwise workaday prose is no longer appreciated amidst the word-drab groves of Academe. For me however, the Roman spice of a peppery Latin phrase adds zing to the bland soup of plain English.

As a boy I was not taught to use the simplest word. My father taught his children to use the most unusual but apt word, especially when you are young, for that way, said Dad, the student increases his or her vocabulary and, when the teacher does not know the word, flummoxes ordained authority, always pleasing to youth.

The citing of a choice extract of Latinity displays to a reader your possible acquaintance with the ancient authorities. Latin's pleasingly terse structure adds variety to English sentences which are often too wordy and diffuse.

Therefore, be bold! Append these ornamental Roman tie-backs to the sometimes glum drapery of an English sentence. See if you like their sound and feel.

Canam mihi et musis

As a writer, I have been at times a little-read author and I have had more popular wordsmiths sneer at my low sales. At such times of potential dejection, I am defiant of low readership and find this Latin tag useful. It means "Then I shall sing for myself and for the Muses."

Ubi apes, ibi mel

"Where there are bees, there is honey." The wide applicability of these four Latin words is pleasing. If others are gaining from some activity, there is perhaps a chance for you too to partake of the "honey."

Aliquando bonus dormitat Homerus

"Sometimes even great Homer nods." The brightest genius can make a mistake or appear to be dull.

Amare simul et sapere ipsi Jovi non datur

Advice that might well appear in an online lonely-hearts website: "To be in love and to be smart at the same time is not granted even to Jupiter."

Apage, Satana

Biblical quotations dressed up in their Latin version from Saint Jerome's translation of the Bible (called *The Vulgate*) can lend a force to words that endless repetition in mere English lacks. This is the famous rebuke by Jesus "Get thee behind me, Satan" from the gospel of *Matthew* 4:10.

Memoria vitae bene actae iucunda est

"The memory of a life well-lived is pleasant."

Acti labores jucundi sunt

Roman orators liked the sound of Latin words like *iucundus* ending with the adjectival suffix of bounty *-undus, -unda, -undum.* It rolled off the tongue with a pleasing orotundity (to use a word borrowed into English with the same ending). The great Roman lawyer Cicero used such words frequently in his courtroom speeches. This one means "Work done abounds in joy."

Qui omnes insidias timet in nullas incidit.

"He who fears every ambush falls into none." In other words, in the long run of reasonable security surveillance, keeping one's guard up is always worth it.

Difficile est modum tenere in omnibus.

This is Saint Jerome's humane admission that we all slip up once in a while.

"It is difficult to keep moderation in everything."

Nulla dies sine linea

"Not a day without a line." This advice to every artist and writer throughout history comes down to us from the Roman encyclopaedist Pliny the Elder, who translates it from the Greek of Apelles, a Greek painter. It is quoted in Pliny's *Natural History* 35.36. Don't let a day pass without writing or reading a line of a language you love and use.

A Latin Tongue Twister

Is all classical Latin written in a mode of grim practicality? Did ancient Roman writers ever cavort in phrases of sportive jest? Of course!

O Tite, tute, Tati, tibi tanta, tyranne, tulisti

"Oh Titus Tatius, you tyrant, you yourself have caused so many of your own afflictions and problems." This tongue-twisting bit of alliteration was written by the Latin poet Ennius in a playful mood. Titus Tatius was an imaginary Sabine king in fables who unwisely attacked Rome.

We'll conclude with three little tags all about the Latin language itself. The first is French but implies that a knowledge of Latin equals useful learning.

Au bout de son Latin

Literally "at the end of his Latin" that is, at the end of his knowledge, at his wits' end.

Rident stolidi verba Latina.

"Only fools laugh at the Latin language."

Non tam praeclarum est scire
Latine, quam turpe nescire

We'll give the great lawyer and orator Marcus Tullius Cicero the last word. "It is not so much excellent to know Latin, as it is a shame not to know it."

How does one say in Latin, "That's all, friends."? ***Omnia sunt, amici.***

Chapter 39

Vernix – A Medical Smear Word

Don't know *vernix*? You ought to know the word. You were born covered with the stuff. It's a greasy, cheese-like slime that coats in patches a new-born baby's skin.

Its full name in medicine is *vernix caseosa,* Medieval Latin for 'cheesy varnish.'

The natal function of vernix is to moisturize the skin of the fetus and to help it slide easily here and there in its "bag of waters," the amniotic sac of the uterus. The fetus is protected and cushioned inside this fluid-filled bag. Vernix then assists the potential neonate to slip along in its passage through the narrow birth canal and possibly protect the emerging babe from bacterial infection by acting as a barrier 'slip cover.' Once upon a medical study, neonatologists claimed that vernix helped to "waterproof" the baby and thus prevent undue heat loss in the moment's right after birth. Now they are not so sure of that particular claim.

Fascinating Etymology

Medieval Latin *vernix* becomes Italian *vernice,* then into modern French as *vernis* and thence into modern English as *varnish,* its precise meaning. Its alternate Medieval Latin forms, *bernix* and *veronix* suggest that Latin itself borrowed the word from Byzantine Greek female given name *Berenike.* Le Robert's *Dictionnaire historique de la langue française* (1994 edition) posits a Queen Berenice of a city in Cyrenaica, the eastern coastal region of ancient Libya, where an odorous resin was first made.

Berenice is mentioned briefly in the Book of Acts in the *New Testament* where she appears as a sister of King Herod Agrippa II. But the Greek term is a fountain from which bubble up dozens of later given names like Bernice and Veronica in English, French Bérénice and Véronique, Slavic Veronika, other Romance languages Veronica and diminutives like Bernie, Bunny and Netta.

Vernissage: from Coating Baby's Skin to Coating Great Paintings

Maybe you know the French art term *vernissage?* It's an invitation, often to friends of the artist and art critics, for a private view of newly completed paintings at an art gallery, usually a day before the official opening. It is frequently used in gallery announcements printed in English too. But originally *le vernissage* was "the varnishing day," when painters, exhibitors or gallery employees could still retouch or varnish the paintings before the public saw them. The word is a derivative of French *vernis* 'varnish' from Medieval Latin *vernix, vernicis.*

Now the Cheesy Bits

The second part of the name *caseosa* means 'cheesy, cheese-like, abounding in cheese,' made up of the common classical Latin noun for cheese *caseus* to which is added one common Latin adjectival suffix of bounty, *-osus, -osa, -osum*, an ending productive of hundreds of adjectives borrowed into English like *glorious* where Latin *gloriosus* originally literally meant 'full of glory.' The other common adjectival suffix of bounty in Latin in *-undus, -unda, -undum* giving eventually English forms like abundant and redundant.

Everybody Borrowed the Cheese

Latin *caseus* 'cheese' was borrowed into many later European languages, perhaps the earliest appearance of the loanword was in West Germanic languages, to give Old High German *kasi*, modern German *Käse, Dutch kaas* and dialect *kees, Old Frisian zise* and finally modern English *cheese.* The word may have travelled to northern Europe as Germanic peoples learned the Mediterranean method of making solid cheese with rennet instead of the more primitive mode using sour milk.

Centuries later the Latin word for cheese, *caseus*, was reborrowed for use in English scientific vocabulary, to give words like *casein*, proteins suspended in milk which coagulate with rennet. The adjective *caseous* is still in use, often humorously, to denote something containing or made of any cheesy substance. The medical adjective *caseous* describes tissue that has disintegrated, as in the phrase *caseous necrosis*, where the dead cells have become cheesy in appearance.

On that tasty note, befitting the scholarly elucidation hereinabove set forth, we shall display a high mode of comportment and silently, sternly take our modest leave.

Chapter 40

Saucy Ski Words & their Naughty but Nifty Origins

Ski Bunny

If a naïve skier were ignorant of the herds of hookers who infest Eurotrash ski resorts, snow-walking floozies and harlots wrapped snugly in shearling coats, tight leather pants, quilted snow jackets and heeled boots last used by SS cross-dressers, one might imagine that North America saw the first use of the term *ski bunny*.

But dankly would one lurk in rankest error. For the term *ski bunny* is a loan translation from Austrian German, *Skihaserl* 'Little Ski Rabbit,' the phrase drawn from the rabbit habit of incessant copulation compared with the coital frenzy of downy-pubed *Schlampen* legs akimbo on duvets in chalets amidst the chilly flanks of mountains in the Republik Österreich. And, hey, just so you know, I'm **not** bitter that I was only once in Kitzbühel for an international Bible-reading conference.

Gorby

Gorby is an insult noun for any outdoors person who is a mere tyro, a clumsy beginner perhaps at camping out. But it is used extensively among winter sports snobs too, where a gorby is a person who sucks at snowboarding. These snooty experts claim that gorby is in origin an acronym for Guy on Rental Board. Probably not. See my etymology below.

Uppity skiers call anyone not dressed in properly expensive ski clothes a gorby. A gorby may be a skiing dimwit with no clue about what's up either on the ski hill or at the après-ski bar. Common gorby attire at a winter resort on weekends sees a hapless, gorboid schnook clad in florescent headbands and giant sunglasses, common attire branding such a person as a yutz of the lowest rank.

True Source of the Word *Gorby*

The cogent origin of gorby lies, I believe, in 1950s campers' and backpackers' slang. G.O.R.P. is an acronym for Good Old Raisins and Peanuts, a trail mix suitable for canoe nibbling and bike food packs, easily packed, and not subject to immediate spoilage.

However, when people who were practically born paddling a canoe across a small lake to a store see a tourist and canoeing neophyte set off on the same trip with thousands of dollars' worth of yuppie camping equipment and three pounds of G.O.R.P.—to sustain them in their fifteen minute canoe paddle across the lake—then it seems natural that gorpy, later gorby, might arise as a mild put-down.

The Dictionary of American Regional English (1991) is quoted by the *Oxford English Dictionary* (3rd edition, 2001) suggesting that the verb *to gorp* is attested in the year 1913 meaning 'to eat greedily' and a later variant (?) *to gawp up* 'to eat like a pig.' But that fact does not preclude my preferred acronymic origin, and besides, the DARE mention includes no substantiating citation.

Nowadays G.O.R.P. is a widely dispensed acronym among mountaineers, long-distance cyclists, snowboarders, skiers and backpackers the world over. *Gorp* is used in German and French. One early summer morning on a mountain road outside Cortina d'Ampezzo in the Dolomites of northern Italy I heard an Italian cyclist laughingly put down a plump fellow rider as "*un vero gorpone*," the gist of the delightful put-down being 'a real trail-mix fatty.' I hasten to add I was walking on a guided alpine tour, not riding at high altitude like those goaty dudes.

Gnar

Gnar is slang among some skiers and snowboarders for the kind of snow ridden on and skied-over in extreme snowboarding or extreme skiing. It is an abbreviation of the surfers' adjective *gnarly*, signifying highly dangerous or extremely cool. Of course, only a – like - totally gnarly dude would kill himself skiing off a razor-sharp glacier. The adjective *gnarly* may derive from an earlier English verb *to gnar* (first attested in the 15th century!) meaning 'to growl, to snarl.' German has a similar verb *gnarren*.

Ski as a Word

Ski is a direct borrowing from Norwegian where in Old Norse *skith* was a length of cleft wood. There is an art to writing definitions of words to use in dictionaries. Anyone who thinks it an easy task ought to take the simplest object near them and attempt to write a brief definition. On your first try, you will surely fail. It's tricky. Here is a definition of the word ski from the *Oxford English Dictionary* that, in its simple aptness, is a masterpiece: "A ski is one of a pair of long slender pieces of wood fastened to the foot and used as a snow-shoe, enabling the wearer to slide downhill with great speed."

English has a rare cognate of Old Norse *skith* in the term *shide* meaning a plank of wood supporting an object or holding it in a useable position.

Slalom

This is yet another direct borrowing from the Norwegian language where *sla* means 'sloping' and *låm* means 'track.' A slalom course is a downhill ski race where the skier must follow a zigzag path between trickily placed artificial obstacles.

Schuss

Schuss is a shot, a blast, a charge, in German. To ski straight downhill very fast with skis parallel is schussing.

And now, perhaps bound in adhesive shellac to a single wide ski as fit punishment, I shall schuss out of here.

Chapter 41

A Roman Boat Afloat in English Words

Did you know that the English word noise comes from Latin navis 'boat'?

Once upon an upchuck, noise made one sick to one's stomach. The English word *noise* comes from a Latin word for seasickness, *nausea.* All forms stem from classical Latin *nausea* literally 'seasickness,' related to Latin *naus, nautis* 'ship,' cognate with ancient Greek *naus* 'ship.' Latin *nauta* meant sailor. A sailor through the stars was and is an astronaut, the first component ultimately from Latin through ancient Greek *astron* 'star.' Cognate with *astron* but a diminutive in form was the Latin word for star, *stella.* Beyond seasickness, nausea came to mean vomiting induced by any cause.

The Oxford English Dictionary explains the semantic shifts nicely: "The sense development is perhaps from 'sea-sickness', the literal sense of classical Latin *nausea,* to 'upset, malaise' (compare figurative senses of classical Latin nausea . . .), then to 'disturbance, uproar', and thence to 'noise, din' and 'quarrel…'"

After 1066 CE, in Anglo-Norman, it was *nois* from Old French *noyse.* Compare similar early Romance language forms like Old Occitan *nauza*, *nausa* around 1150 CE and Catalan *nosa* during the thirteenth century.

Here is the word used in Middle English from around 1325 CE in an early and not very reliable history of England and parts of Europe entitled *The Chronicle of Robert of Gloucester*: "Of trompes & of tabors þe sarazins made þere so gret noyse þat cristinemen al destourbed were." 'So great a noise of trumpets and drums did the Saracens make that all Christian men were disturbed.'

Other English Words from *Navis*: The Nave of a Church

Most of the congregation stood or sat in the nave of a church; the metaphor was naval. The great ship of the church contained the worshippers while other parts of the ecclesiastical building held altars and choirstalls etc.

Classical Latin *navis* was first used in Italian as *nave* to name the body of a church building. Note that the nave or central part of a spoked wheel is related to our belly-button English word *navel*, with its cognates in Old High German *naba* 'nave' and in Old Norse *nöf* 'nave.'

Nef

In the annals of household ornament, a nef is a table piece shaped like a ship and often the product of a silversmith. A silver nef often held small containers of salt, pepper, other spicy seasonings and mayhap linen napkins for milady's lap. Nef is a Middle French reflex of Latin *navis* 'ship.'

Navigate

This, one of our chief sailing verbs, stems from Latin *navigare* = *navis* 'ship' + Latin verb *agere* 'to act, to move, to cause to move, to steer (a boat).'

Navy

A collective noun for a group of ships, this is a French invader from the time of the Norman Conquest. In 1066 CE, it might have looked like *navie* 'fleet, boat' or *nave* or *navee*, all ultimately from classical Latin *navigium* 'voyage on a ship.' Nowadays, *navy* as an English word names all the ships of war owned by one country.

These naval words summon to memory a briny passage from Byron's poem "The Dark, Blue Sea," which shall serve as this chapter's invocation of embarkation.

"Roll on, thou deep and dark blue ocean — roll!
Ten thousand fleets sweep over thee in vain; . . .

Unchangeable, save to thy wild waves' play —
Time writes no wrinkle on thine azurn brow —
Such as creation's dawn beheld, thou rollest now."

Chapter 42

Albedo & Hubbly: Two Winter Words

Albedo

If you doff a white t-shirt and don a black one at summer's end, you'll be somewhat warmer, due to the differential albedo between white and black colors. In the summer, bright white color reflects almost all of the sun's heat and thus helps keep you cool.

Albedo begins its tenure in English as a technical term in astronomy. Sunlight reflected from earth's surface back out into space or diffused in other earthly directions is albedo. Of course, albedo can be measured on planets other than earth too.

A post-classical Latin word for whiteness, *albedo* stems from the Latin color adjective *albus* 'white' from which we get other common English words like album, originally a book of blank white pages.

Italian gives us *albino.*

Egg whites contain a chemical called *albumen* which was the ancient Latin word for egg white.

A kind of surplice worn by priests and clerics is an alb, a vestment of white cloth that touches the wearer's feet, from ecclesiastical Latin *tunica alba* 'white garment.'

Aube, the French word for dawn stems from soldiers' Latin *alba*, the dawn, the "white" part of the day, when light returns. An *aubade* was a song or music originally intended to be sung or played in the morning. An aubade was the opposite of a serenade, music to be performed in the evening (*serenus* Latin 'late in the day, at twilight') when, one hoped, after the cares of the day one could rest serene during an interval of crepuscular repose.

Albion is a poetic name for Britain and refers to the White Cliffs of Dover, a geographic feature noted by the first Roman invaders.

Hubbly

This wintry adjective is strictly North American for "having an uneven surface." Hubbly does not even appear in the *Oxford English Dictionary*, although this exclusion may be part of the anti-American bias still lingering in the British wordbook, part of the OED's Colonel Blimp attitude toward those "damned colonials." Here in Canada I have only heard the word *hubbly* modifying the noun *ice*. Hubbly ice is bumpy. It may have snowed then rained then froze. You might be able to sleigh across hubbly ice but it makes for tricky skating.

Hubbly could be a playful alternative to bumpy. One dictionary suggests it is cognate with a Dutch adjective *hobbelig* 'rugged.' It may be a folk adjective of the English noun *hub* meaning 'bump.' My guess? The form began as *hubby 'bumpy' but that made it a clumsy homograph and synonym for husband, so the coiner altered it to *hubbly* instead.

Homographs are words that are spelled the same but have different meanings, like pole and pole. Confusingly, homonym can be a synonym for homograph.

But, usually, a homonym is a word with the same pronunciation as another word but with different spelling or meaning. Don't you love imprecise grammatical definitions?

Chapter 43

Volcano Words

Know technical volcano words like tephra, a'a, maar, tuya, lapilli, guyot and kipuka

A volcano is inner earth clearing its rocky throat. In November of 2012, the Plosky Tolbachik volcano on the remote Kamchatka peninsula of western Russia erupted anew and brought into world news both familiar and obscure English technical terms in volcanology. These English volcanic labels adopted from other languages are a delightful word upheaval to prod and explore.

First, to help you remember the peak's name, here's a bit of Russian vocabulary. *Ploskii* means 'flat, flat-topped.' It has a brother volcano in the same mountain area called Ostry Tolbachik. *Ostrii* means 'sharp, pointed, peaked' in Russian. Tolbachik appears to be the surname of a pioneer who first prospected a nearby valley of the same name.

Lava

Let's begin with a very familiar volcano word of which few people know the origin. The word *lava* comes into the languages of Europe and into English directly from one famous volcano, Mount Vesuvius near Naples, which blew its top and famously buried the Roman towns of Pompeii and Herculaneum in 79 CE. *Lava* began in Italian meaning 'a "wash" as in a ditch, a rain ditch through soil dug by a heavy downpour.' Neapolitans used the word to refer to a Vesuvian lava stream, for they rightly feared the undulant unguent of molten magma, the lithic pre-lava lurking beneath the rocky crust of Vesuvio, awaiting an urge to erupt. Melted lava was like a 'wash of rock' sliding in a slow obliterative slip of death down the peril-rich flanks of Vesuvius.

Lava's root is the Latin verb *lavare* 'to wash,' cognate with Greek *louein* 'to wash the body' and possibly with West German forms like Old English *lafian* 'to pour water on the body' and modern German *laben* 'to refresh.'

This old Indo-European stem gives English words like *lather* which in its Old English form *léaðor* referred to washing soda, and then came to mean frothy foam of soap and water, cognate with Greek *loetron* or *loutron* 'bath.'

Magma

Magma is one of my pet words in volcanology. Magma is molten rock semi-liquid in nature. After magma is expelled from a volcano it is called lava. The root is a Greek verb *massein* 'to mix, to mingle together.'

Pahoehoe (puh-HOY-hoy)

This is a type of Hawaiian lava that upwells from the fissured rift of its volcano; it is smooth, gelatinous, billowy, unbroken and fluid; then this lava cools into ropy cords. Or as pahoehoe loses heat and de-gasses, a second kind of flow, **a'a** lava, may be formed. *A'a* or *aa,* beloved of crossword puzzle fans, is a rough-surfaced and viscid lava. Some outflows of pahoehoe have been compared to glistening folds of poured taffy.

Hawaiian Etymology of Pahoehoe

Hoe is a Hawaiian noun meaning 'oar' or 'canoe paddle.' *Pā.hoe* is a verb meaning 'to paddle an outrigger canoe.' The single-hulled outrigger was ideal for near-shore Polynesian fishing. Pahoehoe is a reduplicated verb form of *pahoe* meaning 'to paddle a canoe very quickly.' It is a Hawaiian fishing technique, during which canoeists beat their paddles in unison against the gunwales of their canoes or the sides, in order to make a racketing, thumping noise that frightens and then drives fish into a nearby net.

Hawaiians borrowed this word to describe a type of lava because the flow and shiny crust of pahoehoe lava resembled the surface of seawater beaten rhythmically by many canoeists' paddles. (?)

A'a'

As every deft Scrabble player knows, aa or a'a' (pronounced ah-ah) is one of the two kinds of lava that pours forth from Hawaiian volcanoes. As lavas go, aa is rough and looks like slag with bubble holes. As molten aa cools after being exposed to air, gases formed by the melting magma escape, hissing and emitting blister bubbles that burst on the cooling lava surface to give aa its characteristic scoriaceous aspect. The root meaning of a'a' in Polynesian is the eminently descriptive one of 'burn-burn.'

Tephra

Tephra is the classical Greek word for ash or ashes. In modern volcanology, tephra is rock bits and dust propelled into the upper air by the force of an eruption.

Tephra settles in banded layers in the vicinity of volcanoes.

It is a noun often used attributively, that is, like an adjective in appositive clusters, such as tephra layer, tephra cloud, tephra rain. In attribution, nouns are used like adjectives. They add a distinguishing or characteristic quality to the noun they modify as attributive adjectives.

Tephrite is a basaltic rock found in volcanic debris.

Sometimes, previous volcanic eruptions can be dated by studying layers of tephra and this is called tephrochronology.

In olden days, wizards and diviners claimed to tell a gullible person's future by throwing ashes up into the air and observing how such ashes were carried by the wind. This scamming of hapless dupes was sometimes given the fancy name of tephromancy.

Breccia

Breccia names a composite sandy or clayey rock crammed with smaller sharp rock fragments. It is one of the Italian words not from Latin, but borrowed early from some Germanic source, because breccia is cognate with our English verb *to break*, with older German *brechan* 'to break.' French and Spanish borrowed from the same Germanic source to get their words: French *brèche* 'breaking, breach' and Spanish *brecha*. The common English pronunciation is *BRET-she-a.*

Diatreme

A diatreme is literally a through-hole, a modern compound word made up of Greek *dia* 'through' + Greek *trema* 'hole, orifice, opening.' A diatreme is a small vent or pipe-like opening forced wide by volcanic gases during an eruption and then filled with breccia debris (as defined above).

Guyot

A guyot is a flat-topped, undersea mountain formed from a volcano. This word *guyot* is a notorious example of why eponyms are a bad idea in scientific nomenclature. Supposedly the name was given to honor the discoverer of these oceanographic tablemounts, a Swiss geographer named Arnold H. Guyot. How nice. And now that is their legitimate name in science. But — Oh Dear! — Monsieur Guyot did NOT discover them. Their discoverer was Professor H. Hess of Princeton University. Now, Hessless they hiss incessantly, submerged and ashamed. No, they don't hiss but they ought to. English pronunciation follows French, namely *GWEE-oh.*

Therefore the two common synonyms for guyot are much better, more descriptive and more honest names: *seamount* and, even better as a lay name, *tablemount*, because it describes neatly these relatively common features of the Pacific Ocean floor. The flat nature of their level summits are probably due to incessant wave action.

Fumarole

A fumarole is a vent from which volcanic gases escape in vaporous urgency. Fumaroles can occur along small cracks or long fissures. When a fumarole belches forth chiefly sulphurous effluvium, an Italian word is used in English geology to describe such a vent: *solfatara*.

Fumarole was borrowed into English from Italian *fumarola* 'chimney' from a post-classical Latin diminutive form *fumariolum* 'little smoke hole, slit, chimney pot, vent' from a simpler, earlier diminutive Latin noun *fumarium*, originally a small smokehouse used to age wine, itself from Latin *fumus* 'smoke,' source of our common English word, *fume*.

Kipuka

A kipuka (KEE-pooka) is a habitat that supports scant and fragile life forms while surrounded by an earlier lava wasteland. The German word sums it up succinctly: *eine Vegetationsinsel* 'a little island of vegetation' surrounded by lava flows. Kipuka is a Hawaiian word for 'opening.' *Puka* in Hawaiian refers to a 'gap, perforation, blank space in a form.' *Ki-* is a prefix that intensifies or augments the root word. Kipuka's non-volcanic meanings include 'a clearing in a forest' or 'an open space in clouds.'

Lapilli

Lapilli are teeny bits of shattered rock or exploded lava debris smaller than 64 millimeters wide which are propelled from volcanos. The word is a pure Latin plural meaning 'little stones' derived from *lapillus*, one of the Latin words for pebble, itself from *lapis* 'stone.' Lapilli may also stand as a plural of the Italian form of the word, *lapillo.* When the stones of a wall or building have fallen down, the structure may be said to be de**lapid**ated!

Maar

A maar is a shallow volcanic crater that sometimes fills with water and forms a flat-bottomed lake. There are two plural forms: *Maare* and *maars.* The word is a German locative, occurring in German place names to delineate a place with a crater-lake. German Maar looks like a version of *mara*, a Latin word for pond or swamp.

Nuée Ardente

This exotic French term, pronounced aloud, trembles on the English lip. In volcanology *nuée ardente* 'burning cloud' names a luminous cloud of glowing gases, lava debris, pumice and air-borne ash, an incandescing volcanic down-spew, a particulate-dense, roiling cloud of pyroclastic flow from an erupting volcano. One science writer called it "the glow of the flow." To be engulfed in such a poison shroud is doom.

The French plural is used in English scientific writing: *nuées ardentes.*

Etymology of *Nuée*

The common French word for cloud is *nuage*, with both positive and pejorative meanings. Its etymon is Latin *nubes*, with its Latin diminutive form, borrowed directly into English, *nebula*, prime meaning 'vapour, mist.' In early eleventh-century French there was another form of this word for cloud taken from *nuba*, a colloquial variant in street Latin of the time, *la nue* 'cloud.' Eventually, to the simple word *nue* was added a collective suffix *-age* to give *nuage*, prime meaning: a group of clouds, an overcast sky, etc. Then, after existing in written French with a collective sense, *nuage* dwindled in meaning to once again refer to a single cloud.

Nue also had an augmentative form, *la nuée* which signified a big cloud, a cloud full of rain, dark and threatening. That was indeed the reasonable French cloud word to borrow when naming the volcanic nightmare cloud.

Today, in modern French, *la nuée* is almost exclusively negative: *la nuée d'orage* 'the thundercloud or storm cloud'; *une nuée de paparazzi* 'a horde of annoying photographers'; *une nuée de sauterelles* 'a plague of locusts.'

Nuance

One of the most interesting extensions of *nuage* and Latin *nubes* is something originally thought to be caused by clouds, namely, shade, or in French *la nuance.* The developed meanings began in French with *nuance* denoting the hue of a colour, any differentiating qualitative subtleties, the finer points of an argument, the shades of a personality etc. These developed meanings gained the most use in English.

Some Indo-European cognates of Latin *nubes* are: modern German *Nebel* 'mist,' classical Greek *nephos* 'cloud,' Sanskrit *nabhas* 'cloud,' Old Norse *njol* 'shadows,' Welsh *niwl* 'fog, mist' and Old Church Slavonic *nebo* 'heaven.' Nephology is the scientific study of clouds.

Even our word *nubile* 'beautiful, worthy of marriage or able to marry' shared the same root; *nubile* is the adjective of capability from the Latin verb *nubere* which meant in its prime sense 'to veil the head,' that is, in a sense, to becloud the head with a veil, thence to wear the veil of marriage, and thence *nubere* meant 'to get married.'

A nasalized form of the root appears in the Latin word *nimbus*, which meant at first a cloud filled with rain, thunder and lightning, thence a golden cloud circling the head of an Olympian god; later a nimbus was a golden aura glowing about the head of any divine being, such as Christ or Buddha. In meteorology, the word names a type of plump cloud: cumulonimbus.

Outgassing

Outgassing is the release of gases into the atmosphere during volcanic eruptions. During the ancient, violent formation of the world's mantle, some of earth's atmosphere (including some water vapor, nitrogen and argon) originated from outgassing.

Phreatic Eruption

It is a violent eruption of steam when water frazzles and boils to instant steam on hot volcanic rocks. Phreatic first referred to underground water located below the water table. A developed meaning in geology sees phreatic denominate an eruption that involves hot liquid rock, magma, meeting underground water to produce explosive steam and mud that explodes and blasts its way up to the surface through the lava vents. The term was coined as a modern adjectival form of the ancient Greek word for a cistern, reservoir or well, *phear* and its word-forming and stem-containing genitive *phreatos*.

Plinian or Vesuvian Eruption

This is one of the most explosive types of volcanic eruptions, known for producing nuées ardentes and columns of gas and debris that may soar miles-high into the stratosphere. It's named after the Roman writer Pliny the Younger who observed and wrote a description of the famous eruption of Mount Vesuvius in 79 CE, the volcano that buried Pompeii and Herculaneum near Naples. Pliny's uncle, also a writer, of one of the great encyclopaedias in Latin, died in the eruption. Here is part of his nephew's description:

"On the 24th of August, about one in the afternoon, my mother desired him to observe a cloud which appeared of a very unusual size and shape. He had just taken a turn in the sun and, after bathing himself in cold water, and making a light luncheon, gone back to his books: he immediately arose and went out upon a rising ground from whence he might get a better sight of this very uncommon appearance. A cloud, from which mountain was uncertain, at this distance (but it was found afterwards to come from Mount Vesuvius), was ascending, the appearance of which I cannot give you a more exact description of than by likening it to that of a pine tree, for it shot up to a great height in the form of a very tall trunk, which spread itself out at the top into a sort of branches; occasioned, I imagine, either by a sudden gust of air that impelled it, the force of which decreased as it advanced upwards, or the cloud itself being pressed back again by its own weight, expanded in the manner I have mentioned; it appeared sometimes bright and sometimes dark and spotted, according as it was either more or less impregnated with earth and cinders. This phenomenon seemed to a man of such learning and research as my uncle extraordinary and worth further looking into."

- - - Sixth Book, Letter 16, of Pliny the Younger's Epistulae *'Letters to his Friends,' translation by William Melmoth, a translation now in the public domain*

Wikipedia then continues with a summary of what happened next: "Pliny the Elder set out to rescue the victims from their perilous position on the shore of the Bay of Naples, and launched his galleys, crossing the bay to Stabiae (near the modern town of Castellammare di Stabia). Pliny the Younger provided an account of his death, and suggested that he collapsed and died through inhaling poisonous gases emitted from the volcano. His body was found interred under the ashes of the Vesuvius with no apparent injuries on 26 August, after the plume had dispersed, confirming asphyxiation or poisoning."

Pyroclastic

Pyroclastic literally means 'broken apart and reduced in size by fire.' The roots are the Greek word for fire *pyr* + *-klastos* 'thing that breaks up, smasher' from the Greek verb *klan* 'to break.' An iconoclast was originally an infidel thug who broke holy icons. An iconostasis is a screen bearing icons that separates the sanctuary in many Eastern churches from the nave.

One of the deadliest concomitants of a Vesuvian eruption is the pyroclastic flow during which an unstoppable torrent of burning-hot, toxic gases, lava and melting igneous debris cascade down the flanks of an erupting volcano killing all life in its path.

Tuya

A tuya is a flat-topped, steep-sided volcano, as in the picture below of a tuya in Iceland, formed when lava bursts through thick ice or erupts under a glacier. Wikipedia states that "they are somewhat rare worldwide, being confined to regions which were covered by glaciers and had active volcanism during the same period." The word appears to come from Tuya Butte in the Tuya mountain range of northern British Columbia in Canada and was coined by Canadian geologist Bill Mathews.

Etymology of the Word *Volcano*

Volcanus or Vulcanus was the Roman god of fire, the blacksmith of the immortals, his smithy wreathed in clouds of smoke as he honed Jupiter's swords and fashioned winged shoes for flying horses and for Mercury. I think there are possible cognates of Vulcanus in the English noun *welkin* 'a cloud, realm of the clouds, the heavens' and modern German *die Wolke* 'the cloud.' *The Oxford English Dictionary* offers a much less probable Arabic source of the Italian island name. Mount Etna's earliest name in Latin was *Vulcanus mons* 'Mount Vulcan.' The Aeolian Islands north of Sicily still have active volcanoes on islands now called Stromboli and Vulcano. The OED thinks *burkan*, one of the common words for 'volcano' in Arabic, gave the islands their early name. I think the borrowing took place the other way. Arabic borrowed *volcan* and heard it as *bolkan* or *burkan*. My Proto-Indo-European origin of *Volcanus* as a cognate of Germanic *die Wolke* is more etymologically cogent.

A Modest Apopemptic Passage

Now must we leave aside the sunder and rupture of earth's gut, the crust quake, the unsuturing cleft of granitic cones, all such fraught fractures. Instead let us traipse into meadows of lolloping summer, daisy-rich, clover-quilted and bee-choired, to remind ourselves that while the earth may frighten, it also, as summer warms us in the lap of long days, bids fair to delight mortal senses.

Chapter 44

Biblical & Art Terms like Anastasis & Deposition

Having a coffee with a deeply pious Protestant friend, a regular churchgoer, I was surprised to discover that he did not know the meaning of the word *annunciation,* nor did he know to what Christian act the word *deposition* referred. Thus I deem worthwhile a column explaining the Latin and Greek origin of some of these modestly technical terms in theology, many of them shared as terms in the history of European art.

Most Christians know the Nativity and the Baptism but may not be acquainted with terms like the *Ecce Homo*, the Assumption and *Descensus Christi ad Inferos.* Michelangelo's *Pietà* in St. Peter's Basilica at *Città del Vaticano* is well known, given Italy's prominence in European art history and the marble's renown as one of the deftest and most moving Christian sculptures ever carved by mortal chisel.

Fewer know a *Maestà* by name. But, by such egregious lacunae, be thou not befuddled, gentle pilgrim. For this little column, in spite of its taint of lewd sacrilege, will darn up those few holes in the socks of your Christian knowledge. And now, humbly, on bended knee, do we proffer our exemplary verbal bouquet.

Annunciation

In the Latin Vulgate of the *Gospel of Saint Luke* (1:36-39) we read of the *Annuntiatio nativitatis Christi* 'the proclamation of the birth of Christ.' The word was much later Englished as *annunciation*, almost exclusively referring to the announcing by the messenger angel Gabriel unto the Blessed Virgin Mary that she will experience the immaculate conception and bear from her womb the Son of God, Jesus Christ.

The prime etymon in the Latin noun *annuntiatio* is *nuntius* 'bringing news' where *nuntius* perhaps displays a condensation of Latin *novus* Latin 'new' or some earlier form like *noventia 'new announcements, hence news.' Note that we still use the Italian reflex in English when we refer to a papal nuncio, a Vatican ambassador to a foreign court or government.

Annuntiatio has direct components of Latin prepositional prefix *ad* 'to' + Latin verb *nuntiare* 'to bring news, to bear a message.' Think of words in English with the same root like *announce, denounce, enunciate, pronouncement* and *renunciation.*

Bible plus Sex? Eek!

Two saucy paragraphs now follow. They are saucy only for those who wish to bar sex from Holy Writ. *Immaculatus* has only one meaning in the Vulgate. It means "not stained by one spot of human sperm." Latin *im* = Latin *in* = English 'not' + *maculatus* 'stained, soiled' < Latin *macula* 'blemish, stain, spot.' If one needed a Latin word for shot-spot — such as festoon the wallpapers of cheap motel bedrooms whose principal use is found in human anatomical and multiple conjunctions — it would be *macula.* All the prissy evasions and holy moanings claiming that immaculate is a strictly metaphorical word are exegetical balderdash promoted by mincing bishops. Princes of the Church are they, who never permit sex to enter their lives. Lifting an altar boy's robe does not count, of course.

How DID the Holy Spirit Enter Mary?

Remember it took the bearded prelates and assorted latter-day church worthies several years (!) at the Council of Trent (1545-1563 CE) to determine precisely how the Holy Spirit entered Mary. Imagine that. Grown men met in solemn conclave to discuss such trivial nonsense. But, after all, most of darling Mary's bodily orifices were not suitable. We couldn't have the Paraclete tiptoeing into Maria through her vagina! *Dio mio!* An anal welcome was quite out of the question. Through the mouth does not seem at all a cleanly introit. And a nostril besprent with nasal mucus is a lowly corridor indeed down which to make corporeal advent to a saint's classy chassis. The bishops at Trent decided that the Holy Spirit had entered Mary *per aurem* 'through an ear.' Could any frittering away of our brief chatting time here on earth be more idle and inane?

Chapter 45

Wizard's Words of Alchemy

Wizards, adepts of sorcery, stirrers of strange cauldrons, don pointy hats and star-flecked robes, wave wands and hold bubbling beakers high! For today we examine the origin of words associated with alchemy, precursor of modern chemistry and metallurgy during medieval times and the early Renaissance.

Under our etymological microscope and into focus come words like *retort, alembic, crucible, athanor* and the word *chemistry* itself whose root may hark back to pharaonic times.

Alchemy, of course, was NOT scientific, being encumbered with ancient magic, Hermeticism, astrological gibberish and hidden symbols. The pseudo-science's principal fallacy was universal transformation, a proofless notion that base metals like iron could be turned into gold and silver, through the discovery of a preternatural catalyst called a "philosopher's stone" or "the alkahest," a universal solvent.

The Real Name of Paracelsus

I claim a side path here to mention the man who gave us the word *alkahest*. He was a Swiss German alchemist who called himself Paracelsus (CE 1493-1541). He had very little Arabic, but was sufficiently acquainted with Arabic forms to name his universal solvent. So he simply made up an Arabic-sounding word, *alkahest*!

Although Paracelsus dabbled in pseudo-science and utter piffle, the dizzy Swiss did make legitimate contributions to science, especially in early toxicology. I want also to mention him here because he had one of the most resonantly pompous medieval German names ever recorded in print, his birth name being Philippus Aureolus Theophrastus Bombastus von Hohenheim. *Ja wohl!*

Immortality Juice!

Another alchemical fancy posited that a wondrous elixir of life might someday be distilled from dripping alembics into a flask of droplets whose ingestion would deliver to time-bound humans the gift of eternal life. This was but a thaumaturgical whim, that is to say, to speak more plainly, mere capricious mirificence. Okay, I fibbed! I just wanted to use that extremely rare noun *mirificence*, because it is one of the few synonyms for thaumaturgy (wonder working). One of the Indian names for this water of eternal life was *Amrit Ras* which means "immortality juice."

But, in spite of brains chockablock with poppycock, alchemists did develop some basic lab techniques, theories, and procedures of experimentation which are still in use.

Etymology Old when Amarna was New

To suggest that the origin of the word *alchemy* is still in dispute is to indulge in etymological understatement extraordinaire. But the basic evolution is generally agreed upon.

English *alchemy* < Old French *alquimie* < Medieval Latin *alchimia* < Arabic al-kimia < Ancient Greek *chemeia* or *chemia* where it meant 'the transforming' (of gold and silver from baser metals).

Plutarch, a Greek historian (CE 46- 120), uses *Chemia* as a name for Egypt, which may stem from one name the ancient Egyptians called their country, namely Kmt, probably pronounced Kemet, literally 'black land' from the Egyptian hieroglyphic *kem* 'black,' referring to the Nile Valley's rich, dark soil, in contrast to the much paler desert sand.

Later the place name *Chemia* may have become, as some etymologists like to say, "polluted" by another noun, the Hellenistic Greek *chymeia* 'act of pouring or infusion made from plant juices.' The ancient Greek source was *chymos* 'juice, sap,' ultimately from the ancient Greek verb *chein* 'to pour.' Still in use in modern English physiological vocabulary is *chyme*, the noun that names the goopy matter into which food is converted in the stomach before it passes into the small intestine.

Athanor

An athanor was a small lab furnace in which charcoal in a tower was fed down into a fire providing reasonably constant heat for chemical procedures requiring it. It was simply one of the classical Arabic words for furnace, *al-tannūr*; compare other Semitic cognates in Hebrew and Aramaic where the triliteral *nūr* means 'fire.

Crucible

A Medieval Latin form was *crucibulum* or *crucibolum*, prime meaning 'night-lamp,' then a melting pot for metals. Later a crucible was an earthenware vessel used for fusing metals. The original Medieval Latin word may have been *crassipulum* 'grease-burner;' compare Latin *crassus* 'fat' and *crassa* 'grease.' It appears the root became popularly associated with Latin *crux, crucis* 'cross.'

Alembic

An alchemical apparatus used for distilling, consisting of two connected vessels, a typically gourd-shaped cucurbit containing the substance to be distilled, and a receiver or flask in which the condensed product is collected. Sometimes the long neck of the flask receiver was made cold with snow, ice, or cold water in order to hasten the condensation.

The etymology is English *alembic* > Anglo-Norman > *alembic*, Middle French *alambic* > post-classical Latin *alembicus, alembicum* > Arabic al-anbīq (al 'the' + anbīq vessel for distilling < Hellenistic Greek *ambik-*, *ambix* vessel narrow towards the brim for distilling < possibly from ancient Greek *ambon* 'raised lip, edge' + the common object suffix *-iks*. Compare an ancient Greek word for a small cup, *kylix*.

Retort

The retort took the place of the alembic. A retort was a beaker with a long, tubular, downward curving, bent neck used by alchemists, then by chemists, for distillation. Its name refers to the bent neck and is medieval German *Retorte* > Classical Latin *retortus* 'bent back,' past participle of *retorquere* 'to twist, to bend back' from whose base Latin verb *torquere* modern English gets a noun like *torque*. The prefix *re-* is Latin 'again, anew' and indicates that the action named in the verb is repeated.

Cobalt

The metallic element cobalt was named by the copper miners of the Hartz Mountains in Germany after evil spirits called *Kobolds*. Cobalt was also called fools' copper because it bore a false copper ore. Cobalt was considered useless and unhealthy because it is frequently found mixed with arsenic, and because it resembled silver but was not.

Cauldron

A cauldron is a large kettle or boiler with a clear-cut etymological path from Latin *caldarium* Roman word for a hot-bath through French and Spanish forms like Spanish *calderon* and Anglo-Norman *caudron* and doublet derivations like standard French *chaudière* 'kettle.'

As we tiptoe now, Theseus-like, out of the wizard's grotto, past fat vat, sly chalice, odd goblet and mystic grail, fitting it is to recall the witches' spell from Act 4, Scene 1 of Shakespeare's *Macbeth*, for it remembers alchemical days, and is besides rife with the Bard's word-conjuring magic:

"Round about the cauldron go;
In the poison'd entrails throw.
Toad, that under cold stone
Days and nights hast thirty one
Swelter'd venom sleeping got,
Boil thou first i' the charmed pot.

Double, double toil and trouble;
Fire burn and cauldron bubble.

Fillet of a fenny snake,
In the cauldron boil and bake;
Eye of newt, and toe of frog,
Wool of bat, and tongue of dog,
Adder's fork, and blind-worm's sting,
Lizard's leg, and howlet's wing,
For a charm of powerful trouble,
Like a hell-broth boil and bubble.

Double, double toil and trouble;
Fire burn and cauldron bubble.

Scale of dragon, tooth of wolf,
Witches' mummy, maw and gulf
Of the ravin'd salt-sea shark,
Root of hemlock digg'd i' the dark,
Liver of blaspheming Jew,
Gall of goat, and slips of yew
Sliver'd in the moon's eclipse,
Nose of Turk, and Tartar's lips,
Finger of birth-strangled babe
Ditch-deliver'd by a drab,
Make the gruel thick and slab:
Add thereto a tiger's chaudron,
For the ingredients of our cauldron."

Chapter 46

Festina Lente: Roman Emperor Augustus' Favorite Saying

& an ancient Weapon of War Perhaps New to You

Rome's first emperor chose his imperial moniker. Although Julius Caesar was his uncle, before he was plain Gaius Octavius; afterward he dubbed himself Augustus, whose literal sense in Latin is 'he who ought to be revered.' Modest little toga, wasn't he?

The emp, His Augustness, liked to send pert-buttocked slave maidens scampering across the mosaic tiles to fetch and peel grapes. His favorite Latin saying was *festina lente* 'make haste slowly.' Never act rashly. Think. Analyse. Then act. He wanted such forethought in particular from his military commanders.

Emperor Augustus, unlike many of the rash egotists and mad rulers who came after him, may be said to have paid throughout his imperial reign reasonable attention to this motto.

Like many nifty maxims of ancient Rome, *festina lente* was a loan translation from an earlier classical Greek motto, *speude bradeos* 'hurry slowly.'

A Famous Printer of Venice

Much later in Roman history appeared one of the earliest and most renowned of Venetian printers, Aldus Manutius. As early as 1499 CE, Manutius took as his own the somewhat flamboyant Renaissance trademark of the Dolphin and Anchor. Beneath or entwining his symbol he chose the same motto as Augustus, *festina lente*. Take the time to do a thing right.

Why did Manutius select the dolphin and anchor as his insignia? I suggest it was due to an early, secondary meaning of dolphin both in classical Greek and in Latin. Hellenistic Greek *delphinos*, classical Greek *delphis* and classical Latin *delphinus* named not only the sassy marine leaper but also a weapon of war.

Annals of Classical Weaponry

A *delphinus* was a naval assault weapon carried by Greek and Roman war galleys. Essentially a weaponized anchor, a dolphin was a 220-pound lead weight, pear-shaped, bulb-like, with an iron spike thrust into the midst of its molten lead. A dolphin would be hauled up the ship's yard, a spar high on the mast, and then, as the attacking ship approached close quarters to the enemy ship, the leaden dolphin would be dropped or flung down splintering the hull and deck of the enemy vessel in an attempt to breach that hull or smithereen an upper deck. Naval archaeologists have recovered precisely one dolphin of war.

I believe Manutius thought of the important books he was to publish (he rescued many volumes of classical literature from total oblivion) as *delphini*, as counterweights to ignorance, like vast plumbous clods, like swollen boluses of leaden mass, written to smash through unknowingness and unenlightenment and permit the kindly aurae of classical wisdom to shine through to us who would come afterward.

A Symbol Filched by the True Believers

Later still, our old thieving friend, the Roman Catholic Church, also "adopted" the Dolphin & Anchor as a symbol of Christian fortitude. But, like so many stolen signs in a religious context, it is empty, spurious and a bastard device if ever there was one, gaudily displayed perhaps across the braggart cassock of a hunchbacked bishop.

And, on that anti-ecclesiastical impugnment, which, I am certain, will have Saint Peter at the gates wagging the eternal finger of disapproval at my ghost or shabby soul, I shall take my leave, for a moment. But I'm back in the next chapter.

Chapter 47

Horse Sense

Equus caballus is our starting phrase today, the zoological name of the common horse. Both the genus name *Equus* and the species name *caballus* are Latin.

Equus is the classical, somewhat upper-class Latin word for horse, from which descend English words like equine, equestrian and equitation 'the art of riding on horseback.'

Caballus is Vulgar or Street or Low Latin and meant 'nag,' spavined old wretch of a horse, the only kind of bedraggled horse poor people might afford in ancient Rome. *Caballus* is not a native Latin word but was an early borrowing into Latin from a Celtic language encountered during a first incursion by Roman legions into ancient Gaul, heard by soldiers, brought back to Rome as a useful word for nag, and then centuries later exported back to Gaul where it eventually became the French word for horse, *cheval*.

Equine Delvings

An *equus* was a healthy, well-kept mount bestrode by a free citizen or an aristocratic rider, a horse that a Roman knight might ride into battle in a war of conquest. There was indeed a class, an order, a stratum of Roman society, called *equites* 'knights.' They belonged to an order between the senatorial and the ordinary citizen and were the class from which originally the cavalry was drawn. Incidentally, the English word *cavalry* stems from *caballus*, as we explain below. The equites' reward for supplying mounted warriors was exclusive right to certain financial and judicial offices in the government of Rome. However lofty the social heights they attained later under the Roman empire, equites began in the earliest days of the kingdom of Rome as citizen members of a Roman family who could afford, when summoned by their king, to send at least one horse and one rider into military service.

Equus, the classical Latin word, gained currency in present-day English because of British dramatist Peter Schaffer's 1973 play and 1977 film "Equus," an examination of the quite modern madness of a stable boy who blinds six horses. The play is a very dubious defense of schizophrenic excess, here labeled as an act of worshipful ecstasy by the usual perp, an artistic British liberal, namely, playwright Shaffer, busily romanticizing insanity as a brave exceeding of the humdrum bounds of daily life. Such a creaking, 300-year-old Romantic fallacy is pernicious nonsense spread by those who have never watched a loved one's life dissolve in madness, and so, as artists, they can lounge on the comfy couch of non-involvement and fire forth cavalier suppositions about insanity, iron darts untempered in the forge of reality. But for all that, "Equus" is a play worth seeing and reading.

A Nagging Word's Story

So *caballus* was soldiers' common Latin for 'nag,' a broken down horse. Around 500 or 600 CE most Latin speakers who used *caballus* to mean 'horse' would also know the 'upper-class' word, *equus*. So why did they choose to use *caballus* instead of *equus*? They were Roman army grunts. Through all of history, in every language we know of, rough soldiers' slang criticizes and grouses about everything concerning military food rations, their army and its supplies. In that mode of complaint, any army horse is 'a nag,' a *caballus*, never a noble steed. Soon all horses are *caballi* and the word *equus* fades from daily use, left behind and forgotten in the older stalls of the verbal stable and retrieved in modern languages as a strictly upper-class word used by rich riders who, of a morning, equitate.

How the Romance Languages Formed from Latin

The Romans called their best Latin *urbanitas* 'Latin spoken in the city,' from *urbs* 'city,' hence English words like *urban* and *urbanity.* The *urbs*, above all others for Romans, was of course Rome. The word is still heard and seen in our times in the traditional beginning of papal proclamations from the Vatican, *Urbi et Orbi* 'to the city (Rome) and to the world,' originally shouted by a herald before certain Easter and Christmas blessings by the pope at St. Peter's Square.

Latin Transforms into Early French

A Roman general, speaking what the Romans called *urbanitas*, might say in formal Latin, "*Duces equum tuum?*" "Are you bringing your horse?"

An ordinary, uneducated infantryman would speak in the Vulgar Latin of Roman soldiers and he might have asked the same question by saying something like "**Duc's caballu(m) tu(um)*" "You bringin' yer nag?"

A few hundred years later, say, 700 CE, as the dawn of Romance languages approaches, as spoken Latin evolves into Romanz, the earliest French, that question might have sounded more like his: "**Duse t' chavalle*?" and we can see the first forms of what would become the Romance languages where the word horse is: Spanish *caballo*, Italian *cavallo*, and French *cheval*.

Caballus Derivatives

It is of modest ironic interest that the Latin word for broken-down nag gives us such elevated terms as *chivalry*, originally French as *chevalerie* 'ability to ride a horse well.' The great French singer Maurice Chevalier had, perhaps, an ancestor who was a *chevalier*, a knight.

From another French word, *cavallery*, English took the term *cavalry*. The French borrowed *cavallery* from Italian, where it is *cavalleria*, well known in the title of a great Italian opera, an 1890 masterwork by Pietro Mascagni, *Cavalleria Rusticana* 'countryside chivalry.' The Italian word descends from a Late Latin word for horseman, *caballarius*. Mascagni found the plot in a popular short story by Giovanni Verga. About one hundred years later, film director Francis Ford Coppola ended his mafia saga in "The Godfather III" with a long, exquisitely edited opera house sequence in which the concluding scenes and magisterial music of the Mascagni opera are intercut with the deaths of members of the Corleone family. "Godfather III" is a deeply flawed film but this terminal sequence is brilliant, as moviegoers watch Coppola's masterful employment of some of Sergei Eisenstein's 'montage as collision' techniques.

Quebec Note

Canadians will take note that *cheval*, the French word for horse gives *les Québécois* the name of their provincial slang, *joual.* The name of the patois, joual, is a Quebec pronunciation of the standard French word *cheval.*

Equisetum: *Equus* Derivative

Beyond equestrian and equitation, there are few common derivatives of *equus* in English, a testament to how thoroughly *caballus* replaced *equus* in all the Romance languages and in the words English borrowed from Romance languages. But one delightful exception is the botanical name of the marsh horsetail, the widespread 'scouring rush' found in most boggy or mildly damp areas of the northern hemisphere. The botanical genus of horsetail is Equisetum, literally 'horse bristle,' from *equus* Latin 'horse' + *saetum* Latin 'bristle,' or 'hair of a horse's tail.' The common North American English name of scouring rush points to its use by the earliest European pioneers in North America as a pot cleaner. Grease could be cleaned out of iron frying pans by wadding several horsetails together and scrubbing and scouring with the bristly weed.

Three Surprising Horse Etymologies

Bidet

That mainstay of French bathrooms, the bidet, now slowly conquering North America too, comes from a French word for a small pony, that is, an object easily straddled or mounted by the urinating person or during milady's personal cleansing.

Tacky

Now meaning offensive to taste or in disrepair or cheap, the adjective *tacky* began as an American noun *tackey*, a nag, an inferior horse, much like a *caballus*. Tackey first appears in American print in 1800 meaning 'a cheap pony.'

Easel

This word for a wooden frame that supports the canvas as a painter works on it entered English from the Dutch word *ezel* ' donkey' or 'ass.' It is similar to the German *Esel* and the etymology consists of *es, one of the early Germanic words for horse plus the common Indo-European suffixal diminutive *-l*, so that the semantic thrust of *Esel* is 'small horse.'

Is that sufficient horsiness for today, class? Yea or neigh? Neigh? Then how about . . .?

Hippos: the Attic Greek Word for Horse
How Ancient Greek Horse Culture
Affected Naming Customs

Were those ancient Greeks gaga about horses? One has merely to learn the meaning of many aristocratic Greek personal names, while noting that the Greek word for horse is *hippos*. Horses in Homer are described with the formulaic phrase *ookees hippoi* 'swift horses.' As a student of Homer years ago, my translation was 'foot-swift steeds' whose English chain of dental consonants seems to echo stallion hoof-clacks and still pleases me more than the dowdy literalism of 'swift horses.'

Hippopotamus is Greek for 'horse of the river' (Greek *potamos* 'river'). A hippodrome is a place where horses run (*dromos* Greek 'racetrack, running track for men or horses').

Part of the human brain is named after a sea-horse. It is hippocamp or hippocampus, from the name for a much larger ancient Greek sea-monster called *hippokampos.* It had the head and front part of a horse and the tail of a dolphin. First hippocampus became the name of the little aquatic fish cuties, the sea-horses. Then anatomists, picking apart a brain, decided that ridges running along the bottom of the lateral ventricles in the brain looked a bit like little wiggly sea-horses.

Horse & Human Names

As you will see below, the given names of the ancient Greek upper classes were indicative of having enough wealth to be the equivalent of a knight, that is, rich enough to supply a horse or two during wartime. The highest of the four Athenian social classes was composed of persons who could bear the rank of *hippeus*, sometimes translated 'knight' but it meant the family could afford to maintain warhorses in time of conflict, much like the later Latin societal term *equites*.

Hippeastrum

The botanical name of the amaryllis, a large beautiful bulbous flowering plant, derives from the Greek word for knight. It is Hippeastrum 'knight's star' from Greek *hippeus* 'knight' + *astron* 'star.'

Contrary to the scribblings of many gardening amateurs, it does NOT mean 'horse-star' in reference to the flower's large size. That would have been *hippoastrum, an ungainly verbal clumsiness. Hippeastrum was named to suggest the status of the bloom, a flower worthy of a knight. How do we know it is knight's star, aside from the obvious linguistic clues? We know who named the plant. In 1837 the Honorable

Reverend William Herbert, Dean of Manchester, dubbed it hippeastrum.

Wikipedia says "It seems likely however, as William Herbert was both a clergyman and something of an expert on early medieval history, that he chose the name because of the plants striking resemblance to the morning star, a medieval weapon used by horsemen. A version of the weapon was also called a holy water sprinkler, an ecclesiastical object the Dean would have been familiar with."

I think that is a preposterous guess, Wiki. First of all, a flower-loving English parson would have been well-enough acquainted with classical Greek to pluck a Greek term for morning star from his reading both of the classical Greek canon and of the New Testament in Koine Greek. Venus is the morning star and one Greek word for the planet is the lovely *Eophoros*, literally 'bringer of the dawn.' Another term naming the morning star, but one already too widely used perhaps to become the flower name, was *Phosphoros*, literally 'bearer or bringer of light.'

Secondly, the weapon was brutally ugly, invented to shatter human skulls and bore not the faintest resemblance to a flower. No peony-sniffing parson worth his garden spade would ever even think of that hideous weapon while contemplating the glory of a newly bloomed amaryllis. Really! Quite unaccountably stolid of that Wikipedia contributor. Quite *Wik-dick-ulous.*

One-upmanship in Ancient Greece

Horse ownership jibed with ancient Greek social status. History's first, known, great comic playwright was the Greek dramatist Aristophanes. In his comedy "The Clouds" a character named Pheidippides is a pushy nouveau riche and wants to appear of aristocratic origin. So the upstart inserts the Greek root for 'horse' into his peasant grandfather's name, and plain old Pheidos becomes Pheidippos, so that he, the grandson, is Pheidippides, a noble and dulcifluent moniker indeed, and phoney as a chastity affidavit from Zeus.

Aristophanes

This elongation of a personal name by spurious addenda is still with us. *Von* (it means 'of [the family of]') may betoken a German family who were medieval knights. Some of these *Reiterfamilien* had magnificently pompous names for their individual family members who were christened with names like Gotboldus Benedictus Gumprecht von Hohenstolz! An actual recorded German name. Yes, he was a three-foot dwarf who followed mares into the stable, but he owned the castle.

And that little German genitive preposition *von* was important. Consider the German pig farmer who adds *von* to his last name in hopes of elevating his ancestry by means of language instead of noble birth, so that Fritz Scheisskopf becomes Fritz von Scheisskopf. How much more pleasing to a not-very-bright vanity! Many a French *de* in a surname was added to family papers one dark night in a cowshed. In the annals of arriviste duplicity, there is indeed nothing new under the sun.

Greek Personal Names of Horsey Provenance

Philippos - Greek *philos* 'lover' + *hippos* 'horse,' hence lover of horses, and this bestows to posterity the still common given name Phillip, used in almost all the languages of the West and also an element in hundreds of western surnames like Philipson, Phipps, Filipacci, Philippopoulos and de la Philippe.

Hippolyta – literal Greek meaning 'she who looses the reins of horses; developed meaning 'a fine horsewoman, a fine rider'

Hippocrates – The father of Greek medicine has an old horse-culture tribal name that means literally 'he who rules horses.' The acquired meaning implies that he is a good rider or that he owns plenty of horses, a certain sign of wealth in ancient Greece. Another common Greek name that signified similar equine mastery was Hipparchos 'horse-leader.'

Hippias – Greek 'horse-guy'

Dorippe – Greek 'horse gift' from *doron* 'gift' + *hippos* 'horse,' perhaps an early dowry name for a Dorian girl about to marry

Kratippe – Greek *kratos* 'power' + *hippos* 'horse' literally 'she who has power over horses,' a valuable lady in ancient Greece.

Aristippos - Greek *aristos* 'best' + *hippos* 'horse = 'he who owns the best horses'

Xanthippe - That nag of a wife to the philosopher Socrates had a name that means literally 'yellow horse' but the semantic implication is a horse with a notably beautiful off-white coat, so a better English translation of Xanthippe would be mine, 'buttermilk mare.' One of history's most notorious scolds may have been the daughter of a man named Xanthippos or she may have been christened with the name because of fair skin or hair, a modest novelty in ancient Greece.

Extinct Horse Names

The technical names in paleozoology of several extinct ancestors of the modern horse are formed from the Greek root *hippos* too. Eohippus is an early horse (Greek *eos* 'dawn' 'early time'). An extinct relative of the horse is the tiny hipparion (Greek 'pony' from *hippos* 'horse' + *-arion* a common diminutive suffix for nouns, hence literally 'small horse.'

Okay, pardners, Wild Bill thinks we've ridden this pony to the end of the trail. See yuh back at the cookhouse for grub!

Chapter 48

Canadian Occupation Names

Some of these occupational names were coined by Canadians, some we borrowed. A few are still in use; others have gone, worn down by the sandpaper of use or cast aside for newer terms in the techno-rush of history.

Burgess in Saskatchewan

Persistent remnants of colonial vocabulary sometimes linger like sagebrush entangled in a prairie fence. Saskatchewan has a term, unique in Canada, for a citizen who owns property and pays local taxes.

A burgess in Saskatchewan is equivalent to what is called elsewhere in Canada a ratepayer. The English word *burgess* harks all the way back to 1066 CE, when the Normans invaded and conquered England and northern French words poured into English. The Old French word was *burgeis*, its form traceable to a Late Latin adjective *burgensis* 'town dweller.'

Burgess is an Anglo-Norman transformation of what became the French noun and adjective *bourgeois*, whose prime meaning was citizen of a *bourg*, or burg, a fortified town, from Late Latin *burgus* 'castle' or' fort.' *Burgus* traces its lineage to the Vikings, who spoke Old Norse. To them a *borg* was 'a wall,' then 'a wall around a town,' then 'a town.' This wall was at first made of wooden boards, and the related Old Norse word for that slat, *borth*, eventually gives the English term for a piece of lumber, a *board*.

The occupational word *burgess* has had several specific English meanings over the last nine hundred years. It first meant a freeman of a borough or town, one who could vote and enjoy the other full rights of a citizen. By the time of late Middle English, roughly during the fifteenth century, a burgess was a member of parliament for a borough. Later, in early American colonies like Virginia, a burgess was a rep sent by towns to the legislative body of colonial Virginia. In 1619 CE, there assembled the first elected legislative body in American history at Jamestown, Virginia, and it was called the House of Burgesses.

Here's the word in a majestic rollcall written in 1755 by Jonathan Swift: "All persons of honour, lords spiritual and temporal, gentry, burgesses and commonalty."

In England, before the Municipal Reform Act of 1835, a burgess was a magistrate of the governing body of a town.

Early on, German used the *burg* root to mean 'fortress,' as in Martin Luther's mighty Protestant hymn, *Ein feste Burg ist unser Gott* 'A mighty fortress is our God.'

The root is a fertile seed for words in European languages, giving English words like *borough, burglar, burrow, hamburger*, and the common German noun for citizen, *Bürger*, and its elaborations like the usual German word for mayor of a town, *Bürgermeister*. Distantly but surprisingly related are the English verb *to bury* and its noun *burial*, both derived from a supposed Old Teutonic verb **bergan* 'to cover, to protect as a wall does a garden.'

Cradle-Rocker

In placer mining, a cradle-rocker is a trough on a wooden or metal rocker used to separate gold flecks from sand and earth by washing and shaking the muddy gravel in water, and then, if necessary, using mercury to collect the gold. A prospector who performs such a task may also be called a cradle-rocker.

Depot farmer

A depot farmer grew and supplied food to lumber camps, often after the grueling work of clearing a few acres in the bush to produce tillable land. Potatoes for the lumbermen and oats for their horses were the main crops. Outbuildings on the farm might be used by the lumber company to store equipment and supplies. Such a depot farm was often owned by the lumber company itself, and the shanty farmer was its employee.

Donkey Puncher

Donkey puncher? Oh no! Must we traverse the tricky trap of animal abuse? Rest easy, lovers of the domestic ass. A small, auxiliary engine was first called a donkey in the British navy. From ships it spread to mean any of the small engines used in the British Columbia lumber industry. The lumberman who operated these log-pulling engines was the donkey puncher or donkey jammer or donkeyman. For his perpetual safety, let us bray.

A donkey consists of a steam boiler and steam engine connected to a winch mounted on a sled called a 'donkey sled.' The donkeys or sleds were moved by simply dragging themselves with the winch line. They were used to move logs, by attaching lines to the logs and hauling them. A donkey puncher was the machine operator.

There is an obscene meaning of donkey punch, which I do not intend to explicate here and perhaps besmirch these lily-white realms of gentility and innocence.

Draegerman

In the technical jargon of Maritime coal mining operations, a draegerman is a specially trained rescue worker. A draeger was a gas-mask that permitted descent into tunnels where poisonous seepage had occurred. A.B. Dræger, a German physicist and engineer, invented the mask, originally to protect German soldiers during gas warfare in the trenches of World War One. But canny Canadian soldiers brought the idea back to their Nova Scotia mines after the war.

Field Pitcher

In the lingo of prairie harvest terms, a field pitcher is one of the treshing hands. He's the guy who forks sheaves up onto the hay wagon to make a load. Sometimes he's called a stook-pitcher. He's not to be confused with the spike-pitcher who pitchforks sheaves from the load into the separator.

Hog Reeve

This phrase has nothing to do with swine flu. A hog reeve was an historical municipal official in Nova Scotia and Prince Edward Island, whose stern duty it was to collect stray pigs and tote up any damage to property done by wandering swine. The term may have been imported to or exported from our Canadian Maritimes, because we find it listed as an elected office in early New Hampshire township records.

Although he was called hog reeve or hog reefe, he supervised the behaviour of all domestic livestock permitted to graze on town commons or in neighbouring woods. If "estrays" browsed in cultivated fields and did damage, the hog reeve rounded them up and kept them fenced until the owners came, paid a minimal penalty and retrieved their errant beasts. Unfortunately the hog reeve's occupational power was never extended to encompass damage caused by elected municipal officials.

Rock Doctor

Geology abounds with technical terms not generally known to lithic laymen, jawbreakers like geognosy, *Wiesenboden*, and orography. At the other, more playful end of geological jargon is this nugget of Canadian mining slang. A rock doctor is any geologist.

Canadian folk sayings about work

- A man who watches the clock remains one of the hands.
- He could work all day in a bushel basket and still have room to move.
- *Avoir le trou de cul endessous du bras* 'to have your arse under your arm', to be dead-tired.
- Advice to the lazy: Donkeys go best loaded.
- Who will lift the cat's tail, if the cat won't? Immigrants to northern Ontario from Finland brought us this injunction to stop being lazy and get to work. It's word-for-word from Finnish. The obscene implication is that the person addressed with this question is too lazy to go to the bathroom.

Acedia or Accidie

We shall close with a neat word pertaining to the opposite of work, namely *acedia*, a Greek word for sloth, one of the Seven Deadly Sins. The form *acedia* is how the Romans wrote the Latin term having taken it from Greek *akedia* where the negative prefix *a-* means 'not' and *kedos* means 'concern or care' so that acedia signifies carelessness, indifference, apathy, torpor. The form *accidie* entered English in its Norman French form. The medieval Christian church thought that sitting around on your honkers (acedia) was a sin. Therefore: *Arise! Awake! Or Be Forever Fallen!*

Chapter 49

I'll Drink to These Words!

Some Roman booze terms & their derivatives in modern English

Nunc est Bibendum

Here is the Latin text of the first quatrain of a famous poem by the Roman poet Horace, first *Book of Odes*, Poem 37:

Nunc est bibendum, nunc pede libero
pulsanda tellus, nunc Saliaribus
ornare pulvinar deorum
tempus erat dapibus, sodales.

[my translation] Now is the time to drink fine wine; now is the earth fit to be danced upon with free feet, now, my friends and companions, let us furnish the couch of the gods with feasts worthy of Salian excess.

What is the occasion for this ancient Roman celebration? Rome's victory at the Battle of Actium, September 02, 31 BCE, that is, the utter defeat by Rome of Cleopatra! This is Horace, devotee of the first Roman emperor Augustus, writing a public celebration of the defeat by the Augustan army and navy of the forces of Mark Anthony and his lover Cleopatra.

Horace borrowed that famous opening verbal trio *nunc est bibendum*, translating them directly from his favorite ancient Greek poet, Alcaeus, who wrote *nyn chree methusthen* 'now it is fitting to get tipsy.'

In the autumn of 30 BCE, news of Cleopatra's defeat and suicide reached Rome. That was probably the advent of the Horatian idea for this Alcaic poem.

Bibendum is a gerundial form of the verb *bibere* 'to drink.' The verb's most familiar derivative in modern English is an adjective, *bibulous* 'overly fond of drinking alcoholic beverages,' chiefly used in humorous modes, for example, instead of saying a man is a drunkard, a scribe oblivious of cliché might write of his "bibulous propensities." He is still a sodden booze-hound, of course, and shows up most nights "stiff as a fresh-boiled owl."

Even rarer is classical Latin *potator* 'tippler, boozer, drinker,' rare yes, but still in occasional use in modern English.

More common today is *beverage* 'a drinkable liquid' which entered English through Old French *beivre, baivre, beivere, boivre* and modern French *boire* 'to drink,' all from Latin *bibere.* A Middle French form *bevrage* became popular in 15th-century English as *beverage.* Another derivative in extensive modern use is the English verb *to imbibe* 'to drink in.'

Bibunt sobrii, potant ebriosi.

This little Latin tag by Phaedrus displays the exact usage difference in Latin between the two common drinking verbs, *bibere* and *potare. Bibunt sobrii, potant ebriosi.* Sober people drink; drunken people slug it down like parched puppies. The Latin adjective used here for drunk *ebriosus* reminds us of our English getting-drunk verb *to be inebriated.* Gaius Julius Phaedrus was a writer in the first century CE who first translated *Aesop's Fables* from Greek into Latin.

Potables

That semantic difference between the Latin drinking verbs did NOT survive into English where *potare* derivatives came to signify mere drinking of any liquid. Hence there exist phrases like *potable water* 'drinkable water.'

Potion was first a drink, then a kind of special drink, perhaps mixed like a witches' brew with an unsavoury purpose. This extraordinary use of potion led to a powerful variant, also derived from *potio, potionis*: namely the noun *poison*! It too was at first a tainted drink but began innocently enough in Anglo-Norman as *poisoun* 'a draught, a drink' and evolved through manifold forms like *puisun* and *pouson* finally to *poison*. The Proto-Indo-European verbal root is *pōɑh- 'to drink' whose reflexes include ancient Greek *pothi* 'to drink.'

A Roman Drinking Cup

Poculum is the ordinary Latin word for a drinking cup, a goblet, a beaker. It is the basis for one of the extraordinary Roman Catholic indulgences which rich Christians could buy in the Middle Ages. Imagine it. A *poculary* allowed you to get pissed, push your wife over a castle rampart in a drunken rage and still be forgiven, if you had purchased a document forgiving you for getting plastered and absolving you of any small sins committed while bombed, namely, a poculary. No wonder Martin Luther had his work cut out of him!

Your most obedient humble servant, little *moi*, coined a comic synonym for drunk using this fine Latin term. To be wobbling drunk, I wrote, was to be in the throes of "an interpoculary stupor." *Inter*, Latin 'between, among' + Latin *pocula* 'drinking cups,' thus to be, so-to-speak, 'among your cups.'

Yes, it is shameless to quote oneself. I wonder if there's an indulgence for such egotism.

A Mortal Warning

Of course, in this age of political correctness, the sombre drones of temperance remind us that there is nothing funny anymore, anywhere, ever, on earth. Being drunk is bad.

After heavy drinking, men often cannot perform sexually, and this temporary and unpleasant state has been dubbed "brewer's droop."

If you drink, don't drive. Certainly that is a very commonsensical admonition.

All that said, my final word to the abstemious bluestocking is a quotation from a novel *The History of Tom Jones, a Foundling* by Henry Fielding (1749 CE), in which the learned English judge and novelist makes this observation: "It is said strong drink dulls a man. And so it will. In a dull man."

Chapter 50

New & Old Moon Words

like lunain, epigee, apogee & syzygy

A writer whose name I have lost once wrote that the first poem in the first language ever spoken was "O, Moon."

Why, you may wisely ask, do the English words *moon* and *month* both stem from the same Proto-Indo-European root? The thirty-day earth month approximates the lunar cycle of waxing and waning. Throughout history, in some of the oldest calendars, these regular phases of the moon have made it a good timekeeper. Yes, it was superseded by the more accurate solar calendar. But the moon's regularity gave the Romans their words for *measure* and *menstrual* and *menstruate* whose root meaning is "go through the monthly moon time."

*Moon***day**

English named the moon after a month and Monday is moon-day, or, in the oldest English we know, *Monandæg.* French named Monday after the moon too, so French *lundi* is derived from later Latin *Lunae dies* or *Lunis dies* 'day of the moon'. *Luna* is the Latin word for moon. All the Romance languages borrowed that Latin phrase. Compare Spanish *lunes* and Italian *lunedì.*

Hellenistic Greek copied Latin too and called Monday *hemera selenes* 'day of the moon.'

Lunar Etymology

The Latin word for moon *luna* is closely related to other Roman words that mean 'bright light' such as *lux* and *lumen* 'radiance or amount of light' as in the English words *illuminate* and *luminous. Lux* is cognate with the English noun *light* and with the Greek adjective for 'white' *leukos.*

Hematic Matters

Leukos gives English medical words like *leucocyte* 'white blood cell' and *leukemia*, a blood or bone cancer with abnormal increase in white blood cells from a German medical word, itself made up of *leuk-, leukos* Greek 'white' + *-emia* medical suffix meaning 'diseased condition of the blood' from *haima* Greek 'blood.' Compare other blood words like *hemoglobin* and the tricky *anemia* originally meaning 'lack of blood' = *a* Greek 'not' + *-n-* called "nu euphonic" or "nu movable" (a letter *n* inserted into a word to make it easier to pronounce) +-emia from *haima* Greek 'blood.' Nu is the Greek name for the letter *n*. Another scientific word with nu euphonic is *anaerobic* = *a* Greek 'not' + *-n-* nu euphonic + *aer* Greek 'air' + *bios* Greek 'life,' an adjective applied chiefly to microorganisms which can function without oxygen.

Mezzaluna

In the armory of modern kitchen utensils, a mezzaluna is a knife used for chopping herbs. It has a blade curved like a half moon (Italian *mezza luna*).

Hachoir is its French name. It is similar to the Inuit chopping blade, the ulu.

Lunatics & Lovers

There are a number of lunar words we shall not cover here because their meanings are well known. Most know that madmen were first called lunatics because ancient physicians thought they were moon-mad, driven insane by the moon.

Lunain

There is a glorious NASA photograph entitled "Earthrise seen from the lunain." Lunain was a new word coined in 1971 when humans landed on the moon. Lunain was the lunar surface, as terrain is the earthly one. I though it a lovely word for the cold, star-lit countenance of the moon. But no one else did. And so it wisped away and died, in obsolescent desuetude. O regrettable discontinuance! Poor abandoned wordlet.

Sublunary

I like the sound of this adjective, drawn from new Latin *sublunaris* 'taking place under the moon' from *sub* Latin 'under' + *lunaris* Latin adjective 'pertaining to the moon.' Although sublunary (pronounced sub-LOON-ary) began with meanings like 'influenced by the moon,' it came to be used—as the long tongue of English grew fond of the word—to mean 'referring to anything that happened on earth,' then with a pejoration of that sense, sublunary became synonymous with 'gross,' 'earthly' and 'mundane.' I always think it fits best in phrases (my own) like sublunary frolic, or sublunary antics that comprise the cloddish dance of life. In *The Anatomy of Melancholy*

(1621 CE), Robert Burton spoke of "sublunary devils. . . fiery, aerial, terrestrial, watery and subterranean."

Silver was Luna

In the annals of alchemy, ancient cauldron-stirrers gave the names of the seven alchemical metals the names of the seven ancient planets, so alchemists dubbed Sol the sun Gold; Luna the moon was Silver, Venus was Copper, Jupiter Tin, Saturn Lead, Mars Iron and Mercury, of course, was Quick-silver.

Don't Trip over Those Moonbeams!

How many vampire movies feature a nubile sleepwalker, a callipygous cutie, her nightie of diaphanous chiffon abillow in a night breeze, as she lunambulates down Dracula's chill corridor? Lunambulism is a rare and delightful sleepwalk supposedly caused by the moon, from *luna* Latin 'moon' + *ambulare* Latin 'to walk.' So Michael Jackson might have used it to name his moonwalk. Callipygous or callipygian means 'having shapely buttocks' from *kalos* Greek 'beautiful' + *puge* 'buttocks, rump.' Greek *kallipugos* was the epithet of a famous statue of Aphrodite, goddess of beauty, to whom the sculptor had given a superior posterior. Diaphanous is a fancy synonym for transparent, from Medieval Latin *diaphanus* < Greek *diaphanes* < *diaphainein* 'to show through' < *dia-* Greek 'through' + *phainein* Greek 'to show.'

Luna Moth

I will never forget the summer night of my first luna moth, the surprise of my first sighting in Dundas County, Ontario. One teenage midnight I was bolting my uncle's barn doors. Quietly a phosphorescent lime glow loomed in the periphery of my vision. There on the night-black weathered wood of the barn-side, key-lit by moonlight, spread large moth wings, strangely green. American writer Annie Dillard, in her cautious hymn to nature, *Pilgrim at Tinker Creek*, wrote a true description: "Luna moths are those fragile ghost moths, fairy moths, whose five-inch wings are swallow-tailed, a pastel green bordered in silken lavender." *Actias luna*, its zoological name, was given because of two, large, vaguely crescent-moon-shaped, translucent spots on their tapered hindwings, meant to look like large animal eyes and so frighten off moth-hungry predators. The luna moth boasts the broadest wing span and the serenest beauty of all North American moths.

At The Eclose

And we shall add a neat little moth verb, to eclose, a back formation from the English noun *eclosion* 'emergence of an insect from its pupal encasement.' Near the onset of the twentieth century, English entomologists borrowed the word from French *éclosion* 'hatching from an egg' < *éclore* 'to hatch,' ultimately from a Vulgar Latin verb not attested *exclaudere 'to hatch out' = *ex* Latin 'out of' + *claudere* Latin 'to close,' but in etymological reality, a pronunciation change caused a spelling change, for *éclore* actually stems from *excludere* Latin 'to hatch, drive out, exclude.'

Big Moon Monday

So, my moon and luna words having pupated, I must flutter away. But I remind you of supermoons (very large) that occur.

A Couple of Supermoon Technical Words in Astronomy

Once a month the moon is at a position known as perigee, its closest to earth, and apogee, its farthest from the earth.

A syzygy, a lining up of celestial bodies, particularly the sun, Earth and moon occurs rarely. When it happens, earthlings get a full moon. Now, when the syzygy and the perigee coincide, we get the so-called supermoon. Syzygy entered English from French through the late Latin *syzygia* from Greek *syzygia* 'pair, yoking, conjunction' from Greek *syzygos* 'joined up' from Greek preposition *syn* 'together, with' + part of the verb *zeugnunai* 'to yoke.'

The moon's perigee coincides with a full moon. The perigee is the point in the orbit of the moon around the earth when the moon is closest to the earth. Perigee is from Greek *peri* 'around, round about, near to, up next to' + Greek *gaios* or *geios* 'of the earth' from Greek *gaia* or *ge* 'the earth,' an etymon that appears in dozens of English words like geography, geodesic, Gaia 'the earth mother or earth goddess,' geometry and geode. *Peri* is the ultimate prefixal etymon in words like perimeter and periphrastic.

The opposite of perigee is apogee, when its orbit places the moon farthest from the earth. Apogee < French *apogée* < Latin *apogæum* < Greek *apogaion* > apo 'off, away from' + Greek *gaios* 'of the earth.' It is said: the moon is in apogee or at apogee.

Good lunar viewing or Happy Selenoscopy! (Greek, 'moon viewing') but I made the word *selenoscopy* up as a playful neology.

Chapter 51

Words Left out in the Shed

Certainly you know what a watershed is. But what is a walkshed, a laborshed, a megashed, a foodshed, a viewshed? Yes, *-shed* has become a fashionable suffix or second word in about a dozen newish compound nouns, all patterned after the word *watershed.*

Etymology of the Verb *to Shed*

Shed itself begins as an elemental Teutonic verb form with its Old English reflex *sceadan* 'to divide, to separate.' Persistent wee root that it is, the original meaning is still in use in some English dialects, when farmers begin *to shed the cows from the goats* 'to separate domestic flocks into their proper assemblies.' To shed is cognate with modern Dutch and German *scheiden* 'to divide.' One interesting cognate of to shed is to shit and its Germanic partner *Scheisse.* Shit was originally **gescheit* and **gescheissene* 'that which is divided or separated' from the body. English *shed* is distantly related to the Proto-Indo-European roots *skheid- and *skid- which appear in the ancient Greek verb *schizein* 'to split' (think of schizophrenia's original meaning of 'split mind') and the Latin verb *scindere* 'to cleave, to cut' with its modern English derivatives *scissors* and *rescind.*

Watershed

Watershed became popular in English only around 1800 CE. But a German word *Wasserscheide* was four hundred years old that year. *Wasserscheide* first appears in German print about 1400 CE and therefore the English compound *watershed* is very likely a calque, a loan-translation, from the German word which, from its coining, has referred to the drainage basin, the catchment ground from which the waters of a stream or river flow to the body of the stream.

Walkshed

With the word *watershed* in mind, urban planner Alan Durning of the Sightline Institute coined the term *walkshed* to describe the variety of amenities within a one-mile radius of a town or city point. This calibration of walkability is now being studied in a number of American urban sites like Philadelphia and New York City. Walkshed has acquired a secondary related meaning. It is the distance and urban area that a person can comfortably or conveniently cover on foot.

Although Durning may have borrowed the term *walkshed*, it does occur in *The Daily Score* of April 5, 2006, in "One Mile from Home," an article by the man himself, Alan Durning: "A one-mile perimeter, therefore, defines this car-less family's pedestrian travel zone — call it our 'walkshed.' Fortunately, because we chose to live in a compact community, our walkshed turns out to be well stocked." There are earlier printed uses of walkshed. Note that Durning does not specifically claim that he coined the word.

Here are earlier citations:

2005 *Mississippi Renewal Forum* (Mississippi) (Nov. 9) "The Mississippi Gulf Region: A Framework for Renewal" p. 6: A key piece of regional and community livability is walkable access to parks and schoolyards. The walksheds shown here illustrate varying levels of access across the region and within communities (Gulfport is shown using actual walking routes while other municipalities are shown with straight-line radius walksheds).

2005 El Dorado County Transportation Commission *Folsom El Dorado Corridor Transit Strategy Final Report* (Placerville, California) (Dec. 9) "Section 5" p. V-1: Typically, the "walkshed" for transit is about one-quarter mile and, in some cases, as much as one-half mile if sufficient infrastructure is in place to accommodate pedestrians (i.e. sidewalks, safety design and lighting; and land uses that activate the walking environment).

Laborshed

Laborshed is the distance within which live the workers in a factory, a neighbourhood or a city. Its first appearance in print is May 5, 2008 on a Davenport, Iowa website in article written by Jenifer DeWitt: "The first-ever Quad-Cities Graduate Inventory determined that 47,700 graduates are being produced annually within a 90-mile radius, which is considered the laborshed area for the Quad-Cities."

Foodshed

Foodshed is the area of land needed to provide food for a given location or population. It is an older term that either walkshed or laborshed.

1929 W.P. Hedden *How Great Cities Are Fed @ Journal of Business of the University of Chicago* (Apr. 2, 1930) Joseph G. Knapp vol. 3, no. 2, p. 263: Watersheds, Milksheds, and Foodsheds.

Viewshed

Viewshed is the landscape or topography visible from a given geographic point, especially one having aesthetic value.

1970 *Oakland Tribune* (California) (July 7) "Less Spoiling Route OK'd for Briones Lines" (in Martinez) p. 4E: The new route through the park will take the line out of sight about 90 per cent of the park visitors, and cut "viewshed" intrusion to 25 per cent."

Megashed

This is a large, ugly distribution warehouse or big-box store designed to destroy, for example, Mom & Pop hardware stores located within the death-shed of the big-box. Environmental protesters are using this term to decry the wiping out of small neighbourhood shops and their replacement by soulless mega-splorps.

Early Citation:

"First there were the friendly neighbourhood ironmongers. Then came the out-of- town superstore. Now, courtesy of Kingfisher, comes the next generation of DIY outlet, the mega-shed. Called Depot (and appropriately given the American pronunciation Dee Poe), at 70,000 sq. ft. these are twice the size of typical B&Q stores and stock double the number of lines."

—"View from City Road: Plenty of mileage at Kingfisher," *The Independent* (London), September 16, 1992

A Few Other Shed Terms & Phrases

Woodshedding is a playful term among some jazz musicians for practicing and playing in isolated places, like a country woodshed, where you will not disturb neighbours or passersby. The word appeared in the New York Times in October, 2006. Another origin claims that woodshedding "originated from drum practice due to the fact that drum sticks, after hours of playing, start to flake off small bits of wood (usually covering the floor around the drumset). This is referred to as "woodshedding." Although it originated as a drumming term, it is commonly used for any instrument. A shortened form of the word is shedding."

Other -Shed Sayings

"He's not the sharpest tool in the shed" implies that he is stupid.

A shed-dragger is a motoring yoyo who pulls a trailer behind his car that is four times longer than his car.

"Burning down the shed" is low slang for very vigorous sex.

A sheddy is current American public school and high school slang for a student taking "shop" or "industrial arts." Students in academic classes think of building skills classes as fit only for illiterate fools. **Shed builder** is another cafeteria putdown of tech. students.

But at this juncture must we shed all pretense of momentum, for the door of this shed is now closed.

Chapter 52

Roman Kisses

Osculum, basium, suavium & their descendants in English

In creating a puckered repertoire of kissing nouns and verbs, the ancient Romans never got as slangy as Americans, who coined my favorite osculatory verbal phrase. Instead of asking "Would you like to kiss?" a Yankee swain can blurt out, "Wanna suck face?" That vivid invitation couched in eighties' folk speech was popularized in the play and in the film "On Golden Pond."

But dwellers in antique Rome did have a panoply of kissing verbs and nouns, all of which have left their descendants scattered throughout both everyday English and sprinkled in more raffiné realms amidst the technical vocabulary of medicine and other sciences.

No Physiology of the Human Kiss Here

Kissologists elsewhere on the internet have waxed analytical about the physiology and uses of kissing, about the huge number of nerve cells clustered around the mouth and lips, making them a neural furnace of stimulation, but here, in this modest etymological notelet, there shall be no such anatomical disquisition.

Philematology?

By the way, the fancier word for a person who studies kissing is philematologist, from the New Testament Greek word for kiss, *philema*, *philematos* (literal meaning in Koine Greek 'love thing'). That's the 'kiss' noun that New Testament writers used in the story of Judas kissing Christ. It also names the Christian "holy kiss" mentioned five times in the New Testament, as, for example, in Romans 16:16 — "Greet one another with a holy kiss" (Greek: *aspasasthe allelous en philemati hagiou*).

Philema may have been a non-sexual, dry, quick, ceremonial kiss such as men in the ancient Near East exchanged frequently, and thus a translation of the Hebrew nashaq (naw-SHAK) 'to kiss' and its common noun *neshiqah* (nesh-ee-KAW).

***Osculum*, Latin 'Kiss' Word with the Most English Descendants**

In English science, an *osculum* (Latin and English plural *oscula*) is an opening like a mouth, through which, for example, a sponge expels water. Osculum may also name any minute opening.

The related verb is much more common, to osculate, especially as a humorous synonym for 'to kiss.' Its Latin word story is neat. *Os, oris* is the Latin word for mouth. It is the source of our common English adjective *oral*. *Osculum* is the Latin diminutive, meaning 'a little mouth.' When one puckers up the lips in a circular labial muscular constriction, in a cincture of the lips preparatory to kissing, one makes 'a little mouth,' one osculates!

Rarer relatives abound in technical English. Consider the scientific adjective *osculant* 'clinging closely together,' used for example in the study of insects to describe the embrace of caterpillars. The agent noun appears occasionally too, to describe a campaigning senator who, during elections, was an inveterate osculator of small babies and defenseless infants.

Latin's Treasury of Verbal Kisses

Latin had three nouns which meant 'kiss.' Though there is some dispute, in general, it seems as if *basium* referred to a kiss on the lips or a kiss on the hand, *osculum* was a friendly kiss and the rarest Roman term *suavium* (or savium) meant an erotic kiss.

Basium

This is the Latin source of the name of a quite popular Italian candy, *Baci* "kisses." The Latin plural is *basia*. The Proto-Indo-European etymon appears to be *bu 'to kiss' cognate with Persian *bus* 'to kiss' and, of course, with an older English verb, *to buss* 'to kiss.'

Knowers of Latin poetry will think of Catullus' famous love command and the word used in the famous fifth ode of Catullus, all about kissing his girlfriend Lesbia: *da mi basia mille* 'give me a thousand kisses.'

An obsolete synonym for 'to kiss,' last used in 1623 CE, was *to basiate*.

Suavium, the Sweetest of Latin Kisses

This was the erotic, tongue-as-tendril, French kiss of lust, from the Latin adjective *suavis* 'sweet, agreeable.' Here too is a seventeenth-century obsolete kissing verb, namely, *to suaviate.* I like the naughty, salivary sound of this racy verb and we ought to revive its use.

Let us conclude our canoodling smoochirama with four lines I like from Christopher Marlowe's 1592 CE play *Faustus*:

"Was this the face that launched a thousand ships,
And burnt the topless towers of Ilium?
Sweet Helen, make me immortal with a kiss!
Her lips suck forth my soul: See, where it flies!"

Chapter 53

Christian Events as Art Words

Christian theological event names like Epitaphios and Ecce Homo! as terms in religious art history

Ascension

The Ascension of Jesus (Vulgate Latin: *Ascensio Iesu* 'the climbing up' is the New Testament report that, after his resurrection, the Lord was taken up to heaven bodily. A nearby angel told the eleven disciples present that Jesus would return in a second coming in exactly the same mode, in his human/divine body.

Assumption of the Virgin

Blasphemous jest suggests that the Assumption of the Virgin is: *he's wearing a condom*. This is not true, class. Here assumption partakes of its most ancient and prime Latin semantic and means "a taking up to a higher place' from the Latin prepositional prefix *ad* 'to, up to, near to' (assimilating and thus becoming as- in front of the initial s) of the verb + Latin verb *sumere* 'to take up.' The Assumption of the Virgin is the bodily lifting from earth to heaven of Holy Mary, Mother of God. The Blessed Virgin did not accomplish this in a Cessna Skycatcher. Rather, she was wafted to cerulean realms of thrilling wonderfulness by our old flying buddy, *Spiritus Sanctus* 'Holy Spirit' or by lesser divine minions of an angelic nature.

Two technical terms of theology may be of interest here. Mariology is the simple term, the tenets and beliefs dealing with the Virgin Mary. Mariolatry is usually a label of disapproval, referring to worship of Mary that is 'way overboard,' partaking of a pietistical excess which becomes slavish. Protestants sometimes accuse Roman Catholics of mariolatrous indulgence. Mariolatry = Latin *Maria* 'Mary'+ Latin –o- common combining syllable + Late Latin *latria* 'servile worship' < Greek *latreia* 'slavish obedience.' We know the second part of the compound in the familiar word idolatry 'worship of idols.'

Ecce Homo!

These are the most famous words of the great Roman villain of Christendom, Pontius Pilate. Pontius Pilatus was the official judge at the trial of Christ and Pilate was he who ordered Jesus to be crucified. Pontius is known to historical record as the Prefect of the Roman province of Judaea from 26 to 36 CE.

When Pilate presented the scourged Christ to the hostile mob of louts in front of the *praetorium*, his residence in Jerusalem, during that long-ago Passover, the Bible claims that Pontius' uttered the Latin sentence "*Ecce homo!*" There are several translations. But the semantic gist of the Latin is "Here is the guy you want." A literal translation might be "Behold the man!"

Of course, Pilate's sentence (*Ecce homo*) is a translation into Latin in Saint Jerome's Vulgate version of the bible. In the Koine Greek of the original New Testament, Pilate's words to the screaming crowd are reported as "*idou ho anthrōpos.*" The gist of the Greek is slightly more complex than that Latin translation. The sly Greek means: "See. Here is this person. He is merely a human being."

As usual, the cruder Latin translation cannot carry the several subtleties of the apparently elusive Greek. The moment inspired many canvases throughout the history of European painting.

Epitaphios

The Epitaphios is an iconic image depicting Christ removed from the cross and lying supine, while his body is prepared for burial. Its usual form is a tapestry or a richly embroidered large cloth, sometimes laid over the altar during the matins of Holy Saturday which are performed on the evening of Good Friday in the rites of Eastern Orthodox and Eastern Catholic churches. Epitaphios means 'on the tomb or grave' from Greek *epi* 'on, upon' + *taphos* 'grave, tomb.' Think of its more common form in English as epitaph 'inscription on a gravestone.' It is thought to be a short form applying at first to the chant of mourning and thus being an abbreviation of the Greek phrase *epitaphios threnos* 'lamentation at the burial site.'

Two English words are based on threnos: threnody and threne. A threnody is a dirge, a song of lamenting at a funeral, a compound even in its original form Greek *threnoidia* 'dirge' = *threnos* 'grieving' + *oide* 'song.' Likewise the rarer English word *threne* means 'a funeral lament,' but was a quondam synonym for that biblical book called *The Lamentations of Jeremiah*. Once it was also known as *The Threnes of Jeremiah*.

Maestà

Maestà, Italian for 'majesty,' designates an iconic representation of the Madonna enthroned in glory, with Jesus, but with or without angels, saints, flittering attendant putti, and any other winged or armed members of the Blessed Virgin Mary's aerial defence core, comprising what Alexander Pope, in a secular context, made reference to when he wrote:

"Know then, unnumbered Spirits round thee fly,
The light Militia of the lower Sky."

Maria Regina

Maria Regina Caeli or shortened to Maria Regina, Latin 'Mary, Queen of Heaven' is the technical term in art history for any iconic image of Mary on a throne, holding or not holding the baby Jesus.

The Harrowing of Hell

The Harrowing of Hell is not in the Gospels. There is no scriptural reference to Jesus descending into Hell. It is a later addition to the Christian mythos, appearing for example in the Apostles' Creed. Sometimes known by its Greek name Anastasis (literal Greek meaning 'resurrection'), it is credited as an invention of Byzantine Christians and appears in Western ecclesiastical literature for a first time only early in the eighth century. Christ's chthonian descent is taken by some biblical scholars to mean that Christ went down to the dead and came back up as one more proof of his resurrection and his command over death.

But now, until the next time, our pious pinkies, assisted always by angel hands, must close the great tome of Holy Writ.

Chapter 54

Areopagitica

Annals of Rhetoric & Ancient Greek Place Names

Areopagus is a hill in Athens, named in ancient Greek *areios pagos* 'the Martian hill', that is, a hillock in Athens which originally held an altar for the worship of the Greek god of war, Ares. Ares was Mars to the Romans, although Mars as a word is, if not cognate with Ares, at least closely associated with Ares very early in Roman history. Later Mars' Hill or the Areopagus was a meeting place where the most powerful judicial court of the city of Athens held its open-to-the-public sittings. Areopagus was once used in English to mean 'any high tribunal.'

Etymology

Areopagitica < Latin *Arēopagīticus*, < Greek *areopagitikos* 'pertaining to the Hill of Mars [and its judicial assemblies]'

Naturally some of the greatest Athenian lawyers and masters of rhetoric spoke here, including the orator Isocrates who, in the fifth century BCE, after the council had lost much of its power, gave an impassioned speech seeking to restore its ancient importance, a speech known as Isocrates' 'For the Areopagus.'

The word is best known in English to students of rhetorical prose, because John Milton named his famous tract in defense of English free speech after that of Isocrates.

Areopagitica: A Speech of Mr. John Milton for the Liberty of Unlicensed Printing to the Parliament of England is a tract printed as a pamphlet by the poet John Milton against censorship. Milton's 1644 Areopagitica stands as a high prose mark in persuasive argument in the history of English eloquence. Everyone writing English prose in any mode of suasion ought to peruse it for inspiration.

Quotation from Isocrates

(transliteration of the Attic Greek) *Isokrates tes paideias ten rhizan pikran ephee, glykeis de tous karpous.*
(translation) Isocrates said that the root of education is bitter, but the fruits are sweet.

Quotations from Milton's Areopagitica

"As good almost kill a man as kill a good book. Who kills a man kills a reasonable creature, God's image; but he who destroys a good book, kills reason itself, kills the image of God, as it were in the eye."

"Give me the liberty to know, to utter, and to argue freely according to conscience, above all liberties."

"For books are not absolutely dead things, but do contain a potency of life in them to be as active as that soul whose progeny they are; nay, they do preserve as in a vial the purest efficacy and extraction of that living intellect that bred them."

"A good book is the precious lifeblood of a master spirit, embalmed and treasured up on purpose to a life beyond life." This quotation is displayed over the entrance to the Main Reading Room of the New York Public Library.

Miltonic Addendum

From a blog named "areopagitica," posted by K. I reproduce these paragraphs with permission:

Milton "argued for the free exchange of ideas and knowledge. There were limits to his ideas of freedom of the press but he sketched out, in ringing tones, his belief that liberty and progress were dependent on the search for knowledge, truth and understanding.

Milton's ideas came out of that anxious and hopeful period in English history when parliament was at war with the king. He wrote this pamphlet three years before the Putney Debates in which, for the first time, the idea of one man one vote was advanced, and five years before the execution of Charles I and the establishment of the English Commonwealth. It was a period of immense danger, of grief and the separation of families. It was also a time when individuals questioned authority and took responsibility for debating the future of the country.

Areopagitica shows the excitement of debate at the time, when so many people were willing to look outwards and think questioningly about the world, risking their own safety to enter in a debate about the government of their country. Key questions hinged on liberty and what we would now call "human rights":

'Behold now this vast City: a City of refuge, the mansion house of liberty, encompast and surrounded with his protection; the shop of warre hath not there more anvils and hammers waking, to fashion out the plates and instruments of armed Justice in defence of beleaguer'd Truth, then there be pens and heads there, sitting by their studious lamps, musing, searching, revolving new notions and ideas wherewith to present, as with their homage and their fealty the approaching Reformation: others as fast reading, trying all things, assenting to the force of reason and convincement. What could a man require more from a Nation so pliant and so prone to seek after knowledge? What wants there to such a towardly and pregnant soile, but wise and faithfull labourers, to make a knowing people, a Nation of Prophets, of Sages, and of Worthies. We reck'n more than five months yet to harvest; there need not be five weeks, had we but eyes to lift up, the fields are white already. Where there is much desire to learn, there of necessity will be much arguing, much writing, many opinions; for opinion in good men is but knowledge in the making.' [John Milton]

Milton lost and the cause he loved - the Commonwealth - faded. After eleven years, Charles II was invited back by parliament. The leaders of the Commonwealth were hanged, drawn and quartered for their part in the execution of the king. Milton was lucky to survive.

But the ideas of Milton and his contemporaries lived on. In the nineteenth century, working-class radicals were among the most enthusiastic readers of Milton.

Reading Milton was my introduction to Britain's radical past. I read most of Milton for pleasure - I loved the exhilaration of his language as well as his engagement with the ideas of his time. It didn't matter that some was difficult. I took what I could from a first reading and returned later, for more. Milton may have slipped from the public consciousness but I don't think he'll be forgotten forever." [Posted by K.]

Bill Casselman's final reminder

To any who seek examples of authoritative expository prose in English, I recommend reading Milton's poetry too. Close perusal and reading aloud of Milton's epic *Paradise Lost* lets a reader/speaker understand how to imbue semantic thrust and sonic supremacy into English sentences. The stern majesty of Milton's poetic diction surpasses, for suasion and grandeur and splendor, all other English writers.

Chapter 55

At Stool

a learned essay about stool & other fecal words

You may wish to evacuate this chapter, because we now commence a study of the word *stool*, for the elucidation of any who wonder how the name of a chair came to designate a turd.

Please note first that I have always abhorred euphemism, the evasion of simple language by means of sugary evasion, by weasel-word substitutive circumlocution, by replacing stern words with some dinky delicacy of utterance pleasing to the ears of a prissy fop or a bewigged noblewoman of too genteel a birth to have her shapely auricles befouled by gutter talk. What I have to say to such aristocratic word-snobs is "Screw that noise!"

All hail potty-mouthed, low speech!

Proudly do I assert that I am a fan of dysphemism, whereby the varlet wordster (*moi!*) takes a positive or neutral word and replaces it with a loathsome, disagreeable word, the better to awaken the reader from his or her customary doziness and reflective sloth. A dedicated dysphemist would take down the sign that reads "Men's Room" and put up a new sign reading "Drop Fudge Nuggets Here."

Today a (foot) stool is a small tripodal (three-legged) seat, often a mere footrest. But in earlier languages, the common Teutonic root *Stuhl* was a chair of high office, a seat of august authority, even a bishop's lofty throne effulgent with episcopal splendour.

Etymology of the Word *Stool*

In a modern western house, a stool is usually a short stepladder that children and dwarf wives stand on to extend their reach. The Proto-Indo-European root is **sta* 'to stand, to sit, to be located,' an etymon most productive in Western languages giving us in English alone and from borrowed cognates literally thousands of words like: *stand, steady, stay, steer, station, stet, status, circumstance, instant, stasis, ecstasy, hemostat, thermostat, install, epistle, apostle* and *stable.*

Trapeza

Because sportive divertissements and etymological sidetracks from the pathways of wordish duty are not only permissible in language study but often agreeable, I pause to tell you about a Greek word for stool which turns into the modern Greek word for a commercial bank where one keeps money. Trapeza was an ancient Greek word for table, in origin a modest four-legged stool (*trapeza* > *tessares* Greek 'four' + *pezos* 'foot' in compound words > *pous podos* Greek 'foot').

In a Greek Orthodox monastery, the refectory where monks and pilgrims eat is a trapeza, a modest table. Yes, the English words *trapezoid* and *trapeze* stem from the same compound. In ancient Greece, and in the Hellenistic era of the New Testament, money-lenders on the steps or along the porticoes of temples, squatted cross-legged in front of little four-legged tables, exchanging currencies for a fee, taking deposits and receiving interest on previous loans, thence the Modern Greek word for bank became *trapeza*.

By the mid-fourteenth century and perhaps earlier, stool as throne began to disappear in use, contaminated by its newer meaning of *toilet*. We know it meant commode by 1455 because we read of an English king who had in service one "William Grymesby who was Yeoman of the Stoole" and Groom of the Chamber (pot). Now there indeed is a modest regal preferment, if ever one was granted to lowly mortal.

We even have servant bitchiness arising by 1596 CE, in this poisonous little note: "A seventh (whom I would guess by his writing to be groom of the stool to some prince of the blood of France) writes a beastly treatise only to examine what is the fittest thing to wipe withal, alleging that white paper is too smooth!"

The famous diarist Samuel Pepys (1663 CE) was not above informing us of his defecatory habits. On May 24, 1663, Pepys jotted down this fetching notelet: "Having taken one of Mr. Holliard's pills last night, it brought a stool or two this morning." TMI, Pepysie. Too much information, dude.

Consider also the place of stool as a quiet getaway, a spousal retreat, a refugium from household bother. Then must we quote from *Travels into Several Remote Nations of the World, in Four Parts. By Lemuel Gulliver, First a Surgeon, and then a Captain of Several Ships*, better known as *Gulliver's Travels* (1726 CE), in which noble tome Jonathan Swift did write "Men are never so serious, thoughtful, and intent, as when they are at stool."

The House of Easement

Every age has employed vulgar toilet terms like bog, close-stool, commode, crapper, the can, cloaca, earth-closet, water closet, privy, jakes, thunder mug, john, throne room, lavatory, bathroom, shitpot, shitter, dumping ground and the endless chain of syrupy infantilisms like the revoltingly twee "poo-poo-ka-ka-doo-doo place."

Yes, every age has evolved euphemistic ways to avoid saying shithole. My own English favorite is the widely used but now obsolete Tudor phrase "stool of easement." When the Norman word *aisement* first placed its dainty toe upon British soil, easement meant opportunity or ample room to do something. In Old French *eise* or *aise,* which would produce English forms later like *ease* and *easy,* had a similar sense of 'enough room to accomplish a task.' A sixteenth-century history text tells us that "the [Roman] emperor Heliogabalus was killed upon his stool at his easement."

To the Tudors, easement meant the act of voiding excrement and the place it was done, so that the reader of Tudor history finds items like "to do one's easement" or in a Tudor glossary of French *aller à la selle* 'to go to the stoole of easement.'

In modern English, easement is chiefly a legal term naming the right or privilege of using something not one's own, as in the request for a property easement, so that, for example, a few inches of land legally owned by a neighbour may be occupied by a driveway used by you, free gratis or for a fee paid to grant a right of easement.

Where Shit means "To Break a Leg"

In French Theater slang, "*Merde!*" (French 'shit') said to a performer before going on stage is much like "Break a Leg!" among English-speaking actors, obeying the superstitious belief that actually wishing a performer "Good Luck!" before a performance would jinx it.

From 1526 CE comes this information: "It is the King's pleasure, that Mr. Norres shall be in the roome of Sir William Compton, not onely giveing his attendance as groome of the King's stoole, but also in his bed-chamber . . ."

And now, my fecal duty fully discharged, I take my Glade-perfumed leave of you all, in certain hope of your readerly attendance upon my next chapter facilitating the easement of small vocabularies.

Chapter 56

The Names of Rooms in a House & their Origins

The Spider and the Fly

"Will you walk into my parlour?" said the Spider to the Fly,
Tis the prettiest little parlour that ever you did spy;
The way into my parlour is up a winding stair,
And I've many curious things to show when you are there."
"Oh no, no," said the little Fly, "to ask me is in vain,
For who goes up your winding stair — can ne'er come down again."

- Mary Howitt, 1829

I memorized that ditty in Grade Three at Dunnville Public School. When I was a little boy in the 1940s most farmhouses had a "front parlour." Only in town could one find a living room. The parlour was the chamber of the home with the best furniture, where formal guests were received, where close relatives *post mortem* were laid out in their caskets for visitation, often under a problematical painting of a blond Jesus who looked like a Norwegian winkle-gatherer unaccountably clad in a bed sheet, instead of a seedy Jewish rebel. Grandpa could never lie dead in a village funeral home. One was buried from one's home parlour; all other venues were anathematic.

In those etymon-free days I never bothered to wonder about the origin of the words with which the common rooms of North American houses were named. The word *parlour* began in a medieval French convent or monastery as *parloir*, a room in which visitors were greeted, a room where monks and nuns could talk to guests, *parloir* from the French verb *parler* 'to speak, to talk' which gave our *Parliament* 'a speaking place where politicians could talk' and an informal word for a friendly chat or a discussion of terms at the end of a battle, a *parley*. The jargon of a trade or the mode of discourse among a defined group is *parlance*, a noun also derived from *parler*.

In more severe religious orders where silence was enjoined for a virtual perpetuity, a parloir was a mere chink in a wall or an iron-barred grate through which brief words might be exchanged by fleeting visitors, relatives of the sisters and brethren.

Pantry

"Mother's in the kitchen washing out the jugs,
Sister's in the pantry bottling the suds,
Father's in the cellar mixin' up the hops,
Johnny's on the front porch watchin' for the cops."

The members of this Prohibition-era family would never have cared that a pantry was a little room adjoining the kitchen where one first kept the bread, from early Anglo-Norman French forms like *painterie, panetrie, pantere, panterie, pantrie* 'storeroom for bread' from French *pain* 'bread' from Latin *panis* 'bread.' Later, other not immediately perishable food goods might be stored as well in the pantry.

Kitchen

"I cook with wine; sometimes I even add it to the food."
- *W.C. Fields*

Even the unschooled in etymology can sometimes hear that kitchen is the cooking room, the word related to Dutch *keuken* and German *Küche*. But it is not pristinely Teutonic. German cooks borrowed it early from Roman soldiers whose Latin for kitchen was *cocina* from the verb *coquere* 'to cook.'

Attic

The little space under the roof of a house is a pure Greek word, from the same adjective *Attic* that means 'pertaining to Attica, the area of ancient Greece that contained the city of Athens.' At the end of the sixteenth-century was coined a pseudo-classical architectural phrase, *Attic arch*, which referred to a lower story above the main orders of a façade and hence, eventually, an attic was all the rooms immediately below a roof.

Larder

Yet another little storage room off the kitchen was set aside to preserve meat and its derivative fats, like the lard from bacon. In Old French the word for bacon was *lard* from Latin *lardum, laridum* 'pork fat,' possibly cognate with classical Greek *larinos* 'fat' and *laros* 'pleasant to taste.'

Cellar

Cellar began as a small storeroom either above ground or underground. Classical Latin *cellarium* was a storeroom from *cella* 'a small enclosed space.'

Dining Room Surprise

The meaning of dining room is self-evident but its antecedent, the verb *to dine*, contains an etymological surprise in its relationship with our learned adjective *jejune* 'empty, fasting' from classical Latin *jejunus* hungry, dry, barren, unproductive, scanty, meager.' When *jejune* entered English use at the dawn of the seventeenth century its principal sense was 'hungry, fasting' but in the centuries afterward developed senses prevailed. Today jejune usually means juvenile in a bad sense, wanting in substance or maturity.

To dine evolved from a late Latin verb *disjejunare* 'to break a food fast, to breakfast, to consume the first meal of the day, from the negative Latin prefix *dis*, usually expressive of undoing the action of the verb to which it is prefixed, so that Latin *dis* + *jejunare* 'to fast, to go without food. A *jejunium* in Latin was a fasting. The bumpy etymological road leading to the form *dine* looks like this: Latin *disjejunare* > Late Latin *disjunare > Old French *disner* > Medieval Latin *disnare* > Italian *disinare* > French *dîner* > Middle English *dinner* and *to dine*!

Thus English *dine* has the same etymon as the French verb *déjeuner* 'to have lunch, to have breakfast.'

That's our trip through a modest house. Now the night lock must be keyed shut. There's no more room.

Chapter 57

Oxytocin in Childbirth

& other medical & scientific terms
from the ancient Greek word tokos 'childbirth'

In a happy painting of a great lady attended by efficient midwives, by Giovanni da Milano from mid-14th century Florence, we see Saint Anne, just after giving birth to the Blessed Virgin Mary. We are certain those midwives did not have the use of synthetic oxytocin.

Oxytocin is a pituitary hormone in mammals with multiple body functions. Chiefly, oxytocin stimulates contraction of the smooth muscle of the uterus, thus facilitating childbirth. Distention of the cervix during birth triggers the release of oxytocin. Hence the name of this hormone contains the Greek word for childbirth *tokos* whose etymology and whose cognates in other languages we will examine below. A synthetic oxytocin can be used to induce and accelerate labour and to reduce post-partum hemorrhage.

***Disambiguation**: This column is NOT about the dangerous opioid and narcotic **oxycotone** used to treat severe pain and hugely, unwisely, often fatally, over-prescribed by bad, careless doctors under brand names like OxyContin, Oxaydo, Oxyfast, Roxicodone and Xtampza ER. Beware this dangerous poison and its mortal fake versions peddled by criminal drug dealers and medical quacks. Deaths due to overdoses of prescribed drugs are not* *always the patient's fault, in spite of what medical personnel say and write and would have the gullible believe.*

Back to Oxytocin: inducer of childbirth

Upon stimulation of the nipples, oxytocin also helps induce lactation by contracting the smooth muscles of the breasts' milk ducts. Oxytocin was immediately borrowed from the ancient Greek compound noun o*kytokine* 'quick birth' (*okys* 'quick, swift, speedy, sharp' + *-tokos* 'childbirth').

Sexual orgasm also raises the oxytocin levels, promoting a pleasant euphoria and the impulse to fall asleep.

Oxytocic (ox-i-**toe**-sick)

The adjective *oxytocic* is also used as a noun in current medical literature as a general name for agents that terminate pregnancy, that is, abortifacients, showing up in lists like this: ecbolics, oxytocics and emmenagogues. Note that these are usually employed as medical "weasel" words designed to cover up the fact that an abortion is taking place in any place, live or in print where abortion is unpopular.

Are Sociopaths Low in Oxytocin?

Fascinating new studies probe the inability to secrete oxytocin as involved in lack of empathy for others, hence such an anoxytocic lack might be partially causative in criminal behaviour and other sociopathic symptoms.

Etymology of *Tokos* & Indo-European Related Words

Tokos can refer in Greek to the act of childbirth and it can also mean offspring or child. Literally *tokos* means 'something begotten,' being a noun from the verb *tiktein* 'to bring forth progeny, (of trees) to fruit, *tiktein* being a reduplicative verbal form of *tekein* 'to beget.' The more common ancient Greek word for child, *teknon*, derived from the simpler, earlier verb. The Greeks also used the verb to describe the making of interest from money, so that *tiktein* means 'to accrue interest' e.g. from a loan.

Word Relatives in Other Languages

Tokos is cognate with English *thane/thegn*, a servant, minister or disciple of Christ. English readers might remember the word in one of the titles of Shakespeare's Macbeth: *"Hail, Thane of Cawdor."* In that play, thane refers to a retainer who holds land on behalf of a Scottish king. Old English *þegn* meant 'boy, servant, warrior.' In Old Norse a *thegn* was a freeman. Its oldest Germanic sense however was 'boy,' for *thane* is cognate with Greek *teknos* 'boy' and Sanskrit *takman* 'child.'

Other English Words from Greek *Tokos*

These terms are, for the most part, from science, from medicine, particularly from obstetrics. Some are now rare.

A TKD is used to measure uterine contractions. **Tokodynamometer** = *tokos* 'childbirth' + *dynamis* 'power' + *metron* 'measuring device.'

Tocology is still found as a somewhat high-falutin' synonym for midwifery, although it might have been a better synonym for obstetrics with its literal meaning of 'the scientific study and practice of childbirth.'

The occasional psychology text carries the word **tocophobia**, abnormal dread in women of giving birth.

Tocography is the recording of uterine contractions.

Quite rare is **mogitocia** 'difficult delivery of a baby' < *mogis* 'with difficulty.' The more usual obstetrical term today for abnormally difficult childbirth is **dystocia** or **dystokia**. More common is the adjective **ditokous** meaning 'giving birth to twins' with the Greek *di-* combing form meaning 'two.'

There is a manganese mineral called **neotocite** named because it is a product of earlier rocks weathering and thus is more recently 'born' so-to-speak. Greek neotokos 'newborn, recent' < Greek *neos* 'new' + *tokos* 'child.'

Theotokos

In Greek Orthodox and Roman Catholic theology, and in the upper clouds of the Higher Anglicanism, one name for the Virgin Mary is Theotokos 'the one who gave birth to God' < Greek *theos* 'god' + *tokos* 'one who brings forth.'

While we loll serenely upon this unaccustomed nimbus of religiosity, let us take our pious leave and skim aloft on pristine wings, borne upon the zephyrs of an improbable salvation.

Chapter 58

Celibacy

etymology of a contentious word

My brethren and cistern, before we wade into the Vaseline-slippery topic of celibacy and its verbal origin, here are 3 snappers from late-night television comedians of recent decades:

"I read this in the paper this morning: New York City has a priest shortage. So you see, there is some good news in the world. To give you an idea how bad it is, earlier today in Brooklyn an altar boy had to grope himself."

— *David Letterman*

"The Cardinals will be staying at the Domus Sanctae Marthae, the new hotel at the Vatican, where the phrase "turn-down service" means the bell boy isn't interested."

— *Daily Show host Jon Stewart*

"After all these scandals in the church, many Roman Catholics are calling for an end to celibacy. An end to celibacy? How about starting celibacy? Let's at least try it, to see if it works."

— *Jay Leno*

Etymology of the Word *Celibate*

Caelebs, caelibis, third declension adjective 'alone, unmarried, single' is used in Latin to refer to single men only; *nubilis* was the adjective for 'unmarried woman,' hence nubile in English first signified 'able to be married,' then came to mean 'young and lovely.'

A Latin motto, paraphrasing the famous Cartesian statement, has been suggested for these male sex-deniers: *Cogito, ergo sum caelebs.*

A female celibate would have to say in Latin: *Cogito ergo sum nubilis.*

This *caelebs* adjective was different from Latin *solus* 'alone.' *Caelebs* meant the male was alone on purpose, not married for some reason.

Caelebs is akin to the same Proto-Indo-European root, *koilos, that shows up in Old English *hal* 'sound and healthy.' The abstract noun for 'being sound' is from the same root, namely, *hal-th* or *hael-th* = health! A modern English reflex of *hal*, and descendant of PIE * koilos, is *whole*....when whole means "entire, single."

Greetings!

Also from that ancient root are greeting words like Hail! (literally 'be well') and its German equivalent *Heil!*

Wassail began as a Middle English toast. As one raised a goblet of spiced wine or mead, one cried out *Waes haeil!* 'Be well!'

Cælebs and its noun of state *cælibatus* are the only cognate words found in Latin. *Celibacy* is a late coinage, possibly English. The first printed appearance of celibacy in the *Oxford English Dictionary* is mid-seventeenth-century. *Célibat* 'celibacy' shows up earlier in French by 1549 CE, *célibataire* by 1711 CE.

The earliest etymology of *caelebs* is obscure, but the first good guess was made by master etymologist Eric Partridge who drew linguistic attention to the Sanskrit word *kévalah* 'alone.' The uses of the Sanskrit root suggest that, even in Indo-European, the word may have meant "alone by some kind of choice," perhaps equivalent to the Roman Catholic meaning of celibate, in which the choice is supposedly religious. There's a reflex of the root in Old Church Slavonic, *cěglŭ* 'single, alone.'

Don't Have Sex Before the Big Game. Right?

Perhaps an ancient shaman lived celibate so that he had more power to summon the gods? This is a common physiological and psychological fantasy of unmarried monks and nuns and sports coaches: By giving up sex, all that unreleased sexual energy can be redirected to spirituality or the big game tomorrow. Really?

You Will NOT Play Better in Tomorrow's Game!

The redirection of bodily energy argument has **NO SUPPORT** in scientific human biology whatsoever. You have perhaps heard of baseball coaches, those gum-chewing bibles of kinesiological discernment, who tell their male players not to have sex the night before the big game. Do subsequent performance studies corroborate this notion? **Not one**. Of course, there are vast squads of string-around-the-dick lunkheads who believe it. Unfortunately, gullible ignorance of physiology does not constitute proof. Human males denied human females will mount inflatable sex toys, boys, girls, goats, larger domestic pets and knotholes in oak trees.

Celibacy: Legit Life Style OR Creepy Avoidance of Sex

Once in a while, wacky old maids dismount from their gear shifts to proclaim harangues defending celibacy. But does history teem with celibates? Florence

Nightingale was single. Sir Isaac Newton never dipped his stick. And dig those scandalous Vestal Virgins of old Rome. But most people screw. It's fun. The abstainers are almost all psychotically afraid of sex or twisted into a cankered, bitter knot of loathing because some man or woman abused, thwarted, undid or deserted them.

According to preponderant psychiatric orthodoxy, male celibacy is a pathetic attempt to disguise fear of sex or avert being labeled a pervert, an attempt almost always doomed to seedy failure.

Unless you were born as a large head with nothing below the neck except a hideous waving field of teeny millipede legs, lifelong sexual abstinence is a disease. Celibacy, say the majority of psychiatrists, does not work. Offering your genitals to God is a sign of deep sickness, not a token of corporeal piety.

Anatomical Contamination is the Diagnosis

The term for this malady in psychoanalytic literature is often "anatomical contamination." The sickness may begin quite early in childhood, due to incompetent parenting, bad toilet training or any number of mommy-and-daddy screw-ups. The child beset with anatomical contamination comes to loathe his or her body, to unduly dwell on bodily exudations like pus and mucus and sperm and rheumy droolings. The AC body is felt to be a cesspit of filth and rot. Sex partakes of this rot and must be avoided at all costs. There's a creepy fastidiousness in their thinking about sex. Irish poet W.B. Yeats' lady friend complained through all of their relationship that William would not go down on her. In a letter to her, Yeats actually wrote (and later also in a public poem!) that his reluctance to engage in cunnilingus had to do with one fact: "Venus has pitched her tent in the house of excrement." Yikes! Perhaps the apter expletive would be: Holy Shit! I guess W.B. never heard of Irish Spring soap.

Another causative agent sometimes promoting anatomical contamination is a child's developing awareness of his or her homosexuality. This must be hidden forever! Celibate nunnery and monkery then beckon. By giving up a troublesome sexuality, the worrier can postpone announcing homosexuality. The western-world's epidemic of moppet-diddling by priests suggests just how effective a deterrent that ploy is!

From a book defending and glorifying religious celibacy edited and contributed to by Carl Olson (*Celibacy and Religious Tradition*, Oxford University Press, 2008) here is one of the classic Roman Catholic fear-of-sex statements shrouded in pro-celibacy gobbledygook: "Celibacy is an excellent example of exerting discipline and control upon the human body." Wee Carl does not go on to say that sexual need leaks out in many sick ways: not merely upending altar boys but also the unappetizing spectacle of monks in their lonely cells masturbating with stainless-steel scouring pads "so it will hurt." Penile abrasions, anyone? How sick is that? "Yes, my brethren in Christ. Surprise! I'm leaving our religious order. I'm getting married next week — to a Kurly Kate!"

Poor, old, feminist-assaulted Sigmund Freud had a sense of humour. Siggy wrote that "everything repressed returns — usually at 3 a.m. and in a bad mood."

All of science tells us celibacy is unnatural, sick and — mainly — impossible.

The Celibacy Test

Three young candidates for the priesthood are told by the Monsignor they have to pass one more test: The Celibacy Test. The Monsignor leads them into a room, and tells them to undress, and a small bell is tied to each man's penis.

In comes a beautiful woman, wearing a sexy belly-dancer costume. She begins to dance sensually around the first candidate. Even before she has begun to remove her veils, his little penis bell jingles. Ting-a-ling. Ting-a-ling.

"Oh Patrick," says the Monsignor, "I am so disappointed in your complete lack of self-control. Go take a long, cold shower and pray about your carnal weakness."

As Patrick leaves, the dancer then continues, slowly dancing around the second candidate and peeling off her layers of veils. As the last veil drops: Ting-a-ling goes his bell.

"Joseph, Joseph," sighs the Monsignor. "You too are unable to withstand your carnal desires. Go take a long, cold shower and pray for forgiveness."

The dancer then proceeds to dance her sensuous dance around the third candidate. Slowly around him she dances, now devoid of all of her veils, but the third candidate remains unmoved. His bell does not ring.

"James, my son, I am truly proud of you," says the Monsignor. "Only you have the true strength of character needed to become a great priest. Now, go and join your weaker brethren in the shower."

Suddenly James' bell goes ting-a-ling, ting-a-ling.

Final Cheap Celibacy Joke

After a lifetime of hand-copying ancient texts, an elderly monk became abbot of his monastery. Realizing that for centuries his order had been making copies of copies, he decided to examine some of the monastery's original documents. Days later, the other monks found him in the cellar, weeping over a crumbling manuscript and moaning, "It says *celebrate*, not *celibate*."

Chapter 59

Hunchback Words like Kyphotic, Lordosis & Quasimodo

Were I naught but an insensitive churl, fain would I plummet to the pitiless nadir of telling hunchback jokes. But did you hear that the Hunchback of Notre Dame has retired? He received two years back pay, a lump sum, and a case of Bells.

Before his demise, Quasimodo was in the kitchen when his mother walked in carrying a wok. The hunchback said, "Great, I love Chinese food." His mother shook her head, "Chinese food? No, no, my dear son. I use the wok to iron your shirts."

Gibbous & Other Hunchback Words

Nowadays the word gibbous means hunchbacked. Gibbous is not pronounced *djibus.* Unlike most Latin-derived words in English that begin with gi-, gibbous has a hard g sound, as it had in classical Latin. Used in English by the onset of the fifteenth century CE, gibbous first meant 'sticking out' or 'rounded,' then, three hundred years later, English astronomers could speak of "a gibbous moon," when the bright part of the moon is more than half its circumference but not a full moon. Gibbous is still used in reporting lunar status. It's a humpbacked moon.

Gibbous did not refer in English to human hunchbacks until the late 1600s. About that same time, two related Latin terms were borrowed directly into English scientific vocabulary. Gibbose came from *gibbosus* 'having a hump' and from the same Latin adjective but formed as a French noun came *la gibbosité*, Englished as gibbosity 'the condition of having a hunch back.'

Etymology

From Latin *gibbus* 'hump,' the word is certainly cognate with Latvian *gibbis* 'hunch-backed' and probably cognate with Greek *kûphos* 'hump' and *kuphós* 'bent forward, all descended from an Indo-European root *kub- and *kup 'to curve, to bend.' Latin had an even simpler reflex of the root too: *gibber, gibbera, gibberum*, an adjective meaning 'hunchbacked.'

Note that the English noun *hump* is NOT cognate with *gibbus*, instead hump shares origin with Indo-European words like Latin *incumbere* 'to lie down,' ancient Greek *kymbē* 'drinking cup, bowl, hollow part of a vessel, boat' and Sanskrit *kumbha* 'pot.' Among the English derivatives from such roots are *incumbent* from a Medieval Latin meaning of *incumbere* 'to seek, to obtain, to hold any ecclesiastical office.' In the technical English vocabulary of formal anatomy *cymba* names the central empty part of the external human ear.

Quasimodo

The most famous gibbous person in literature is the title character in *The Hunchback of Notre Dame*, an 1831 novel by Victor Hugo, whose French title is *Notre-Dame de Paris* 'Our Lady of Paris' referring to the famous Seine-perched cathedral around which the plot revolves.

How did Quasi get his modo nickname? Neat story. Victor Hugo based the fictional character on a real-life hunchbacked stone mason who worked on the 1830s restoration of Notre Dame, a restoration promoted by Hugo himself and one of the reasons that Hugo wrote the novel, because Notre Dame was not the ecclesiastical showplace of Paris that it became. Bats pissed in its belfries and birds shat upon its altars until in 1832 Hugo's novel helped draw attention to Notre Dame's state of shabby disrepair and a massive, decade-long renovation commenced.

In the novel, a little Parisian boy is born frighteningly ugly, hunchbacked and warty-faced. On a Sunday after Easter, the grotesque runt is abandoned, left on the flesh-chilling stone steps of the cathedral, awaiting any vagrant mercy arising in the heart of a passerby. An abbot sees the boy, takes pity upon him, and brings the lad into the life of the church. He grows up to be a jack-of-all-trades and the chief bell ringer and he is named Quasimodo.

Now the Sunday after Easter is called Low Sunday and still in some European countries called Quasimodo Sunday. Is it Low Sunday because the pious are still in a crucifixional funk after Christ's Easter demise? Or it is merely lower, being postcrucifixional? We don't know.

But we do know the first words of the antiphonal introit, the hymn once sung in Latin by the choir and congregation as they wend up to the altar (Latin: *introibo ad altare Dei* ' I shall go in now unto the altar of the Lord.') Those Latin words are *quasi modo geniti infantes, rationabile, sine dolo lac concupiscite* 'as newborn babes desire the sincere milk of the word that ye may grow thereby.' So says *The King James Version* of the *New Testament's* First Epistle of Peter, chapter 2, verse 2.

In Hugo's deft writerly invention, the kindly abbot hears the choir chanting the very Latin words 'newborn babes' as he stoops to rescue the little child.

By the way, I'm sure I saw the Hunchback of Notre Dame this morning. If it wasn't him, it was a dead ringer.

Other Hunchback Words in Medicine

The 'crookback' nouns of English medical vocabulary are kyphosis, scoliosis and lordosis. Their adjectives are kyphotic, scoliotic and lordotic. Herewith, a small but useful note about the disease names that end in –osis: they all take an adjective in –otic. Consider more familiar pathological nouns like neurosis and its adjective neurotic, thrombosis and thrombotic, sclerosis and sclerotic, necrosis and necrotic, cyanosis and cyanotic.

Kyphosis or Cyphosis

In classical Greek kuphosis meant 'condition of having a hunchback' from kuphós 'crooked' or 'bent.' Kyphosis is the classic hunchbacked condition, backward curvature of the spine.

Scoliosis

Derived from another Greek adjective *skolios* 'bent, curved, crooked' comes scoliosis, a condition in which the spine is curved from side to side, lateral curvature of the spine.

Lordosis

In Greek *lordos* means 'bent backward. The lordotic patient suffers a spinal curvature that pushes the chest out. It is a severe deformity.

Let us give the last word to the fictional bell ringer, Quasimodo: "My misfortune is that I still resemble a man too much. I should have liked to be wholly a beast like that goat there." - *The Hunchback of Notre-Dame*, Victor Hugo, 1831 CE

Chapter 60

Farce

Farce once meant a sausage; later it named a musical insert into a Gregorian chant and finally a mode of theatrical comedy.

The Playful Roots of the Word *Farce*

Farc-, farct-, fars - a Latin verbal stem or root that means 'to stuff.' This Latin verbal stem descends from the compound Indo-European root **bhareku*, made from two simpler roots: *bheu* swell + **reg* stretch, bind = *bhareku

This double meaning of 'swelling and binding or stretching out' suggests that even in Proto-Indo-European, the verb concerned stuffing fowl and other meats, and perhaps the making of Paleolithic sausages!

When IE roots begin in *bh-*, they often enter Latin as *f*. Thus *bhareku* appears in Latin as the stem *farc-* in the verb *farcire* 'to stuff.'

The principal parts of Latin verbs are often listed like this: *farcio, farcire, farsi, fartum (farctum, farsum, farsitum)* here displayed to show the different forms borrowed by later languages like French and English.

Some Latin Uses of the Verb

Farcire in Classical Latin meant 'to stuff, to cram, to fill full.'

1. For example, Pliny, writer of Rome's first encyclopedia, wrote of a mason who set out
   medios parietes farcire fractis caementis
   'to fill the interior of the walls with crushed stone.'
   You can see the ancestor of our English word *cement* in the Latin *caementis.*
2. The passive form of the verb *farcire* was used to describe gagging as part of torture:
   in os farciri pannos imperavit
   'he ordered rags to be stuffed in the [person's] mouth.'
3. In Latin, the verb was associated with food too, as it could be used to mean 'to fatten an animal':
   gallinas et anseres sic farcito
   'therefore let him fatten chickens and geese!' (for a future feast).
4. A related noun, *farcimen*, meant 'sausage, something stuffed.'
5. A *fartor* was a poulterer, one who fattened fowls as an occupation, while the adjective *fartilis* meant 'able to be stuffed' when applied to fowls being prepared for a meal.

Explanation: Use of the Asterisk in Word Study

*An asterisk placed before a word or root means it is a supposed form, a hypothetical form, not backed up by printed evidence, but thought by linguists to have been a spoken form based on the printed evidence of a later word seemingly derived from such a hypothetical form. Why is the symbol * called an asterisk? It's the Greek word for 'little star.' Greek *aster* 'star' + *-iskos* a common diminutive suffix of Greek nouns = *asteriskos* 'little star.'

There was a transmissive form in Latin too, *asteriscus*. The frequent mispronunciations of the word, atrocious attempts like 'ass-trick' and 'ass-crick,' arise from speakers not looking squarely and carefully at the word. Asterisk is simple. The chief stress is on the first syllable (ASS-ter-isk) and every letter of the word is pronounced. Asterisk's earliest printed appearance in English is in a commentary paragraph of the Wycliffe Bible in 1382 CE.

The Farce Root in Romance Languages, Descendants of Latin

In Vulgar Latin or perhaps later in early and medieval Church Latin, forms like *farsa,**farsia,* and *farsura* existed. For we have in early French *farsse* (1447 CE) and in early English *farse* (1530 CE) with a liturgical meaning.

A farse was a word or phrase inserted or 'stuffed' into the ordained words of prayers and of the Roman Catholic Mass. From the 9th to the 12th centuries, tropes (extra phrases) began to be added to the music and the texts of the Latin liturgy.

For example, there is a short prayer called the *kyrie eleison*, which is Greek for 'Lord, have mercy.' The syllables of these two words are stretched over many notes of music in plainsong and its later form, Gregorian chant. The choirs chanting these beautiful prayers sometimes improvised, as all true artists are compelled to do, but within strict bounds of astute musical judgment.

Personal Aside about Musical Improvisers

I can briefly abide musical improvisers except the arrogant scatty-wadda-wadda-doodoo- *artistes* who, for example, burble their way through the metamorphic destruction of an exquisite Cole Porter song. What impudent jazz singers do not seem to realize is a simple truth: Cole Porter wrote the tune, not you, the scat singer. When you, jazzbo, have shown the listener that you can reproduce what Porter so brilliantly composed and lyricked, then and only then, my gulping gargling crow, shall I permit you to assault my ears with your raucous or bluesy scatting, but only once shall I pollute my velvet auricles, before returning to a rendition of the master's work that has not been defiled by upstart unmusicality of the most abject and vulgar mode.

More Farse

One common farse in the kyrie consisted of inserting one of the Ten Commandments between each kyrie and eleison. The words of the commandment were often in the vernacular or native language of the singer. Another form of farse recorded in marginalia on a medieval manuscript of prayers has the farses written in thus:

kyrie genitor ingenite, vera essentia, eleison
'O Lord, unbegotten begetter, true being in all things, have mercy.'
The 'unbegotten begetter' referred to Christ's birth of the Virgin Mary.

Medieval Mystery Plays & the Birth of Theatrical Farce

Farses spoken or sung in vernaculars like Early French also served as a gloss on the Latin of the Mass, of prayers, and of epistles and readings, to make the congregation, who knew little or no Latin, aware of the meaning of the texts. Lessons and Epistles so altered were called in early French *épitres farcies* ('stuffed' epistles), used especially at important times in the church calendar, such as Christmas Day, to ensure the laity understood the story of the birth of Christ.

The next development in the meaning of farse saw the word applied to parts of mystery plays. Also called miracle plays, these religious dramas arose during the 13th century, when French trade guilds put on plays based on Biblical stories. At first performed inside churches, early medieval church authorities quickly forced the somewhat vulgar plays to be performed outside the church, often on stages built on wagons, so the players could move from town to town. The most famous mystery play in English is *Everyman*.

Once outside, players felt freer to include more outrageous and audience-pleasing theatrical devices: devils emerging from fiery hells to round up the damned with pitchforks, acrobats, indecent clowning with groping, stuffed codpieces, and gigantic dildos, plus satire of local authorities and bits of more innocent tomfoolery. These gags inserted or stuffed into a Biblical play, as one might stuff ground meat into a sausage, were called *farce* in Old French by 1420 CE when, in a manuscript of miracle play texts, we find "*Miracles de plusiers malades/ En farses pour être mains fades.*" 'Miracle cures for several diseases [are shown] in our little acts [but they are only] to gain the applause of tasteless peasants.' *Pour être mains fades* means literally 'to be vulgar hands.'

In 16th century Italy, these farse formed the basis for *commedia dell'arte* with stock characters like Arlecchino, Punchinello, Colombina, and Pantalone who influenced comedies by Ben Jonson and Molière, and gave rise to characters like Harlequin and Mr. Punch of Punch and Judy shows.

Bye-Bye, Bible!

Eventually some of the plays lost all their Biblical content. By the 15th century in France, by the early 17th century in England, such plays 'stuffed' full of buffoonery were called *farces*, their sole and noble purpose being to make the audience laugh. But laughter may induce free thoughts about a status quo. In 1447, at Dijon in France, a lawsuit was brought against the performers of a miracle play called *Mystère de St Eloi*. Royal prosecutors alleged that a farce had been inserted into the play to excite political ridicule of the king of France and his religious bum boy, the Dauphin.

We are NOT Amused

The Vatican, true to its innate, pompous, religious fascism, has never been amused by farces lampooning clergy with sex jokes. Given the huge number of Roman Catholic priests busily buggering little children all over the world, one can perhaps understand if not sympathize with their collective Holinesses deep concern about truth-revealing humour. Nothing seems to annoy fascists more than being mocked.

Then too, church officials cast a cold eye on ordinary people having fun. Jesus wept, but—if we are to believe Holy Writ—Jesus never laughed. Ha! And Oy!

The Wagging Finger of Puritan Disapproval

In any case, with vulgar farces lampooning church officials in scurrilous and sexually suggestive language, the Vatican boiled over into many a hissy-fit. In 1570, Pope

Pius V banned farce. In the middle of the 17th century, a sour Puritan grump named Oliver Cromwell, after beheading King Charles I, likewise tried to destroy English theater, an action as futile as Pius V's ban. These funny romps were not called farces in England until after the Reformation. Before that, knockabout comedies were stage-jigs or drolls.

From Vaudeville to "Fawlty Towers"

Farce grew in popularity during the later 16th century in England and France, and never looked back, as it sailed through British music halls, vaudeville, and into early silent films as pie-throwing slapstick. It is with us still in timid, debased, politically-correct television sitcoms and in the much more robust and uproarious genius of modern playwrights like Joe Orton, whose splendid farces include *Loot, What the Butler Saw*, and an unjustly neglected British television farce, *The Erpingham Camp*, one of the funniest plays I have ever read in English. Beside Joe Orton in my personal list of farce favourites I would put John Cleese in the exquisite BBC hotel comedy series *Fawlty Towers*. Orton however took far more giddy, over-the-top, anti-societal chances than John Cleese ever did.

Medical & Culinary Meanings of the *Farce* Root

Farce that sausage then, but beware of myocardial infarction (which term we explicate below).

The culinary meaning in French of *farcir* and in English of the verb *to farce* 'to stuff foods,' continued parallel to the religious and theatrical uses of the verbs and nouns derived from Latin *farcire*. An English vowel gradation gave the noun *forcemeat* (initially *farcemeat)

'meat, vegetables, etc. chopped and spiced and used to stuff fowls and sausages.'

In France, a veterinary noun arose to name a disease of horses called *farcin*, a chronic form of glanders, being a congestive inflammation of a horse's lymph vessels. *Farcin* derived from a Late Latin name for the disease, *farsiminum*.

Farcin entered English unchanged, and then was shortened to *farcy*, in terms like button farcy and cattle farcy. In button farcy, small tubercular nodes called buds form in the skin of a horse's legs, thorax, and abdomen.

Further French elaborations of *farce* gave *farceur* and *farceuse*, the former borrowed into English to denote an actor skilled in low comedy and slapstick. In Old French *farceur* also meant 'sausage-maker' or *patissier* who made paté and fancy stuffings. From this occupation, several French surnames arise: Farce, Farcé, Farcis, and Farçat.

The intensive Latin verb *infarcire* is the root of a contemporary medical term. Most medical nouns in English stem from classical Greek and Latin words. For example, *myocardial: mys, myos* Greek, muscle + *kardia* Greek, heart

Thus, myocardium is heart muscle, cardiac muscle that surrounds the heart in a tough, thick layer. So follows our etymology of the medical phrase: *myocardial infarction*.

Myocardialis Scientific Latin, of the heart muscle + *infarctio, infarctionis* Latin, stuffing a sausage until it is full

A myocardial infarction is a heart attack due to the closing off of a coronary artery that causes an infarct of the heart muscle.

In an infarct, part of the heart muscle dies from lack of oxygen because blood supply via the coronary artery has been interrupted. The artery may be said to have been occluded, obstructed or stuffed by a thrombus, that is, a blood clot.

Infarction is a 17th-century coinage belonging to the discredited theory of humours, and so the word is not truly appropriate to modern cardiology. But some old words die slowly. Originally, infarction referred to a 'stuffing together' of bodily humours.

I hope you have derived etymological benefit from my farcical excursus. Let's wrap up with a pun from the "Star Wars" movies: May the farce be with you! May the infarct not be!

Chapter 61

Autopsy: Dissecting a Word

Let us begin with the word's semantic weight. The word *autopsy* has borne three different meanings in its trip through English.

1. The word's first meaning in English was very simple: "seeing for oneself," exactly what its Hellenistic Greek etymon *autopsia* signifies: Greek *autos* 'self' + Hellenistic Greek *-opsia*, a combining form of ancient Greek *opsis* 'appearance, sight, view, the act of seeing.' Think of English words with the same root like *myopia, optical, optometrist* and *synopsis*. This English meaning appears as late as a 1901 history textbook in which G.B. Grundy wrote — somewhat redundantly — of an ancient author: ". . .that he is describing from personal autopsy the scenes of the great events which he narrates is overwhelming." I label the sentence redundant because his words "personal" and "aut-" of autopsy share a meaning that did not have to be expressed twice.

2. Then, in a second semantic shift, autopsy came to mean *close diagnostic examination of a living patient.* One must remember the thousands of years when mobs of ignorant religious lunatics, Christian and otherwise, thwarted the advance of scientific knowledge by preventing dissection of any corpse because "God didn't like it." Thou, miscreant, must not tear asunder what the Almighty has labored all day Saturday to confect.

Better to deny science and spend millennia ignorant as a pious slug leaving its pathetic slime trail of devotion across the rich, green, potentially explicable leaf of life! (End of author rant)

3. Finally, today, autopsy means medical examination of a corpse and its organs, to discover the cause of death, whether by misadventure, natural aging or disease. Sometimes autopsies are conducted to reveal how disease afflicted the human body interiorly and if applied therapies were efficacious. One remembers Leonard L. Levinson's sly and punny definition of an autopsy as "remains to be seen." This third meaning of autopsy arose by early in the 19th century, as scattered clouds of scientific enlightenment scudded over France and Germany — but not without an autopsying doctor or two being burned to death as Satan's warlocks, with pious Christians standing around the bonfire smirking their approval.

Eventually a corpse could be examined and dissected and a new English forensic term was needed and so borrowed from French terms like *autopsie cadavérique* and *autopsie cadavéreuse*, which were lying around in medical French for a hundred years before being shipped over to England.

The German word *Autopsie* was in print by 1750 CE. Autopsy entered English by means of French through a Roman version of the Greek, namely Latin *autopsia* 'seeing with one's own eyes.'

Galen used the Greek word frequently to mean close visual inspection of a patient for diagnostic purposes. The doctor Galen (131-201 CE), like many of the best physicians of the Roman empire, was a Greek who wrote in Greek. His writings summarize ancient anatomy and medical procedure, adding new observations based on his own practice. For fourteen hundred years, Galen's writings were the authority on medicine in the Christian world and their virtual worship as the only medical truth held back and stunted the advance of anatomical research.

Related Word Study

Some obsolete synonyms for autopsy are: *necropsy, necroscopy, sectio cadaveris, thanatopsy, necrotomy, ptomatopsy,* and *ptomatopsia. Nekros* is the ancient Greek adjective that meant 'dead.' A cemetery or 'city of the dead' is a necropolis. *Thanatos* is a Greek word for death, most commonly seen in the English term *euthanasia* 'inducing a comfortable death.' Sigmund Freud used the Greek noun by itself to name what he called 'the death instincts or Thanatos.' One ancient Greek word for dead body or corpse was *ptoma, ptomatos* 'fallen body, corpse, carcass' (stem of the noun from the verb *piptein* 'to fall, to drop'). It appears this Greek word for dead body may have referred originally to a soldier who had "fallen" in battle.

Ptomaine, often a cause of food poisoning, was named because the toxic amine was first isolated in decaying animal bodies and in decaying vegetables. Check out the chemical names of some of ptomaine's fellow amines: cadaverine and putrescine.

There's a lot of stiff competition in writings about autopsy, but I think we've buried most of the contenders. In any case, in respect to the autopsied verbal cadaver on my etymologist's table, I think that's a wrap.

Chapter 62

Cabiria

In our Annals of Onomatology, the scientific study of the origin of names, we trace the exotic source of an Italian female given name that is also a Fellini movie title.

Cabiria is best known to English speakers in the title of Federico Fellini's 1957 film *The Nights of Cabiria* (Italian: *Le notti di Cabiria*) starring his wife Giulietta Masina as a prostitute, a petite, wandering waif traipsing through the streets of Rome seeking true love and finding only abuse and disappointment.

The American Broadway musical and movie *Sweet Charity* is very loosely based on Fellini's screenplay of "The Nights of Cabiria." But the raucous, outer-space-queen, garish blatmouthedness of that screeching vulgarian actress Shirley MacLean bears no comparison with the delicate screen artistry of Giulietta Masina.

Although I cannot name chapter and verse, I believe that in some print interview Fellini said he got the unusual feminine given name from the title character in a famous silent movie made in Italy in 1914 entitled "Cabiria." Anyone studying Italian cinema seriously is certain to screen this early silent film, since "Cabiria" stands out in excellence from the mediocre shlock Italy usually produced early in its movie history, tedious orgy tales of ancient Roman decadence, spindly chariot races, with a creeping-looking Ulysses sword-fighting with papier-mâché monsters, choppy scenes in which the actor playing Ulysses has bigger tits than the female temptress. One of Cabiria's instantly and widely adopted innovations was a moving camera, a camera pushed on wheels and dollies and carts, to relieve the "static frame" of most early silent films.

Etymology

But *Cabiria* as a word is perhaps 3,000 years old. 2,000 years ago or more, the word arrived in ancient Italy from a Greek mystery cult centered around subterranean earth deities with the non-Greek name 'the Kabeiroi' (probable Semitic meaning: 'the mighty ones'). They seem to have been associated with fire worship of Greek god of fire, the lame blacksmith Hephaistos.

From the Greek isle of Samothrace, this worship of Vulcan-like forces of the ocean spread rapidly during the Hellenistic Age, to be introduced eventually by Greek slaves and settlers into southern Italy (eventually called Magna Graeca because so many Greeks speaking Greek lived there). The Cabiri were represented as an old man and his son whose chief divine function was the protection of sailors. Cabiria might easily have been a name given to a daughter by a fisherman father who worshipped the Cabiri.

But there is no root in Greek or Latin for this word, while there is a most probable one in the Semitic languages of the ancient Middle East.

Probable Semitic Roots of the Name

In the Hebrew word *kabir* and in its *shoresh* or triliteral root: *k-b-r*) and in Arabic *kabir* or *kebir* the inherent meaning is 'big, great, large.'

The word is common in the Old Testament, for example in The Book of Job 36:5 "Behold, God is mighty (kabir), and despiseth not any: he is mighty (*kabir*) in strength and wisdom."

In Arabic, *al-bait al kabir* means 'the big house' and *al bait kabir* means 'the house is big.'

In the very well-known Islamic pious phrase *Allahu Akbar*! 'God is greater [or greatest],' one sees *akbar*, the comparative or superlative form of the Arabic adjective *kabir* 'great.' This common phrase of praise is said aloud upon fortunate occasions: upon receiving a blessing from Allah, upon hearing good news, upon escaping from danger or achieving victory in a battle, upon business success, upon hearing of a relative giving birth, upon learning that a loved one has had successful surgery, etc.

So, in a quaint Italian rural given name, there echo chthonic sonorities like the quondam glide of unguent lava's rock jelly, like the redundant undulance of sea swell whose waves beach-taste the island sands of Samothrace.

Chapter 63

Rhapsody, Scrotal Raphe & Wrap

A simple Greek root is the key to understanding and knowing forever these seemingly complex medical words: palatorrhaphy, episiorrhaphy and herniorrhaphy. In this little essay, learn these terms and rhapsody's musical and literary sources too.

Rhapsody

Educated North Americans know the word in the title of composer George Gershwin's "Rhapsody in Blue," a brilliant, breezy transforming of jazz riffs and motifs into orchestral concert form, a musical rhapsody on the sounds and feelings of New York City living, everything from squawking taxi klaxons to the exultant joy of skyscraper viewing via neck-crane, to spinning in the Scylla and Charybdis of Manhattan's whirling, oceanic Roaring Twenties.

Rhapsody as a free-form single composition or fantasia based on some Romantic inspirational topic belongs to German and English musical criticism of the 18th, 19th and early 20th centuries, for example Liszt's "Hungarian Rhapsodies" or Delius' rhapsody "Brigg Fair" based on an older English folk-tune.

But the word harks all the way back to Homer where a rhapsodist was one who stitched songs together and recited or chanted them for an audience, thrumming a lyre as he intoned the tale. Yes, the *Iliad* and the *Odyssey* were chanted or sung to the audience.

Rhapsody's Aptness

This stitching word (related to the Greek verb *rhaptein* 'to sew') fits perfectly with the mode of acquisition of tales that eventually produced the ancient Greek poem of an epic homeward journey, *The Odyssey.* Scholars now think each episode of Odysseus' travel tales may have begun as a factual, realistic account of some extraordinary happening passed as oral history around a distant Hellenic campfire. Soon travelling bards heard these fireside adventure stories and improved them, adding wonder, magic, monsters and awe, then wove and stitched them together as a rhapsody (*rhaptein* 'to sew') into a longer narrative.

One theme in the *Odyssey* was a *nostos,* Greek 'a set of daring adventures lived through on a long voyage home.' Consider the original meaning of our word *nostalgia* 'painful memories of home' from Greek *nostos* 'home' + Greek *-algia* 'pain.' Nostalgia is not an ancient Greek coinage. It is a modern, New Latin neology arising from a scholarly loan translation or calque of the German word for homesickness *Heimweh* (literally in German 'home-pain') into its Greek-root equivalents.

Stately Measures Indeed!

These ancient rhapsodists cast the derring-do of the hero into poetic metre and commenced slowly through generations to produce what we possess today: one of the great polished epics of humanity, to sit beside our reverence for Homer, who was, as another poet,

Tennyson, said of Roman Virgil, "wielder of the stateliest measure ever moulded by the lips of man."

Ancient Greek *rhapsoidia* 'epic poem recitation at one hearing and sitting' is literally a weaving together of different songs, from *rhaptein* 'to sew, stitch together' + *aoide* or *oide* 'ode, song' from the verb *aeiden* 'to sing.'

Cognate words include Greek *rhepein* 'to bend,' *rhapis* 'rod,' the Viking word *orf* 'handle of a scythe,' Old High German *worf* 'handle of scythe' and Lithuanian *verpti* 'to spin.'

Cognate in a Modern Anatomical Name

A related form that appears in Modern English includes the anatomical term *raphe* 'seam, suture' from ancient Greek *raphe* from the verb *rhaptein* 'to sew, to stitch, to suture.' For example, the seam-like ridge that runs around the scrotum with one testicle on each side of the seam is in English anatomy the scrotal raphe.

The scrotal raphe is part of the perineal raphe, visible evidence of humans being bilaterally symmetrical. Wikipedia continues the definition: "In men, this raphe continues through the midline of the scrotum (scrotal raphe) and upwards through the posterior midline aspect of the penis (penile raphe). It is the result of a fetal developmental phenomenon whereby the scrotum (the developmental equivalent of the labia in females) and penis close toward the midline and fuse." Many a boy — and quite a few girls — have seen the seam-line under the penis.

Here's another informative quotation: "This is called the scrotal raphe and every boy has one which extends from his bum (perineal raphe) up to the tip of his foreskin (penile raphe), though it is more prominent in some boys than others. When you are developing in the womb, you start off with all the cells to make you into a girl. About 7 weeks after conception, the Y chromosome kicks in and this converts your ovaries into testicles. The clitoris and inner labia become your penis and the outer labia fuse together to form your scrotum. The raphe is the seam where these parts fuse together."

Rockin' good news! That ought to make a few sexist, dick-wagging studs quiver!

Other English Medical Terms from this Root

Several other medical terms for suturing procedures are known to some patients, like episiorrhaphy, herniorrhaphy, palatorrhaphy and rhinorrhaphy.

Quail not at the complex appearance of these medical words! I'm going to explain them so you will always know their meanings and how to pronounce them in English.

The ancient Greek etyma or roots are *raphe* 'seam, suture, a line showing where items have been sewn together' from the basic verb *rhaptein* 'to sew, to stitch together' giving the longer action-noun suffix *–rrhapia* 'a stitching, a sewing, a mending of tears and rips.'

Episiorrhaphy

[i-pees-ee-ORR-afee]

Most common, known to many mothers, is episiotomy, a surgical cutting of the perineum to permit easier passage of an infant's head during childbirth and crowning, when the baby's head is first visible. The subsequent repairing of any perineal cuts may be referred to as an episiorrhaphy 'sewing up wounds in the pubic area.' Episiorrhaphy may also refer to sewing in place a prolapsed uterus. From Greek *episeison* 'groin, pubic region' + *rafee* 'seam, suture'

Herniorrhaphy
[her-nee-ORR-afee]

Also commonly known is herniorrhaphy, the surgical repair by suturing of a hernia, that is, any abnormal hole in a body cavity.

Palatorrhaphy
[pal-ah-TOR-afee]

Palatorrhaphy is the surgical correction of a cleft palate by suturing.

Rhinorrhaphy
[rine-ORR-afee]

During a "nose job," one of the operations performed by plastic surgeons may be a rhinorrhaphy in which excess nasal tissue is cut out and the wound edges are sutured (sewn) together.

Common English Verb Cognate with Raphe & Rhapsody

The Germanic cognate of Greek *raphe* appears in a common English verb *to wrap*, seen in Middle English *wrappen*, in Danish *vravle* 'to twist together,' Middle Dutch *lappen* 'to wrap up,' Middle Low German *wrempen* 'to wrinkle, scrunch the face,' and Greek *rhaptein* 'to stitch together, to sew," ultimately from Proto-Indo-European *werp- 'to turn, wind' from PIE root *wer-'to turn, bend.'

So, my eager verbivores, we have journeyed from epic poetry to lowly scrotum; and now must we stitch our tale together in order that it may cohere during recountings yet to come.

Chapter 64

Syringe, Syrette and Syrinx, the Nymph Who Said No to Horny God Pan

Increase your understanding of English vocabulary by examining the origin of syringe, whose first meaning was "flute," the source of WWII's morphine syrette, how the Greek god Pan was named and the tale of the reluctant nymph Syrinx, as well as the root among ancient domestic livestock of our word panic!

An excellent definition of our most common modern meaning of the word *syringe* is provided, as so often, by the *Oxford English Dictionary*: "an instrument that consists of a glass barrel fitted with a plunger and a hollow needle and is used for the injection of medicines or for aspiration of fluid from body cavities…"

The ultimate source of syringe is ancient Greek *surinx* or *syrinx* meaning 'panpipe, tube, channel, wooden flute.'

As we look at how a term for flute came to mean hypodermic, we shall retell a founding Greek myth, and a salty little romp it is too, all about randy Pan chasing comely nymphs through the Hellenic boscage.

Mythic Cavortings

Like many another evocative Greek noun falling into the thicket of myth, the word *syrinx* was at some date personified by the ancients and became Syrinx, a pert woodland nymph. Nymphs were benevolent, sexy young female spirits who guarded and haunted freshwater streams, fountains, wells and springs. Nymphs were, if you like, female "spirits of place." The word *nymph* is related to an ancient Greek word for 'bride,' suggestive of their nubility and sexual ripeness.

From Thing to Person

This semantic metamorphosis, of syrinx 'panpipe' to Syrinx 'nymph.' was an ancient etymological ploy, a mode of explaining how the word came to mean 'set of pipes' or 'wooden flute.' *Easy,* said early Greek word-nuts. Syrinx, they posited, must have taken its name from a flute player of long ago! Such personification often happened in ancient Greek when, in the vocabulary of the day, there was not a great number of words similar to the term whose origin was being sought. In short, such a personification befell words suffering a dearth of likely cognates.

Hunting for Cognates

Now *syrinx* in ancient Greek had only two common look-alikes: *syrizein* 'to pipe, whistle, hiss,' an obvious derivative of the noun,' and Greek *solen*' 'channel, pipe.' But it is not clear if the ancient Greeks even made a connection between *syrinx* and that last cognate *solen*, hence the explanatory myth.

Eric Partridge says the Greek *syrinx* meaning 'panpipe, tube, channel, wooden flute' is cognate with Sanskrit *surunga* 'tube.' Highly dubious. I think the Sanskrit or Prakrit word looks like a late borrowing from Greek — perhaps through Persian?

From a Medieval Latin form *syringa*, medicine named a catheter for cleaning wounds with a water wash. This meaning was not transferred to hypodermic needles until 1884.

Pan-ting for Nymphs

Let us return to our Greek folktale. One afternoon, amidst the ferny dells of Arcady, the goaty god Pan, in his usual state of hysterical concupiscence, thought what a pleasant interlude would ensue should the goat-hooved deity be able to subdue one of the slower, less agile nymphets before lunch. A nooner with a nymph! Eureka!

Who then was this Pan? His name Pan stems from the Greek verb *paien* 'to pasture animals.' Pan began as a rustic fertility deity of the fields, guardian of shepherds and divine custodian of flocks. Thus he frequented high pastures and mountain meadows, hunting and playing "country" music on his panpipes as he danced a horny jig. Pan was also a lustful little bastard who would screw anything on two or four legs. He survived well into the later history of Europe. In Great Britain, for example, he became a medieval fertility figure called The Green Man, whose terra-cotta or leafy face one can still buy to nail up and guard one's fields and help insure an uberous abundance of crops.

Panic!

Imagine now a peaceful afternoon lolling sweetly over an ancient pasture in the Peloponnese. While a cowherd daydreams, gentle kine browse in meadows. Suddenly, unaccountably, the cows stampede and moo in terror. The cowherd chases them and brings them back to the meadow. Just as suddenly as it began their terror abates. What got into those cows? Why, a panic, of course. The god Pan chased them, sporting with them briefly. The cowherd remembers another time, following a stray calf into a cave and suddenly being overcome by rapid fear. Pan had darted nearby, causing that panic. The word came into English from French. Rabelais in 1546 had written in medieval French *terreur Panice. Panikos* became a Hellenistic Greek adjective that meant 'pertaining to a groundless fear.'

The Green Man

In some parts of the English countryside known as Jack-o'-the-Woods, the Green Man was indeed a kind of northern Pan, a spirit of bounteous fruitfulness for crops, domestic animals — and humans. The Green Man was invoked on wedding nights. Often depicted as a tree spirit, his forest eyes peering through a facial cloak of oak leaves, the Green Man himself is only glimpsed briefly after his fleet feet rustle dried leaves on a warm August day. This potent herald of fecundity surges up from spermy earth, anoints those nearby with his green benison and assures all living things of teeming seed and mellow harvest. In feudal times, British female serfs entering a field to mow hay, often kissed the Green Man's wooden face nailed up on a fence, thereby insuring they would get pregnant before winter and give birth in springtime. His breedy, procreant duty done, the Green Man then vanishes, vacuumed back down into chthonic subterrane as mysteriously as he appeared.

Hereby Hangs a Greek Tale and a Tail

Our little myth begins with Pan falling in love with one of the most beauteous nymphs, Syrinx. He spotted her early in the vernal bloom of her young womanhood as her breast buds swelled and narrow hips grew round.

Pan lusted for her. After weeks of stalking, Pan glimpsed the svelte nymphet flitting through sylvan glades. He gave chase. As she ran, Syrinx brushed back slender, tendrilling lianas pendulous and asway from overarching branches. At length, Syrinx came to the bank of a forest brook and invoked the help of her sisters, the naiads or stream nymphs. Rising from their watery haven, the naiads saw the huffing and salivating Pan in lecherous pursuit and heard the obscene clack of his goat hooves on the pebbles of the creek's embankment. Then, fins aflutter, the naiads rose from the stream as a chorus and said "No!" By their most potent magic, naiads transformed Syrinx into a hollow reed, such as already grew along the shallowed marges of the brook.

When, erect and puffing, Pan reached the stream's bank, he could not see Syrinx at all, merely an undulant bed of water-cradled reeds. Pan sighed in disappointment and his mournful breath blew through the reeds making a sad sound, at that point congenial to Pan and reminding him of the unattainable nymph Syrinx.

Nimbly Pan scampered to the pliant reeds and cut off some of their tops and hollowed out these top stems, all to make a new panpipe, seven hollow reeds tied together with a thong of goatskin. When he played it, Pan would be reminded always of Syrinx.

But, of course, one of the reeds Pan cut was Syrinx herself! In a somber, amoricidal twist at the end of this Freudian story, Pan killed his love to make his music, and that is why, forever afterward, the notes of his Pan flute would be chiefly long and dry and full of mourning, a tristful tune for a denied amour or, at the lowest estimate, a fluted lamentation for a forfeited lust.

Hollow river reeds were the building tubes, so-to-speak, of panpipes, hence their name Syrinx, honouring the nymph who escaped Pan, only to be slain by him. The classical Latin plural *syringes* later gives English our medical instrument name, the syringe.

English Poetical Reference

Here is a poem written in 1860 by Elizabeth Barrett Browning (1806-1861 CE) whose opening two lines are still quoted, both seriously and more often satirically.

A Musical Instrument
What was he doing, the great god Pan,
Down in the reeds by the river?
Spreading ruin and scattering ban,
Splashing and paddling with hoofs of a goat,
And breaking the golden lilies afloat
With the dragon-fly on the river.

He tore out a reed, the great god Pan,
From the deep cool bed of the river:
The limpid water turbidly ran,
And the broken lilies a-dying lay,
And the dragon-fly had fled away,
Ere he brought it out of the river.

High on the shore sat the great god Pan
While turbidly flowed the river;
And hacked and hewed as a great god can,
With his hard bleak steel at the patient reed,
Till there was not a sign of the leaf indeed
To prove it fresh from the river.

He cut it short, did the great god Pan,
(How tall it stood in the river!)

Then drew the pith, like the heart of a man,
Steadily from the outside ring,
And notched the poor dry empty thing
In holes, as he sat by the river.

"This is the way," laughed the great god Pan
(Laughed while he sat by the river),
"The only way, since gods began
To make sweet music, they could succeed."
Then, dropping his mouth to a hole in the reed,
He blew in power by the river.

Sweet, sweet, sweet, O Pan!
Piercing sweet by the river!
Blinding sweet, O great god Pan!
The sun on the hill forgot to die,
And the lilies revived, and the dragon-fly
Came back to dream on the river.

Yet half a beast is the great god Pan,
To laugh as he sits by the river,
Making a poet out of a man:
The true gods sigh for the cost and pain,—
For the reed which grows nevermore again
As a reed with the reeds in the river.

*

Pan was shown in antiquity as both a young boy playing reed pipes, breathing creativity to the human soul and delight to his flocks and as the coarser, goat-footed, insistent seed-spreader of fertility.

Other Injectional Queries & Tidbits

1. Why is the genus to which lilac trees belong called Syringa?

You can guess. The hollowed-out stems of some species were once used to make primitive pipes and flutes and even syringes.

2. In ornithology, syrinx names the vocal apparatus of a bird.
3. "Syrinx" is a short piece of music by Claude Debussy, composed in 1913 for solo flute, an obbligato composition in the repertoire of any classically trained flautist. It was originally entitled "*Flûte de Pan.*"
4. **Hypodermic** syringe is a small syringe used with a hollow needle for injection of material into or beneath the skin. The word is a mid-nineteenth century coinage, arising with the spread of vaccination, cobbled together niftily from Greek *hupo* or *hypo* 'under' + Greek *derma* 'skin.'

Syrette

In their personal med kit, almost every Allied soldier in World War II carried a few ccs of morphine in an easily injectable form called a syrette. It was invented and named by the Squibb pharmaceutical company by taking the first syllable of *syr-inge* and adding a French diminutive suffix *–ette.*

Syrettes had a tube like toothpaste at the end containing the chemical (in Squibb's syrettes often morphine tartrate) and a wire loop one pulled to break a seal. Then one shoved the needle at a shallow angle into an arm or leg and then squeezed the tube to inject the morphine. The idea was that perhaps even a wounded soldier in the field could self-administer the pain-killer. But if a medic performed the function, he pinned the empty tube to the collar of the soldier victim so subsequent examination by army doctors would include the amount of the injected field dose.

One Hollywood film shows the compassionate use of a morphine syrette and that's a moving scene in Steven Spielberg's World War Two movie "Saving Private Ryan." A young medic gets blown apart by a Nazi machine gun. He's alive enough just to suffer screaming agony for a few hours then he will surely suffer a painful death. With a telling nudge, he knows enough to ask a wise soldier companion for "a little morphine." His friend rips open some Squibb syrettes and plunges two or three of them into one thigh of the dying medic. It is an overdose and the medic dies.

Almost every soldier on fatal battlefields of the Second World War knew what one used morphine syrettes for: yes, to alleviate physical torment, but also to end unbearable pain. Thankfully, most of those stories were left on the battlefield. The savvier infantrymen knew that pious committees of busybody Christian do-gooders waited back home to punish any soldier or medic who gave an overdose of morphine to a dying, screaming man. These pacifist Quaker virgins, who had never so much as seen what a bomb can do to a man's body, clucked in disapproval at euthanasia. After all, Jesus wants us to suffer. Just ask these morons of mercy, as they push severely retarded children in wheelchairs through death wards.

I'll never forget seeing one of those "mothers," lips pursed in spiritual superiority to everyone else on earth, saying to a documentary camera crew, as the lens showed us her child writhing in 24-hour pain, "Vern and I have decided to dedicate Little Timmy's pain to Jesus." Oh yeah, what about asking Little Timmy what he wants?

I hope her Mother-of-the-Year medal gets lost in the mail.

Now I don't want to needle you, but, if you've no objection, I'd like to inject a bye-bye into this arm of the discussion.

Chapter 65

Family

Its surprising origin as a word in Latin where it first meant 'house full of slaves'

In Latin, *familia* began as a collective noun meaning 'all the slaves belonging to one master' based on a common Latin word for slave-servant, *famulus*.

The Romans appear to have borrowed the word from their Italian neighbours, one race of whom were the Osci. By 350 BCE Rome had conquered the Osci. The Oscan word for 'slaves of the household' was *famelo*, while Oscan for household slave was *famel*.

The Oscans, justly or not, had the reputation among the stern early Romans of being a degenerate race of sexual profligates who held naked orgies nightly upon the rolling pasturelands of Campania. As *l'heure bleue* of twilight settled like a pestilential fog on the Oscan fields, depraved lewdness ran amok; debauched games during which gauze-clad damsels scampered screaming through tepid porridge were spoken of, and — oh my! — moans of lust rose loud, drowning out susurrous devotions lisped by shy virgins on temple steps; tales of repugnant cavortings in vats of warm lard (!) and lascivious slitherings nude in mud reached the shocked ears of innocent Romans, who, horrified and disgusted, immediately begged for more details. Perhaps not too different from today's Vatican emails of nun-to-nun chatter?

A little later in Latin, *familia* came to mean all the people over whom the *paterfamilias* (Latin 'head of the household') held sway. That included his wife, his sons and his daughters. So even in Latin *familia* sometimes meant 'members of one's immediate family,' and sometimes the extended circle of one's blood relatives out to second and third cousins, as well as all the slaves and servants and workers on the estate of a *paterfamilias.*

Romans Who Abused Slaves were Roman Trash

Every Roman did not treat slaves badly. Here's a satirical comment on cruelty to servants from that deft comic epigrammatist, Martial (circa 39 CE to 103 CE). Born in Spain, Marcus Valerius Martialis arrived in Rome as a new boy and viewed the eternal city's shenanigans from a witty immigrant's dry perspective. This is from his third book of epigrams, a rebuking couplet about punishing a kitchen slave (# 94):

Esse negas coctum leporem poscisque flagella.
Mauis, Rufe, cocum scindere quam leporem.
"You deny that your rabbit is cooked and call for the whip. You'd rather cut up your cook, Rufus, than your rabbit."
Casselman addendum: The implication is: Rufus, you are a sadistic lout.

Dominus Illuminatio Mea 'The Lord is my Light'

Paterfamilias was not the most common Latin word for 'master of the house.' That was *dominus*, based on *domus* 'house, estate.' Dominus gives the Latin Bible the name for Jesus, *Dominus* = Lord, and gives English the verb, *to dominate.* For those into S&M, it also supplies an occupational name for Brenda, Queen of Pain & Whips. She is a *dominatrix*, feminine form of dominator. The Biblical quotation that heads this paragraph is the motto of the University of Oxford and appears frequently as part of the printer's device which is the emblem of Oxford University Press.

Other English words from the same root are: *domain* through French *demaine* and, perhaps surprisingly, the term *dame* meaning 'lady' through Old French from Latin *domina* 'mistress, lady,' feminine of *dominus* 'master of a *domus*' Latin 'house.'

Getting Too Familiar?

The first Latin meaning of the adjective *familiaris* was 'belonging to one's own household.' Extended meanings followed in Latin, most of them borrowed into French and English along with the Latin adjective. *Familiaris* referred to anything private and personal, as opposed to public. Further semantic generalization occurred to render *familiaris* as meaning 'well-known, customary, welcome, suitable, etc.' — all senses familiar in English.

In his play, *Henry the Fifth* (Act 4, scene 3) William Shakespeare, in Henry's famous St. Crispin's Day speech, writes a line that almost quotes an early Latin manual and strongly suggests that Shakespeare is remembering one of his sixteenth-century Latin classes:

"King Henry: . . .
Old men forget; yet all shall be forgot,
But he'll remember with advantages
What feats he did that day. Then shall our names,
Familiar in his mouth as household words. . .

Be in their flowing cups freshly rememb'red."

Household Words was a weekly London magazine edited by Charles Dickens in the 1850s which took its name from the lines above.

Of course, familiarity, they say, breeds contempt. Let us forestall such scorn, by an abrupt egress from this little essay about one family of words.

Chapter 66

Rare Words like Iiwi & Yapok

One of the aspects of our language I most cherish is unfathomableness, in its prime meaning of 'not being able to reach the bottom.' One can never sound the sea floor of the study of English words. There are millions of them. Nobody, not even multilingual snooty phuds (Ph. Ds), can plumb the sweet abyss of etymology. Let down into the verbal waters the heaviest lead sinkers you have. Never will they fathom Lake Word. All the merrier reason therefore that I lay out upon the gutting table of the wording room rare and startling forms for your delectation.

1. Cucking-stool

This obsolete English punishment was visited upon disorderly women or cheating tradesmen. The cucking-stool might serve to tame an unruly wife or a scolding harridan. The offender was sentenced to be tied to a chair or what was called in medieval Latin *cathedra stercoris* 'a shitting chair,' a board chair with a hole in the seat to facilitate defecation. The punishment consisted of being fastened to the chair for hours so that passersby could jeer and humiliate the offender. The cucking-stool could also be taken to a river or pond and dipped in and out of the water, an earlier and less lethal version of waterboarding such as madman and quondam U.S. Vice President Dick Cheney once advocated.

Sir William Blackstone in volume 4 of his *Commentaries on the Laws of England* 1765–69 writes of a 1769 CE punishment: "She … shall ... be placed in a certain engine of correction called the trebucket, castigatory, or cucking stool … now it is frequently corrupted into ducking stool."

Other sentencing quotations from the annals of British jurisprudence include these—

1534 CE: "… the two women to be placed in the coqueen stool and dipped to the chin."

1633 CE: "She was committed to being ducked in a cucking-stool at Holborn Dike."

Cucking here means 'shitting,' from the now obsolete English verb *to cuck* = to cack = to shit, derived from the widespread Proto-Indo-European etymon */kVk/* that gives words and phrases like *kucker* Yiddish 'shitter,' to *cack*, to *kack* 'to shit', Latin *cacare* 'to defecate' and even the reduplicative English nursery noun *kaka* = shit.

A ballad, dating from circa 1615 CE, called "The Cucking of a Scold," illustrates the punishment:

Then was the Scold herself,
In a wheelbarrow brought,
Stripped naked to the smock,
As in that case she ought:
Neats tongues about her neck
Were hung in open show;
And thus unto the cucking stool
This famous scold did go.

2. Rixatrix

Rixatrix is a very obscure Old English legal term. It is Latin for scolding woman or shrewish female quarrel-maker. It is the Latin feminine of *rixator* 'contentious person.' From the Latin verb *rixare* 'to quarrel' derive a number of other rare terms, some English, some manorial Latin:

rixation = 'brawling'
rixa = 'debate, contest'
rixor = 'contestant, disputer'
rixosous = 'quarrelsome,' from the Late Latin adjective *rixosus*

3. Wittol

A wittol is a husband who knows of his wife's infidelity but does not care that she has become unfaithful. He's a contented cuckold. Wittol is from Late Middle English *wetewold*, formed in imitation of *cokewold* or cuckold, with *wete* (that is, in its modern spelling, *wit*) replacing coke. It is probably based on a misconstruing of the correct etymology of the word *cuckold*. The Middle English spellings *cokewold* and *cukeweld* were adaptations of Old French *cucuault* or *cucuald. *Cucu* was the bird *cuckoo* in Old French, to which here was added the pejorative suffix *-ald, -auld, -ault, -aud*. The cuckoo is a bird that lays its eggs in other birds' nests; in a similar manner the cuckold suffers that another male sleeps in his 'nest' with his bird/wife.

4. Desman

Up now scurries another entrant in our rare English animal words contest. The desman is a long-snouted, aquatic, insectivorous, musk-secreting Russian rat. The little mammal is endangered. The name is of Swedish origin where *desman-råtta* means 'musk rat.' The wee, odorous desman dwells chiefly along the banks of the Volga and Don Rivers of Russia.

5. Iiwi

This beautiful, red-feathered honeycreeper *Vestiaria coccinea*, is a Hawaiian bird whose red feathers used to be collected to make cloaks for fat-assed native chiefs. The name is pronounced *eevee* and is an imitation of one of the bird's distinctive calls.

6. Yapok

The yapok is an amphibious opossum of South America, whose name is taken from the Oyapok River which flows between French Guyana and Brazil. This water-opossum, *Chironectes variegatus*, has webbed toes to facilitate its swimming and pursuit of prey. These sleek and slippery marsupials do most abound and pullulate upon the slidy banks of the river after whom they were named. O moist clay, never dry!

7. Embiggen

Warren Clements, the quondam but always fascinating *Globe & Mail* word columnist, reported years ago (March 28, 2009, page R14) that a reader sent him this: "the Yahoo picture-sharing website's options menu informed us that, with a few clicks of the mouse, we could 'embiggen' the photo."

Love that coinage! Sometimes even a marginally literate bonehead site like Yahoo stumbles upon a novelty that adds to the word stock of a language. *To enlarge* is the customary verb. But *to embiggen* adds a clumsy, funsy swelling that teeters and totters and threatens to implode with a feeble, susurrant sssffffffft! — due to "enlargile dysfunction." Such an enormity may well befall this very column, should I not now absquatulate.

Chapter 67

Vadose & Phreatic: Water Table Words

Two Hydrology Words I was Forced to Learn

Never, until the frost of age grayed my beard, had I encountered technical terms about the water table. Hydrology had remained to me mercifully dehydrated. *Vadose* is said of water occurring above the water table and thus available to plant roots. *Phreatic* is water occurring below the water table in the so-called zone of saturation and thus water usually able to flow, to move. The water table itself is sometimes called the phreatic surface. The water table is the level below which the ground is saturated with water; that is, the soil pores and rock fractures are soaked in water.

I had to learn these terms when a giant, bully corporation building a hospital extension dug so deep into the soil of the block in which my house stood that the water table was altered by the hospital construction and, after 50 years of bone-dry basements, all the dwelling houses in that block became damp and wet and we had to put in sump pumps, drains and all manner of devices to keep rising water at bay. The board of governors of the hospital laughed at our plight – until we got two lawyers versed in dealing with corporate bullies. Our lawyers threatened to sue their pompous asses off. Then the noble elders gently relented and paid the entire cost of assorted sump-pumpery for every single dwelling house on our block. Bastards!

Phreatic (free-**ATTIC**)

English borrowed the word *phreatic* from French *phréatique.* Byzantine Greek had the adjective *phreatikos* 'of, pertaining to, or from a well or cistern.' That stemmed from ancient Greek *phrear, phreatos* 'a dug well, a water source not natural, a cistern, a reservoir, a water tank.' That had entered the very earliest form of the Greek language, called nowadays Proto-Hellenic, as *p^{h}rḗwər, and *phrewar* came from the earliest ancestor of Greek and English that we know, from a root very ancient indeed in Proto-Indo-European and its descendant languages. In PIE its putative form was *bhrehwr 'source of water, well.' That etymon for 'water well' had reflexes in many ancient and modern languages, such as Sanskrit *bhúrvan* 'movement of water' and Old Armenian *ałbiwr* 'fountain, water source.'

A Short Note on a Special Asterisk*

When in this column you see an asterisk (*) placed in front of a word root, it means there is no printed proof of such a word root ever existing. The asterisk means the form is a hypothetical or conjectural construct, not an historical, attested word. Yes, even etymologists have to guess sometimes. The asterisk makes clear that, in the study of a word's history, fact of origin remains distinct from mere theory of origin.

Vadose

This geological adjective stems from Latin *vadōsus* 'pertaining to a *vadum* 'a shallow area of water.' Vadose in English describes underground water circulating in subterranean shallow conduits and caves above the water table. Latin *vadum* means 'shallow water, fording place in a stream, shoal, and shallows (as a noun). In Latin *aqua vadosa* was a stream or brook or any water course able to be forded by humans or crossed by domestic animals.

Both words, *vadum* and *vadosus*, derive from the Latin verb *vadere*, 'to go quickly, to walk fast.' Remembering that Latin *v* was pronounced like our *w*, many will guess correctly that a close cousin, a reflex of *vadum* occurs in our English verb, *to wade*, and in its modern German counterpart, *waten*. Ditto Swedish and Norwegian *vada* and even in the language of the Vikings, Old Norse *vað*.

Familiar Uses of the Latin Verb *Vadere*

Vade-mecum

An English synonym for guidebook no longer in common use is still encountered when reading Victorian and Edwardian English novels, namely, a vade-mecum. Since early in the seventeenth century a vade-mecum has meant a small manual compact enough to be carried, for instance, in a traveller's pocket as a travel guide. It is a simple Latin sentence and means literally "Go with me."

Quo Vadis?

The Acts of Peter is a gospel NOT included in the canonical texts of the *New Testament* and so is branded apocryphal. But, as a text, it is no more or less dodgy than any other fanciful gobbet of Holy Writ. In this little tall tale from the ancient Near East, the apostle Peter is wisely running away from possible crucifixion in Rome. On the Appian Way, a highway leading south from Rome, Peter encounters a strange figure who turns out to be Christ risen from the dead. In the surviving Latin translation of this Greek gospel, Peter asks Jesus "*Domine, quo vadis?*" 'Lord, wither goest thou?' Jesus replies, ""*Romam eo iterum crucifigi*" 'I am going to Rome to be crucified again.' This bold reply puts a little iron in Peter's resolve and he returns to Rome, eventually to be crucified upside down.

Down through the pious ages, the phrase became popular among doubting Christians. In 1895 a Polish novelist, Henryk Sienkiewicz, wrote a best-selling novel about the encounter, translated into many languages, including an English so monosyllabic that some Hollywood producers could actually read it and turn it into a 1951 movie. Just to show that some Swedes cannot read Polish, Sienkiewicz was granted the Nobel Prize for Literature in 1905. It would not be the only time that glutinous, pietistic drivel was awarded a prize. My fave passage in *The Acts of Peter* informs the reader that Peter himself performed miracles. In the text, so help me God, Peter resurrects smoked fish and makes dogs talk. If ever you need help at your deli, Holy Pete is your man!

Phreatomagmatic

As our obscure polysyllabic vocable today, as a gift to true questers after recondite vocabulary, we present the wonderfully explosive adjective, *phreatomagmatic*, a relative newcomer to the coinage-gallery of modern geology.

Phreatomagmatic has this terse and apt definition in *The Oxford English Dictionary* "designating or relating to a volcanic eruption in which both steam from groundwater and an aerosol of magmatic gases and particles are expelled." *Scientific American* magazine tells us that "phreatomagmatic eruptions … take place either when magma heats and cracks rock close to an underground water table or when sea-water somehow gains entry to the magma chamber."

Magma is one of my especial pet words in geology. Magma is molten rock semi-liquid in nature. After magma is expelled from a volcano it is called lava. The root is a Greek verb *massein* 'to mix, to mingle together.'

And so, as we lie here prone, perhaps on a spring day, our ears pressed to earth's peaty bosom, listening to the nurturing gurgle of subterranean waters, let us, however briefly, specify our beatitudes.

Chapter 68

Gregory

One of the world's most common given names suggests 'watchful shepherd'

Etymology of Gregory

Gregory is such a popular given name and surname all around the world, and particularly common throughout Christian countries that speak languages of the Indo-European family, because *Gregorius* 'watchful' was the name of three great saints and many popes. Our Gregorian calendar is named after one of those, Pope Gregory XIII, who introduced it in 1582 CE.

In classical Greek its adjectival form *gregorikos* meant 'watchful,' as a shepherd watches over his flocks. The Greek verb from which the adjective stems was *ageirein* 'to gather together' as a shepherd gathers sheep together and then watches over them. One ancient Greek cognate noun familiar to us named the plaza or town square in which people gathered together to vote and to speak, the *agora*.

A related word, a cognate of the Greek *gregorios*, was the Roman word for flock, herd, animal gathering, namely *grex, gregis* from which derive English words like *gregarious, congregation, segregate* (to separate into different groups), *aggregate*, and of course our given name under discussion, Gregory, from the agent noun from *grex*, Latin *gregor* 'one who tends flocks, shepherd.'

Something really bad that stands out in its badness is *egregious*. This negative sense developed in English. In Latin *egregius* meant the exact opposite: literally standing above or outside the common herd because of its excellence, from Latin *ē* or *ex* 'out of, above' + Latin *grex, gregis* 'flock, herd.'

Of course the idea of shepherd as a Christian description of Jesus perfuses the New Testament, where the Latin shepherd word is *pastor*, appearing, for example, in Saint Jerome's Latin version of the Bible called The Vulgate. Here is one famous passage which begins at John 10:11 "*Ego sum pastor bonus. Bonus pastor animam suam dat pro ovibus*" 'I am the good shepherd. The good shepherd gives his very life for his sheep.'

The original is of course in the Koine Greek of the New Testament: *ego eimi ho poimen ho kalos*. "I am the good shepherd."

Latin *grex* 'flock' has cognates throughout Indo-European, such as Old Irish *graig* 'herd of horses,' Lithuanian *gurgulys* 'swarm,' Gaelic *greigh* 'stud horse' and Sanskrit *grama* 'herd, crowd, community of people.'

Although it pains a person of my stature, beyond measure, to indulge even a nano-second of vulgar jest, I feel it may be permissible here to utter one low crudity: Now let us make like sheep and flock off.

Chapter 69

Trammel

Caught in a word net

From humble start as a word among fishermen to name a certain kind of fish trap (described below) trammel acquired new and more elite meanings. Today, residing in the upper reaches of word frequency lists, trammel is chiefly a written noun used by educated people, less often a verb.

The Snob Factor

As one might imagine, words highest in an English frequency list are terms in daily use, e.g. *and, the, to, be, is, you, them, eat, walk, love,* and *hate.* It is said that with 500 common words from the top of our spoken frequency list, one could communicate most needs in simple English. Pocket travel guides to English often include these 500 most-heard English words. In sum, use of the word *trammel* or related forms usually indicates a post-secondary-school education.

"The first principle of a free society is an untrammeled flow of words in an open forum."
Adlai Stevenson, 1900–1965 CE, U.S. Democratic politician quoted in the New York Times (Jan. 19, 1962)

Possible Etymology

At first in English, a trammel was a particular kind of fishnet. Here's a reference written about 1440 CE, "Tramayle, grete nette for fyschynge." The word we now spell as *trammel* entered Middle English from Middle French *tremail*, from Medieval Latin *tramaculum*, perhaps a variant of earlier *tremaculum* or *trimaculum* from Latin *tres* 'three' + Latin *macula* 'spot, mesh.' A melodious Italian noun is still is use: *trimaglio.*

Nifty Latin Word Lore of *Macula*

Macula's basic import in Latin was 'spot, stain, dark mark,' hence the im**macula**te conception (the not-stained conception), where Mary was impregnated without the hideous "stain" of Joseph's human sperm, but instead endured only the divine, dove-dainty spritzings of the Paraclete. Immaculate can mean 'spotless' or 'very clean' too. Ophthalmology's anatomical term, *macula lutea* Latin 'yellow spot,' names the cell-dense spot which is the center of the retina and upon which the lens focuses eye-entering light. At the macula, light is transformed into neural signals which tell the brain what we are seeing.

Even in classical Latin *macula* extended its meaning from 'spot' to 'hole in a net' or 'mesh.' Two Roman writers on agriculture use *macula* with this common transferred meaning. Varro writes about *rete grandibus maculis* 'a fishnet with big holes' that is, with a wide mesh. Columella describes *reticulum minutis maculis* 'a net with small-holed mesh.' The net bag that your British punter used to take to market to bring home the fresh vegetables was called a reticulum or a reticule. My own farm-raised, Ontario, Canada, maternal grandmother, born at the end of the nineteenth century, used the word *reticule* and took one with her when she went grocery shopping "in town."

What is a Trammel?

So what does this three-meshed fishnet look like? *The Oxford English Dictionary* has a superbly worded definition: "A long narrow fishing-net, set vertically with floats and sinkers; consisting of two 'walls' of large-meshed netting, between which is a net of fine mesh, loosely hung. The fish enters through the large mesh on one side, drives the fine netting through the large mesh on the other, and is thus trapped in a pocket or bag of the fine netting."

In Today's Speech & Script

Trammel's most common semantic extension in modern English, that is, *trammel* as noun meaning 'hindrance, restraint, check, impediment' is not seen in print until the mid-seventeenth century. In modern English, the word's negative adjective *untrammeled* is more used than the plain noun *trammel*, most commonly in the adjectival phrase 'free and untrammeled,' a phrase that arose because many hearers and readers did not know the meaning of untrammeled, so a synonym 'free' was placed in front of the less common adjective to assist comprehension. These adjectival explanatory pairs are common in English prose.

After fifty years of hard labor, the prisoner was free and untrammeled.

I am always glad to think that my education was, for the most part, informal, and had not the slightest reference to a future business career. It left me free and untrammeled to approach my business problems without the limiting influence of specific training.
Alice Foote MacDougall (1867–1945), U.S. businesswoman in *The Autobiography of a Business Woman*, ch. 2 (1928)

I deign to add a usage note, perhaps elitist, as the prime meaning of 'deign' dictates. To say of something that it is untrammeled is to imply that in some of this thing's "modes" it is trammeled, hindered, dense with rules, clotted with bureaucratic fussiness. "Free and untrammeled" is such a tawdry cliché that I would never use it.

In Shakespeare's play *Macbeth*, the titular Scot is musing on how to murder King Duncan.

"If it were done when 'tis done, then 'twere well
It were done quickly: if the assassination
Could trammel up the consequence, and catch
With his surcease success; that but this blow
Might be the be-all and the end-all here,
But here, upon this bank and shoal of time,
We'd jump the life to come."

What Macbeth is saying here is: *If we could murder Duncan and if his assassination were at all popular, why then we could probably get away with the murder. Heh-heh-heh.*

Other Sample Uses

1. Too often indoor trees are allowed to grow untrammeled and soon look messy.

2. Trial courts now have untrammeled discretion to impose any sentence within the statutory range.
3. "Reading is merely a surrogate for thinking for yourself; it means letting someone else direct your thoughts. Many books, moreover, serve merely to show how many ways there are of being wrong, and how far astray you yourself would go if you followed their guidance. You should read only when your own thoughts dry up, which will of course happen frequently enough even to the best heads; but to banish your own thoughts so as to take up a book is a sin against the holy ghost; it is like deserting untrammeled nature to look at a herbarium or engravings of landscapes."
   Arthur Schopenhauer, 1788–1860 CE, German philosopher, from Aphorisms on the Wisdom of Life: Parerga and Paralipomena *(1851) English translation from Essays and Aphorisms, Penguin (1970).*

Trammel then is a useful noun and verb, worth adding to your armamentarium of words, worth carrying into any verbal joust to whose combat lists you may be summoned.

Chapter 70

The Names of Baroque Dances

How those dainty toe-tappers were christened

With a fleeting nod to Terpsichore, Greek muse of dance, we quickstep forward with the etymology of a few named dancing modes from the baroque era, like *pavane* and *gavotte*, not listed alphabetically nor comprehensively but rather in a brief scroll of delight, judged by how pleasing to the ear and to the word-soul I found the terms.

Terpsichore

Speaking of delight, the very name of the Greek muse Terpsichore (terp-SIC-oree) means approximately 'she delights in dancing' from *terpein* 'to delight in' and *choros* 'dance.'

In Frank Sinatra's swinging 1959 recording of "Come Dance with Me," the name of the muse is memorably mispronounced as "TERP-si-cor." The error was either lyricist Sammy Cahn's Hollywood ignorance (my bet) or Frank Sinatra's dick-wagging bravura stance which stated hoods like Frank could mispronounce academic words because, like Sinatra, they are major-league studs. In any case the precise *causa erroris* is now lost in time, a mere reverberant historical echo in some Capitol recording studio of the past. But—damn!—Billy

May's big band bounce still puts the wax on my dance floor.

My interest in the names of these Baroque dances began while listening to J. S. Bach's four orchestral suites and finding I was ignorant of some baroque dances which comprise Bach's and coeval suites, for example: *allemande, bourrée, sarabande, gigue, réjouissance* and *gavotte.* I did vaguely remember an Ascot Gavotte from the musical "My Fair Lady." And through the orthographical veils of the French *gigue*, I could discern our English *jig* — although apparently jig may not be derived from French. In any case, when the word is used to name the last movement of a Baroque suite, as French *gigue* or Italian *giga*, it's a snappy dance-tune in lively triple rhythm (usually 6–8 or 12–8).

Pavane

The European Renaissance bestowed upon us this stately courtiers' processional dance for couples. Pavane is one of my favourite words — British pronunciation please: peh-VAN or — the even snottier Oxfordian version that I prefer — peh-VAWN (to rhyme with lawn).

From the savoury plosiveness of its initial letter, pavane flows forth from pronouncing lips like forest water slipping over stones in a summer stream, each aqueous rill delayed by filaments of moss whose wavering tendrils subdue the water's rush.

The sedate dignity of the pavane's leisurely steps appears to have evolved from a fifteenth-century northern Italian dance, probably *danza padovana* 'dance typical of the Italian city of Padua.' The word's first printed use was in 1535 CE.

Having appeared variably as *pavan, paven, pavin, pavian, pavine* or *pavyn*, the eventual modern English form was borrowed from Middle French *pavane*, itself from Italian dialect *pavana*, feminine of *pavano* 'of Padua,' from a dialect version of the city's name *Pava*; compare the name of the city in Tuscan dialect *Padova*.

A False Source

An alternate, more colourful, and quite probably spurious origin is *pavón*, the Spanish word for 'peacock,' from Latin *pavo, pavonis* 'peacock.' Choreographic historians do believe that the decorously sweeping pavane, to music in 2/ 2 or 4/ 4 time, grew popular in part because it permitted lushly gowned and bewigged aristocrats to preen and mince, showing off their gaudy raiment, much as a male peacock flaunts his startling tail. Says one writer, "Until about 1650 the pavane opened ceremonial balls and was used as a display of elegant dress."

Encyclopedia Britannica says, "The pavane's basic movement . . . consisted of forward and backward steps; the dancers rose onto the balls of their feet and swayed from side to side. A column of couples circled the ballroom, and the dancers occasionally sang. By about 1600, livelier steps like the fleuret (a brief lift of each foot before a step) made the dance less pompous. The pavane was customarily followed by its afterdance, the vigorous galliard."

Several notable later composers wrote instrumental works using the stately measures, such as Fauré's "Pavane for Orchestra" and Ravel's 1899 solo piano piece "*Pavane pour une infante défunte*" 'Pavane for a Dead Princess.'

Gavotte

In the southern French province of Provence, a town name for a citizen who dwells high up in the Alps is *un gavot.* In the language of Provençal *gavoto* names a mountain dance of the Gavots. The gavotte is a minuet-like dance but in quicker time. *Un gavot* may derive from a pre-Roman Gallic form like *gava or *gaba that meant goitre, one of the afflictions of mountain people removed from any convenient source of iodine.

Allemande

Allemande does mean "a German dance" from French *allemand* 'German.' It has devolved into an American square dance call, for example allemande left and is mistakenly believed to stem from French *à la main.* Allemande named a Baroque courtly step in which the couple's arms were interlaced.

Bourrée

This was a rustic dance of the French Baroque period originally a lively country two-step in common time, two beats to a bar, first seen in the Auvergne, once a province of south-central France and now a larger administrative region. *Un pas de bourrée* is, as defined by *The Oxford English Dictionary*, "a sideways step in dancing in which one foot crosses behind or in front of the other."

One source claims the name stems from eighteenth-century French *bourrée* 'a bundle of sticks chopped for firewood.' It is said the vivid rural two-step was first danced around the perimeter of a small rural bonfire.

Réjouissance

It means 'rejoicing, merrymaking or celebration' in French. In baroque orchestral suites, it named a spirited and lively dance tune which might accompany such revels.

Sarabande

This stately Spanish Baroque court dance resembles the minuet and was perhaps first encountered during the Crusades by Christians from Spain watching a Saracen dance, noting that *sarraceno* was a Spanish word of the time for an Arab or Muslim. Saracen was picked up from Hellenistic Greek and Latin as a dismissive name for nomadic tribes who fought the Romans, then by racist extension it named any Arab or Muslim.

Written in slow triple time, its Spanish and Italian form is *sarabanda* or *zarabanda*, probably from a Persian word *serbend* 'a song.' Other possible Persian sources include a dance named after an old region of Iran called Saravand, or a Persian place name Saravana 'clump of reeds,' or even a Persian word imported or acquired in India, where one of the native names for the month of August is Sravana. One might then perhaps posit a dusty-footed sun dance to invoke rain during a dry spell. Remember too that when dance modes were taken up by the elite of court, the faraway magic of a foreign name added to the exotic delight of a new dance.

Sir Osbert Sitwell, in his poem ""On the Coast of Coromandel," liked the word's music and wrote: "Saraband and rigadoon / Dance they through the purring noon."

Waltz

Although not in Bach's orchestral suites, this dance-word's elemental husk is tantalizingly ancient. Its root in Proto-Indo-European is *wel 'to turn,' mother of a thousand words or reflexes in later languages. *Walzen* in early German means 'to turn, to turn together, to spin round, to roll, to revolve, and then finally to dance the waltz. One thinks of our English borrowings from the cognate Latin verb *voluere* 'to turn' such as *involve, revolve* and *convolve* and of the French pickup from German, *la valse.* Most apt is *Walzer* to name the twirling, whirling ecstasy of waltz-time. Best Waltz title? Robert Stolz may be proud of his operetta title *Zwei Herzen im Dreivierteltakt* 'Two hearts in three-quarters time."

Yeah, Zeke, But What Makes 'em Do that there High-Steppin'?

A terminal note about the psychological impetus to dance may not be out of place. The old myth about dance being a socially acceptable form of intercourse used to be mocked. But – heavens to Freud! – it may be true! Some shrinks and neurologists and anthropologists who have done preliminary studies of dancing suggest that dance first was body signals as part of natural selection during extended courtship rituals. The more risk-taking gestures and leaps of male dancers are said to have attracted women seeking sturdy mates. Darwin thought this, but he also knew the sheer joy of traipsing around the campfire in time to rhythmic thumps on a hollow log was part of dance's hold on humans. Videos of men watching women dance, and men watching women dance, seem to confirm this mate-evaluating origin of dance.

Say, Bobby-Sue, I ever show yah muh two-step?

Chapter 71

Digital Anomalies

Congenital malformations of the fingers and toes

You, reader, exhibit all the symptoms of pentadactyly. Nor can you evade this condition, short of cutting off a toe or a finger, for it is merely the medical word for the possession of five fingers or toes per limb. Far better the genetically ordained five digits a limb than to fumble through life as a glum monodactyl, letting fall the condom just when you ought not to! Had your existence been delayed, you might, with leathern flap, have flitted o'er antique skies as a wing-finger or pterodactyl. You were spared the sorrow of this entry in a 1998 number of *The Journal of Hand Surgery*: "Another case of the monodactyly type in which we tried to lengthen three transplanted proximal toe phalanges ended in failure."

The chief and relevant etymon is *daktylos*, the Greek word for finger or toe. In poetic meter, dactyl is the name of one metrical foot (long-short-short or ¯ ˘ ˘. It was named after the finger because, beginning at the knuckle, a dactyl is one long bone or syllable followed by two shorter ones. For example, the first line of Henry Wadsworth Longfellow's Acadian poem "Evangeline" is a dactylic hexameter: **This** is the / **for**est prim- / ***ev***al. The / **mur**muring / **pines** and the / **hem**locks . . .

The first five feet of the line are dactyls; the sixth a trochee.

The English word *poetry* is metrically a dactyl.

Anatomical Anomalies

The medical terms naming congenital malformations of the fingers and toes merely add familiar Greek roots to the *–dactyly* base.

Polydactyly (Greek *polys* = 'many') is a congenital excess of fingers and/or toes.

Syndactyly (Greek *syn* 'with, together) names webbed toes and/or fingers.

Brachydactyly (Greek *brachys* 'short') is abnormal shortness of the digits, as when the fingers have only two joints.

Arachnodactyly (Greek *arachnis* 'spider') names a condition of abnormally long, thin digits.

Macrodactyly (Greek *makros* 'big, wide') is abnormal enlargement of one or more digits.

Clinodactyly describes a bend or pronounced curvature of the little fingers toward the adjacent fourth fingers. It is a fairly common isolated anomaly which often goes unnoticed, but also occurs in combination with other abnormalities in many genetic syndromes, and in approximately 80% of individuals with Down syndrome.

Oligodactyly (Greek *oligos* 'few') is the presence of fewer than five fingers or toes on a hand or foot. It is a rare congenital malformation.

The words also appear as part of larger compound names in the annals of teratology (study of fetal anomalies) such as the serious deformity of *acrocephalosyndactyly*. This is a congenital syndrome characterized by a peaked head due to premature closure of the skull sutures and associated with fusion or webbing of the fingers or toes. In cruel street speech, victims are called pinhead or conehead. *Akros* is Greek for 'pointed, sharp' and *kephalos* means 'head, skull.' Almost all cases are sporadic, signifying fresh mutations or environmental insult to the genome. The offspring of a parent with the syndrome has a 50% chance of inheriting the condition.

A similar but not exactly similar cephalic malformation is oxycephaly (Greek *oxys* 'sharp, pointed'), also known as turricephaly or high-head syndrome.

Teratology is the scientific study of congenital abnormalities, from Greek *teras teratos* 'monster, marvel, thing to be stared at.'

Ectrodactyly is total congenital absence of digits. The word began as a modern Latin coinage, *ectrodactylia* based on Greek *ek* 'out, out of, away from normal' + *troma* or *trosis* 'damage' + *dactylos* 'finger, toe.'

If now I offer to tiptoe away, it is not, *Gott sei Dank*, due to brachydactyly.

Chapter 72

Elf as a Word

"Airy elves by moonlight shadows seen"

– Alexander Pope

When long ago the first European ships disembarked their brutish cargo of scruffy immigrants on North America's pristine shores, those more picayune members of the European fairy world, to wit, brownies, goblins, sprites and, in particular, teeny-weeny elves, with their sorcerous and occult endowment, did not stand a chance. Large, thuggish aboriginal spirits had already landed with an oafish thump, frowsy supernatural beings like the northwestern trickster Raven or his eastern counterpart Nanubush, mere buffoons who played cheap tricks on humankind. To some southwestern tribes he was Coyote, to southeastern peoples Rabbit and Hare among the Sioux. He had many names: Iktomi and Winabojo. But he was a big, cloddish prankster, a petty snickerer of the night world, who, instead of bedazzling humans with bounteous slight-of-hand was the kind of imp who preferred to place a fart-cushion under the chief's blanket. What a loss to fairydom that we never welcomed clever elves to our continent!

Oh sure, Santa's elves survived in fairy lore, but what an ugly crew of shrunken, peevish munchkins they turned out to be, slavishly carving wooden toys for nasty, ungrateful little children who never thanked them. Ever hear of a kid leaving out milk and cookies for Santa's elves. No. Only Oreos for the fat man.

Fascinating Etymology of Elf

To undo the unjust desuetude into which the elfin realm has plunged, today we celebrate that neat word: *elf.* It appears to be a reflex of an odd and wonderful Indo-European root whose chief meaning was 'evil white,' white as a symbol of magic belonging to the night. In Old English it was *ælf,* with its West Saxon adjective *ylfig* 'of the elfish world' that did not make it into modern English. But see my word coinage below.

English *elf* is cognate with words in modern German. *Der Alp* is a goblin that squats on a sleeper's chest and causes nightmares, featured in Henry Fuseli's most famous painting, *The Nightmare,* a 1781 oil painting by the Anglo-Swiss artist Fuseli *(1741–1825).* Folk belief said *der Alp* was a whitish sprite. The same 'evil white' root names the mountainous Alps in German, *die Alpen.* The Vikings knew these tiny terrors in their language of Old Norse, *alfr.*

Some of the other ancient words related to elf bear the glow of white magic. Consider Old English words for swan, *ælbitu* and *ielfetu* and Old High German *albiz* and *elbiz* 'swan,' or Latin *albus* 'white,' and Greek *alphos* 'a white skin disease,' along with Welsh *elfydd* 'earth, world,' and Russian *lebed* 'swan.'

The root appears in a common English given name as *Alfred,* in Old English *Ælfraed,* literally 'elf-advice,' originally perhaps a shaman or Germanic wise man who prudently took night counsel from the little people who dwelt in acorns and hid behind mushrooms during the day. Even an English monarch held the name, King Alfred the Great.

With All Due Lack of Humility, I Coin a New Word

Here do I proffer a new word for you, from the Old English adjective *ylfig* which, had it come down into modern English through use, would today appear spelled /*elfy*/. In the admittedly bursting hoard of English words, there is a modest lacuna where *elfy* might serve. *Elfy* differs from the adjective *elfin* which nowadays chiefly denotes diminutive size and is appreciative. Elfy could be a solid synonym for *pixilated* 'possessed by elves,' 'spellbound by fairy power.' And here is one of my exemplary sentences for your perusal: *The elfy tendrils of madness were already, by their dense neural thatch, obscuring the clear light of her reasoning.*

The early Teutons thought elves did both good and evil. They exchanged "good" children for evil changelings. In an age before child psychology and before any knowledge of neurological deficits, this elf-exchange was a primitive attempt to explain why a normal child might suddenly "go mad" and do bad things.

In *A Midsummer Night's Dream*, the spritely Puck is an elf whom Shakespeare introduces to us in Act 2, Scene 1. A fairy says:

"Either I mistake your shape and making quite;
Or else you are that shrewd and knavish sprite
Call'd Robin Goodfellow: are not you he
That frights the maidens of the villagery;
Skim milk, and sometimes labour in the quern
And bootless make the breathless housewife churn;
And sometime make the drink to bear no barm;
Mislead night-wanderers, laughing at their harm?
Those that Hobgoblin call you and sweet Puck,
You do their work, and they shall have good luck:

Are not you he?
Puck:
Thou speak'st aright;
I am that merry wanderer of the night."

A Personal Favorite

Mickey Rooney made a surprisingly good Puck in the 1935 Warner Brothers movie of *A Midsummer Night's Dream.* Max Reinhardt's hugely successful European stage production was transferred to Hollywood and bits of movie magic were added by veteran director William Dieterle. One outstanding cast member was long-time movie villain Victor Jory as Oberon in **the** performance of his entire film career. Rent this old gem some night and be enchanted.

To conclude we cannot resist one final Shakespearean snippet, also from *A Midsummer Night's Dream*, taken from Oberon's valedictory at the end of the play:

"Now, until the break of day,
Through this house each fairy stray. . .
Trip away; make no stay;
Meet me all by break of day."

The rushy waterfall of English dramatic poetry never flows ampler than cascades which pour forth in *A Midsummer Night's Dream.*

Chapter 73

Quorum

As a foreign word *quorum* is an inflected pronoun in Latin and a genitive plural of the relative pronoun *qui* (cognate English *who*) and means literally 'of whom' or 'whose.' The only English plural is *quorums.*

Quora is not Latin and is not an English plural form. Eschew such a plural. Shun it as a dowager clad in black bombazine might view, through her tortoise-shell lorgnette, a beetle defecating on her orchid corsage.

Quorum began in English at the end of the fourteenth century as part of a Medieval Latin sentence at the start of court documents or statements by a commission. A quorum listed the number of appointed or ordained persons who had to be present during deliberations and subsequent statements of formal bodies for such statements to bear the force of law, at first with councils of justices of the peace in Norman England. It appeared in initial Latin sentences which began, let us say, with a list of the names of two necessarily present justices, followed by this Latin: *quorum vos duos esse volumus* 'of which we wish [and command] that you two be [necessary and present.'] In other words, for the council to be legislatively potent, to issue a legal judgment or command, these two members, this quorum, had to be present.

Quorums were instituted to prevent an unrepresentative small number of committee members from acting in the name of a much larger body, to stop a minority of group members from voting against a majority.

Partial Jewish Source

But I also think there seeped into the pompous political assemblies of later European councils knowledge of the quorums required in many religions in order for prayer or religious conduct to proceed. I think especially a knowledge of the Jewish *minyan* was known by politicians and they wanted the prestige of religious quorums to rub off on their less noble political shenanigans.

A *minyan* is a quorum of ten Jewish adults required for a religious obligation such as public prayer. In modern Judaism a minyan can mean the prayer service itself. The triliteral Hebrew verbal root is *maneh* 'to count, to number.' Its cognate in Aramaic *mene* 'numbered,' appears famously at Belshazzar's Feast in the biblical "writing on the wall" in the Book of Daniel 5:25 where God writes words that Daniel reads as MENE, MENE, TEKEL, PARSIN and interprets them for the king: MENE, God has numbered the days of your kingdom and brought it to an end; TEKEL, you have been weighed and found wanting; and PERES, the kingdom is divided and given to the Medes and Persians. Due to the weighty solemnity of that occasion I can only remind the pious reader of comic writer S.J. Perelman's apt pun: "One man's Mede is another man's Persian."

The Most Renowned Minyan?

The original number needed for a minyan was 12, said to derive from the traditional twelve tribes of Israel. Some say the 12 Apostles of Jesus constituted a minyan or quorum permitting many Jewish rituals to be performed. Some say Jesus, as rabbi, chose an itinerant minyan to accompany him during his travels and travails in earthly ministry.

Some Uses of *Quorum* in Latin, with text and my translation

To lessen the oddness of the word *quorum* and show its common, homey Latin use, I present below sample Latin sentences with translation. Roman orators and lawyers like Cicero loved the orotund sound of the Latin word *quorum* and so it appears frequently in Cicero's court speeches.

1.
C. Julius Caesar, *De Bello Gallico (The Gallic War)*
hominum milia decem, undique coegit, et omnes clientes obaeratosque suos, quorum magnum numerum habebat. . .
[he] drew together from all quarters to the court, all his vassals to the number of ten thousand persons; and led together to the same place all his dependents and debtor-bondsmen, of whom he had a great number…
2.
quorum garrulitas si patienter accipitur,
whose chattiness if it is patiently accepted…
3.
quorum per ripas nebuloso lumine marcent . . . flores.
upon whose riverbanks in the dim light flowers wither.
4.

Quæque ipse misserrima vidi, et quorum pars magna fui.
All of which misery I saw, and a great part of which I was.
5.
Haut facile emergunt quorum virtutibus opstat res angusta domi.
It is not easy for men to rise whose good qualities dire childhood poverty thwarts.

Quorate

This is a learned adjective used more often in England than elsewhere. A quorate assembly counts the number of attending members requisite to conduct official business.

Having concluded what I have to tell you about quorum, now therefore I declare this meeting adjourned *sine die.*

Chapter 74

Proper Terms for the Droppings of Animals

Just Dropping By

In presenting my modest feast of fecal terms, my scat sheet, my *cacata carta* (Horatian Latin 'shitty sheets'), my scatologue, my selection of the proper words for animal droppings, I abhor the giving of the scantest offense. Fain would I stab with pointiest quill my hand, were I to induce even a maiden's blush or to cause milady's jabot to slip down into the heaving heaven of her poitrine and be forever embosomed. But, gentles, we are dealing with words about animal shit. So look out!

Merds & Other Droppings

British novelist Anthony Burgess once suggested in print that English possessed no good term for dog shit. Using French, as, years ago, some Park Avenue matron might—"*Mais no! Une merde de chien on le sidewalk!*" is simply too precious, too macaronic, too much a foolish mix of languages. Also symbolic of simpering preciosity are hobby farmers who insist on referring to "bovidung" instead of cow shit. Burgess wanted a term less vulgar and less crude than dog shit but less namby-pamby than evasive euphemistic phrases like 'doggie do-do.' The great writer demanded a phrase solidly representative of the unpleasant object to be denominated. A novelist and essayist with broad etymological scope, Burgess stepped forth with the aptly drab but perfect coinage *dog merd*. Unfortunately it has not been taken up by the general populace and 'dog shit' still abounds on the cloddish tongues of low-born persons.

Merd *& Merde & Merde Alors!*

Meaning excrement or turd, *merd* was already in Anglo-Norman by the twelfth century, a direct borrowing of classical Latin *merda* 'shit,' origin of the now common modern French exclamation "*Merde alors!*"= an emphatic, sometimes sarcastic "Oh, well then!"

Some uses of the *merde* word in twentieth-century English exist. British theatre slang demands that, when a backstage wish of "Break a leg!" is offered to the actors about to go onstage, the proper response, obeying long-standing British thespian superstition, is "*Merde!*" It is used as a minced oath, instead of saying "Oh shit!"

Be Gone, Thou Merdivore!

One rare adjective I like, useful in the tiny quiver of insult arrows that English possesses, is *merdivorous* 'eating shit.' I think we could back-form a noun from that excellent adjective and address a cowardly and odious person as "You loathsome merdivore!"—a neology coined on the analogy of the voracious words like carnivore, herbivore, omnivore and locavore (the now ecologically discountenanced term for one who eats only local food) Locavores do not save the planet; local food does not spare us toxins or help save the earth. Much like the "organic food" mania, it is largely a scam, designed to extract more food dollars from our already thinning purses.

Let us not confine to the dank oubliette of forgotten words the rare but lovely *ranivore* 'eater of frogs,' said to be common in France. Nor must we pass over, in a prissily democratic attempt to avoid obscurity, the delightsome *piscivore* 'eating fish' and its splendid Hellenic equivalent, *ichthyophage* from *ichthys* Classical Greek 'fish' + *-phagos* Greek 'eating.'

One of the neat *–phagos* borrowings in English is a word for coffin, *sarcophagus*, literally flesh-eater, from Greek *sarkophagos*, from *sarx, sarkos* 'flesh' and *-phagos* 'eating.' Ancient Greeks believed the limestone used to make the sarcophagus would help to consume or "eat" the dead flesh of corpses buried in such a limestone box.

Much Needed Synonym for Republican

Long needed in English has been a proper delineation of the moronic hoards who populate the outreaches of our right-wing political spectrum. I propose, when we tire of the label Republicans, that we summon back an adjective from the 1880s, *autocoprophagous* 'eating their own shit,' the central ancient Greek etymon being *kopros* 'excrement, feces.' One of my favorite words in paleontology bearing the same root is *coprolith* 'a fossilized turd.' Long ago, in dusty high-school classrooms, I was taught by several coproliths.

Dropping Some Other Terms

Now I present orthodox English terminology for the feculent depositions of other animals. The go-to authority on such words is C.E. Hare's magisterial and still regnant *The Language of Field Sports.*

The Billets of a Fox

What an elegant choice to name vulpine ordure! This billet is from Old French *billette* 'piece of wood cut for fuel,' a diminutive form of *bille* 'tree trunk.'

The Crottels of a Rabbit

The tiny little balls in piles of hare scat are crottels, a diminutive form of French *crote,* except that no printed evidence of such a derivation has come to scholarly light. So we must be content to happen upon the crottels and then whisper to our inner huntsman, "Bunnies are near!"

A word related to crottel is still operative in modern French. There is a widely available French cheese named *crottin de chèvre* 'goat turds.'

The Fiants of a Wild Boar

Who knows when next you may be hot in pursuit of a collared peccary scampering its frightened way through arid scrublands of Arizona? Suddenly you must reference their scat. You may point to and speak of their fiants. Fiants also name the dung of foxes and badgers. But I like to think of the tusked javelina snorting and oinking its way to nearby cover while followed by four brave hunters in a Jeep with the sixteen rifles, all of them required to kill one wild wee piggywig.

Taken from French hunting vocabulary, the word *fiant* was firmly ensconced in English by 1575 CE when gentleman author George Gascoigne used it about badgers: "The Badgerd pigges at comming out of the earth do commonly. . . cast their fyaunts." In the same book, Gascoigne also used the new word as a verb: "They fyaunt within it [sc. a burrow or hole] and hide it." Modern-day sales analysts would call Gascoigne "an early adopter." He read all manner of continental poetry and prose and then introduced new literary modes into Renaissance English both by translating and by adapting, among them a French hunting manual.

In the mode of sixteenth-century books, Gascoigne favoured florid and lengthy titles. Now I happen to love long titles and so I reproduce with delight his total title: *The Noble Art of Venerie or Hunting: Wherein is handled and set out the vertues, nature, and properties of fifteene sundry chases, together with the order and manner how to hunt and kill every one of them. Translated & collected for the pleasure of all noblemen and gentlemen, out of the best approoved authors, which have written any thing concerning the same: and reduced into such order and proper termes as are vsed here in this noble realme of Great Britaine.*

Fiant stems from *fient* French 'dung' from a supposed Medieval Latin form like *femitum ultimately from classical Latin *fimus* 'dung, dung hill.' Another French version was *fiens* from a Latin variant *fimum*.

Scat

This all-purpose term for animal droppings is apparently quite modern, although its etymon is ancient. Scat's first known use in print is the year 1927. Scat is a direct short form borrowed from a common ancient Greek word for dung, crap or shit, namely *skor, skatos*. The word is still around in Modern Greek too, ó *skato*, pl. *skata* meaning 'feces.' Of course it's the source of our modern English literary word scatology and its adjective scatological and someone else's neology *scatalogue* quoted in the first sentence of this essay.

Some musicians say it is also the source of scat singing, doodle-oodle-doodling when the singer has forgotten the lyrics to a song. Or, when, like pompous windbag jazz singers, you the singer think you know the music better than Cole Porter who wrote the music. Hint to scat singers: You do NOT know the music better than the composer. You the singer are not a composer but a poseur or a *poseuse.*

Uncle Billy's Free Amendment of a Vulgar Error

Willingly do I offer a corrective note — without prejudice, as is ever my wont — to the oh-so-dainty housewife, trying to be snooty and upper-class but managing only to be illiterate, the mistress of the house who referred to a solitary glum dog merd deposited on her verandah by saying "The dog made a fece [sic] on our front porch." Not possible, I'm afraid, your ladyship. The word *feces* is plural only, dear madam. There is no singular form in the English language, perhaps on Mars where your nose is usually pointed, but not here on earth. Feces is a plural form in classical Latin where *fæces* is the plural of *fæx* meaning 'dregs.'

The mistake is similar to persons who imagine *kudos* 'praise' is a plural word and speak incorrectly of "the just kudo [sic] bestowed upon the hero." No, indeed. Kudos is singular, both in its native language Greek, and in its adopted one, English.

A Mass of Frass

Frass is the excrement of larvae or any excrementitious ejecta voided by plant-and wood-boring insects. From German *Frass* 'animal fodder,' 'repulsive food,' its origin is the German verb *fressen* 'to devour, to stuff your food in like an animal' itself an intensive form that began as *veressen* 'to really eat a lot.' Yiddish still has the noun *fresser* for a human glutton or piggy eater. German has *Fresserei* to name a guzzling, gut-stuffing pig fest, 'a real feed' as bloated 400-pound obesity victims say, while drool and sundry lipids course down their double chins in goopy rivulets.

Fumets

Deep in the forest primeval or deep in the forest defecatory, one could get into trouble following deer scat. You might begin to stutter during a sentence like "Did the doe do do-do?" At such tongue-rippling moments it is always reassuring to have synonyms at one's fingertip if not at one's tongue tip. Deer scat is fumets. The word is rare and always plural. There are bizarre orthographical variants including strange spellings like fewmets. There is no trace in print or parchment of the Anglo-Norman version of this word. But it must have been something like *fumets or *fumez from French *fumer* 'to put manure on fields' from Latin *fumare* 'to give off smoke,' so that the secondary sense of 'to fertilize with dung' arose from the odorous steam issuant from fresh manure.

Lesses Are No More

Although the word is, as an old professor of mine used to say, "crystalized in obsolescence," bear scat may still be called the lesses of a bear. The dung of any animal dubbed ferocious can be the lesses. Wolf lesses are spoken of. But, usually today, the word scat has replaced lesses. Borrowed from now obsolete French *laisses*, the word probably arose as *laissées* from *laisser* French 'to leave,' so that its prime meaning was 'the leavings [sc. of the animal].'

Spraints on Your Ankle?

As yet another token of its excellence, English is among the few world languages that has a specific word for otter turd. In the slang of British hunting, otter droppings are *spraints*. O most excellent wordlet! Derived from Old fourteenth-century French *espraintes* 'things squeezed out,' from the French verb *espraindre* 'to squeeze out' ultimately from Latin *exprimere* 'to squeeze in order to expel something.' For example, the Romans used *exprimere* to name the action of squeezing water out of sponge. The modern French noun plural is *épreintes* and the verb *épreindre*. Words squeezed out of one's mouth are *expressed* and groups of such words make up *expressions*.

But now, enough of vile feculence, say I! Enough of dwelling unduly upon lowly excreta. We may be born in the stable but our eyes, our brows, even our eyebrows, must lift ever toward the starry welkin and the upper ethers where do cavort, hover, and in general helicopter about, the sweeter-smelling angels of our nature.

Chapter 75

Ten Latin Epitaphs

to give your drab tombstone a little class

1. If you favour the snotty epitaph, as I do, this little line of Latin terseness may please you:

Tu fui, ego eris
(Implied words not expressed are between brackets.)
"What you are (alive), I was. What I am (dead), you will be.

2. This may be too portentous for an ordinary epitaph, but a strong personality might indeed think that visiting a person's tomb induces a reminder of death's finality.

Taceant colloquia; effugiat risus. Hic locus est ubi mors gaudet succurrere vitae.
This is a common and very apt statement at the entrance door of a coroner's laboratory: "Let idle babble be silenced. Let laughter be banished. This is the place where the dead teach the living (their secrets)."

3. You might wish to repeat what gladiators shouted to the Roman emperor as they entered the arena to probably be killed by fellow gladiators or by wild beasts. You might wish to change imperator to Deus, so that it would read: "We who are about to die, salute you, God" (and thanks a lot for our mortal nature)

Nos morituri te salutamus, imperator! "We who are about to die salute thee, O emperor!
Or, for pouty Christians, ***Nos morituri Te salutamus, Deus.***

4. ***Non fui, fui, non sum, non curo.***

Literal meaning: 'I was not; I was; I am not; I care not.' Extended meaning of the terse Latin: 'Once I did not exist, then I was born and existed, now I do not exist and I don't give a damn.'

5. Perhaps you want to show off and have a "deep thought" about death on your tombstone. Ancient Greek then is much more impressive than mere homey Latin. How about this little brain stretcher, originally written in Greek by one of the smarter Roman emperors? "Think not disdainfully of death, but look on it with favour; for even death is one of the things that Nature wills." *Extracted from the Meditations of the Roman Emperor Marcus Aurelius. ix. 3.*

6. On a long-ago visit to Rome, to read some Latin epitaphs out on the once-cobbled roadway of the Via Appia, I happened across one tombstone whose naïve and gentle kindliness touched me. As I recall, the Latin inscription began: ***Siste, viator. Tibi gratias ago ad sepulcrum meum visitare.***
"Pause briefly, traveller. Thanks for stopping by, to visit my tomb."

7. ***Sit mihi terra levis.*** "May the earth lie light upon me." The implication has nothing whatsoever to do with the possibly heavy clay soil of a cemetery. The line means that, even if a few sinful transgressions blot my earthly record, I hope that, after my death, these paltry

infractions will not count too heavily against me, should a moment of divine judgment occur. I, Bill Casselman, always liked the way the ancient Egyptians symbolized this common mortuary thought. The departed's soul (his Ba) was weighed by the god Anubis in a scale against the feather of truth.

8. ***Vivamus vitam in totum, ita ut mors cum noctu ad vitam furandam nos visitet, furari nihil relinquatur.*** "Live life so fully that, when death comes for you like a thief in the night, there will be nothing left for him to steal."

9. ***Firmum in vita nihil est.*** "Nothing in life is permanent."

10. ***Requiescat in pace.*** "Rest in peace."
R.I.P. This is the most common Latin epitaph. The verb form is an optative subjunctive whose sense, spun out to a more pleasing amplitude, might be: I hope and I wish that she or he may rest in peace.

But no Latin epitaph equals my favorite one in English. It is on the tombstone of the American poet Robert Frost composed by himself. Frost is buried at the Old Bennington Cemetery in Vermont. His epitaph reads, "I had a lover's quarrel with the world."

Chapter 76

Diploma Words

Archive, protocol & other terms derived from the names of ancient documents

Just as we today have laptops, e-readers, notepads and ring-binders, in the same way scribes scribbling scripts of yore had papyrus and lambskin parchment and scrolls in which they wrote down records of important things. It is generally agreed among scholars that writing itself began in simple practicality as a method of keeping business records, like amounts of grain in a warehouse or how many vats of oil awaited loading on board a ship.

During early December of 2010, I and many other citizens of the world read the Wikileaks of American diplomatic emails and were aghast at the low deception and the weasel disregard of truth endemic to diplomatic communication.

So it is natural that I began wondering about the root of the words *diplomat*, *diplomacy* and *diploma*. Every year, earliest summer is the season in the western world when students reap the just guerdon of their winter labours, namely, the diploma, a very old word whose etymology intrigues the questing wordnut.

The defence of the creepy world of diplomacy by the world press and by high-mucky-muck politicians startles even a cynic. Daily, through the fecal pool of untruth, wades diplomacy, neck-high in evasion of honesty, its once-clean face now stained brown with lying, stealing secrets, and all manner of prevarication from little white fibs to felonious subterfuges of criminal cunning.

All diplomats are sneaks.

Not so long ago in my own country of Canada we endured ten years of an entire, far-right-wing, federal government dictated by the sneakiest, creepiest prime minister who ever had control of my once-honest country. His inglorious name was Stephen Harper.

Diploos Greek 'folded in two'

As you might expect of diplomatic words, all three terms arise from flimflam and hocus-pocus. The original meaning of diploma is not surprising. Diploma in ancient Greek was 'a letter folded in two' so passersby could not read it and it remained secret.

Di- meant two or double in Greek and *ploos* meant 'folded.' Even in ancient Greek diploma came to mean things like 'a letter of recommendation' or 'a communication between princes or important persons,' containing information that mere grubby peasants should never know, even if they could read. Diploma also meant 'a letter granting permission to perform certain acts.' Today we'd call it a licence. From diploma came later extensions, first in French, like *diplomat* and *diplomacy. Diplomate* appears first in print as a French noun in CE 1792.

Protocol

protos Greek 'first' + *kolla* 'glue'

In medicine, a protocol is a detailed plan of treatment. In ancient times the first sheet of a papyrus was glued to the scroll. This *protokollon* or 'first glued sheet' displayed the title and summary of the scroll contents. It acted as a table of contents and an index. All other meanings, like diplomatic procedure and protocol's use in computerese, arise from this original meaning of 'first glued sheet.'

Archive

Archive began as the name of an ancient Greek office building where significant documents were stored. The word for government in ancient Greek was *arche* and the word for government office was *archeion.* That term was borrowed into Late Latin as *archivum* and thence into early French as *archif* and thence into English as *archive.* Its first use in English was in the plural form, where by CE 1645 archives meant 'the public records office.'

Document

In medieval Latin, *documentum* was 'any official paper or charter', before that, in Old French, it meant 'a lesson,' that is, something taught, from Latin *documen, documentis* 'lesson, specimen' from the common Latin verb *docere* 'to teach,' the same root as its familiar agent noun *doctor*, literally 'one who teaches, teacher.'

Diary

Dies is the Latin word for 'day.' In Medieval Latin appeared the form *diarium.* First it was a military paymaster's word. It was a daily fee paid to a soldier for extraordinary duty. This payment was duly recorded in a journal. Quite soon *diarium* came to refer to the journal itself with space for sundry memoranda, daily jottings, records of events, payments due etc. By CE 1581 the English form *diary* was established.

Another word that began as a term for soldiers' pay was salary, originally *salarium,* a precious measure of salt doled out to serving military personnel, the only way of preserving meat in ancient times, from Latin *sal, salis* 'salt.'

Script

In Middle English, the word *script* started with this spelling: *scrite*, an aphetic borrowing from an Old French form like *escript* or *escrit*. The English spelling underwent what is sometimes called an etymological respelling, where someone who knew Latin wished to renew the Roman orthography. In classical Latin *scriptum* meant 'something written' being the perfect past participle of the verb *scribere* 'to write,' among whose future reflexes one finds words like *scribe, to scribble, scribbler, conscription, to describe, prescription* etc.

Manuscript

Manus is the Latin word for 'hand.' Think of manual labor, requiring hand work, the rules of which might be contained in a training manual. Therefore a manuscript is originally 'something written by hand.'

Personal Opinion concerning Julian Assange

Julian Assange, the noble founder of Wikileaks, releases secret documents so that ordinary citizens can view the tissue-thin pond scum of deceit upon which the fragile peace of our world is so deceptively and precariously maintained. Assange is a hero to me. But he is a profound danger and embarrassment to the fib-fat swine, the scheming herd of current politicians. These moral lepers, these cowardly slime balls, believe we the people are stupid and MUST be lied to. Nonsense! It seems we have only to confront their treasonous sneakery, hold it up to the exposuring light of common sense and they fold like cheap lawn-chairs. But if we keep silent, what is our reward? The shit pie of fraud square in the kisser.

In the proctoscope required to observe the current political interior of the USA, we see a president's sucking lips firmly pressed to the foul, polluting anus of the American corporation. Remember that, when we of the world have been delivered like sheep into the claws of the fascist, know-nothing monsters of the American night, our deliverer to Hell's Mouth, our scapegoat, our patsy up the slaughterhouse ramp, our stumblebum messiah, will have been the Do-Nothing Non-Voter. Western persons of good will must vote lest the choice-deniers, the grade-three-drop-out homophobes, the Tea Partiers, the Neo-Nazis and other sewer-life of modern times continue to infest the halls of our government.

Chapter 77

Amusement & the Muses

Musing on the origin of such terms

The Origin of *Amuse* is Not Amusing!

The English verb 'to amuse' came into common use after Shakespeare. Its original sense was entirely negative, namely, 'to gaze stunned at something.' It is perhaps from French *à* 'to, at' + *muser* 'to stare stupidly.' Maybe amuse is a direct borrowing from the Italian verb *amusare*? But to muse or *muser* was in use in the earliest French with a pejorative meaning, for example from CE 1086 the adjective *musart* 'absent-minded, foolish.' *-Art* or *-ard* was an active pejorative agent suffix in older French. Thus muse is originally descriptive of a gaping, staring look; likewise *muser* had the Anglo-Norman sense 'to gape, stare, wonder, marvel.'

A Misguided Seeking of Novelty

In a desperate attempt to be innovative — even when the abandonment of etymological reason results — the *Oxford English Dictionary* has taken to manufacturing, quite out of the vaporous ether, word roots that never existed. Being in need of a primitive French noun, the OED etymologist has sat up all night knitting a new word *mus, an unattested form (philological gobbledygook that means 'never existed'). States the

OED, in an utter delirium of neological frenzy, that this wee root means 'the snout of an animal.'

What has happened is that the OED, without acknowledging the theft, has "borrowed" this etymological suggestion from Earlier French and Italian amateur wordsmiths who first posited this supposititious flapdoodle, based on the fact that there is an early Italian word, *muso* that means 'the snout of an animal." There is also still in modern French the common word for muzzle, snout or nose of an animal *le museau*. Thus, according to this putative origin, if you "mused", you sat dumbfounded looking like a stupid animal. One must remember, as certain frantic dictionary-rifflers apparently cannot, the present existence of a form like *museau* does not automatically imply that a preceding form, *mus, ever existed.

The Muses' True Root

All that bother! When a perfectly traceable origin of *to amuse* leads ultimately through early French and Latin back to ancient Greek where the nine muses were the tutelary goddesses of the arts, from *mousa* a Greek word that meant 'song' and 'the arts' and even 'music,' often in its Greek plural form *mousai*. That Greek form may be an Attic reflex of an earlier Proto-Indo-European root *men 'thought, mind' and thus be cognate with Latin *mens, mentis* 'mind, brain' and with Greek *menos* 'spirit' and with Greek *mnasthai* 'to remember' and with Sanskrit *manas* 'mind' and Sanskrit *manyate* 'he thinks.'

To muse then, quite naturally, quite following its etymology, means to be reflective, to sit calmly inspired by the ancient Muses of art, even to cogitate philosophically, musing on life and its meanings.

More Amusement

The 'idle' semantic hue in the meaning of the word *amusement* was helped by early senses of 'to muse.' In Anglo-Norman and Old French *muser* meant 'to waste time in idle thought.' We still hear it in English in bad poetry: "Idly sat he, musing by the river's flow." In 1889, Robert Louis Stevenson in his novel *The Master of Ballantrae* wrote of a listening person: "He would fall into a deep muse over our accounts."

Music in the Museum

Two common English words derived from Greek adjectives based on *mousa* are *museum* and *music.*

Museum is a direct borrowing from classical Latin where it meant as the OED aptly defines it "a place holy to the Muses, a building set apart for study, especially the institute for philosophy and research at Alexandria." Latin in turn borrowed the word from ancient Greek *mouseion* 'haunt of the Muses' or 'art school.'

All the languages of Europe and some other tongues adopted the term: French *musée*, Italian *museo*, Portuguese *museu*, Spanish *museo*, Dutch *museum*, German *Museum* and Swedish *museum.*

Music began as a Greek adjective *musikos* 'of or pertaining to anything to do with the Nine Muses.' Then, as a noun, it came to mean a person devoted to or composing poetry sung to music, a lyric poet, and then the musician who played the music that accompanied the poetry. Sometimes the lyric poet himself played the lyre.

With an old Russian adage we shall pipe this musing to a close. "When the cannons are silent, the muses are heard." What does that proverb mean? Simple. A peaceable kingdom is the best seed-bed of art.

Chapter 78

Puffling

A common bird not mentioned in most dictionaries

A puffin is an auk-like seabird. The puffin is pelagic, that is, it spends most of its life on the open sea, eating fish. One ancient Greek word for the open sea is *pelagos*. The puffin comes ashore to lonely northern coasts only to breed and raise its pufflings in a colony called a puffinry.

A puffling is a puffin chick.

Puffling was obviously formed by ornithologists or birders on the analogy of duck/duckling and goose/gosling to mean the young of the bird.

Today the headword *puffling* is not found in *The Oxford English Dictionary* nor in *Merriam-Webster's Third New International Dictionary, Unabridged*, 2002. Yet there is no excuse whatsoever for the exclusion of the word *puffling* from such modern dictionaries. Is puffling too new a word to brashly enter the hallowed precincts of the OED? Certainly not. The word is centuries old! 200 years ago, puffling was used to describe the young of another seabird, the Manx shearwater.

Always a valid sign of a word's vitality, puffling is being used to form new compound words. A Scottish society for the protection of birds had a "puffling cam" watching a puffin nest in a rock crevice which always holds but one teeny puffling.

Citations

Has the word been widely used over the last hundred years? Yes. Birder books and ornithological literature are rife with the word. Here are but a few modern instances:

2012 – It is in published book titles, e.g. *Puffling Patrol* by Ted Lewin and Betsy Lewin, hardcover, published March 2012 by Lee & Low Books.

2012 – " Saturday, July 14th, 2012. Pufflings get disoriented at times and are often attracted to the light in nearby towns."

2000 – "The puffin chick is called a 'puffling.'"

Suffixal History

Is *–ling*, the common Germanic appurtenant suffix too obscure to etymologize? Certainly not. It's been around for 2,000 years. Even in Old English it made a few bird names, like a blackbird called a *swertling* (think of swarthy 'dark') and our still used *staerling* or starling. In Old Saxon and Old English *–ling* denoted a person associated with a particular thing, as in words like *hireling, darling* and *sibling.* In early modern English, -ling served as an affectionate diminutive giving us words like *nestling, nursling, sapling* and *suckling.* Then it took on a negative, pejorative sense and produced terms like *groundling* and *worldling* and *starveling.* The suffix's chief use in modern English coinages is as an abusive suffix in words like *princeling, godling, kingling* and the rarer *sissyling.*

Etymology of Puffin

No cogent source of the word *puffin* exists. With a damp guffaw, the goddess Etymology has shrouded its origin in the sea fog of history. There is a plenitude of silly folk etymologies that your humble deponent (*moi*) chooses not to encourage by listing. The two genera to which puffins belong do have traceable names. They are Fratercula and Lunda. Lunda is explained below. *Fratercula* is Latin and means 'little brother' because some early ornithologists thought that puffins looked with dwarf monks waddling around looking for a leaking wine barrel or a free food handout. The Latin word for brother, a cognate of brother, is *frater*, hence English words like fraternal, fraternity and fraternize.

Names for Puffin in Other Languages

Lundy Island in the Bristol Channel off the coast of Devonshire was named by Viking invaders, with an Old Norse phrase, *Lunde Ey* or *Lundi I*, which means in Old Norse 'puffin island.' That Old Norse word for puffin is still flapping about in all the Scandinavian tongues and several neighbouring languages. The Icelandic word for puffin is *lundi*; Danish and Norwegian *lunde* and Finnish *lunni*. The Swedish name for puffin is *lunnefågel*. *Fågel* in Swedish means '(little) bird.' Compare a common but abusive word for homosexual in Yiddish, *faygl* from German *Vögel* 'bird' and *fogele* or *faygeluh* with a Germanic diminutive suffix –*le* or –*el*, so called from the supposedly birdlike, too-dainty, effeminate bodily movements of some homosexual men.

Warning! Neology Ahead

I shall cease these flighty sourcings by coining a word. The puffin chick waddles. So one could refer to the waddling puffling. But I think the waddlesome puffling presents, to the attending ear and reading eye, a superior audiovisual sense of a wee puffin chick as it shuffle-toddles along a rocky outcrop clinging to its cliff-home or natal puffinry.

Chapter 79

Guttersnipe

& other drippy words

The Latin word for a drop of liquid is *gutta*. From *gutta* stem English words like gout, gutter and guttersnipe.

Pharmaceutical Confusion

When doctors and pharmacists knew Latin well, prescriptions and their instructions were written in Latin shorthand, some of which survives to cause drug mix-ups to this day.

There is no excuse to write on medical prescriptions confusing Latin short-forms. For example, a drop can be written as gt. or gtt., standing for the Latin singular noun *gutta*. A posological instruction like "drops" may be abbreviated as gts. or gtts., standing for the Latin plural *guttae*. What does "three drops in a glass of water" actually mean to some palsied sclerotic or paretic yoyo wearing a Batman mask slumped by the bedside and trying to dose himself? A drop may mean to him a slosh of water from a large glass or half a liter poured out in dementia. Still seen in the more recondite medical literature is the Latin dispensing adverb *guttatim* 'drop by drop.' That can be abbreviated as gttt. Three ts! What needless bother! *Just write 'drops' for corn sakes*! you might object. But there is a problem too with the simple instruction "by drops."

That's a Real Poser

By the way, posology is the branch of pharmacy or medicine that deals with the administration of doses, the quantity and frequency of dosage. Its root is the ancient Greek interrogative adjective *posos* 'how much,' akin to its Latin equivalent *quotus* 'of what number, how many,' from which English gets the word *quota*.

What's Wrong with Writing "Drops"?

'Drops' is utterly unscientific — especially sloppy and dangerous as a chart instruction for IV medications, as we are reminded by this warning note from *Taber's Cyclopedic Medical Dictionary* (F.A. Davis Company; Philadelphia, PA; 1993): "Gutta, plural guttae — a medical/pharmaceutical term. But not an accurate measurement of liquid. The amount in a drop varies with the nature of the liquid, its viscosity, its temperature, its specific gravity, its elevation above sea level, etc., etc. It is, therefore, not advisable to use the number of drops per minute of a solution as anything more than a general guide to the amount of material being administered intravenously."

Guttate

In botany, a leaf may be guttate, that is, dotted with drop-like spots of colour.

Guttus

It was a narrow-necked Roman terra cotta cruet or oil flask by which liquids could be poured out drop by drop, hence its name. A *guttus* was used in sacrifices to dispense sanctified oil and also to store scented olive oil used to anoint Roman bathers after they emerged from the baths.

Latin proverb

Gutta fortunae prae dolio sapientiae.
'A drop of luck is better than a vat of wisdom.'

Gutter

From Latin *gutta* 'drop' the word entered the earliest Old French as *gute, goute*, modern French *goutte.* In French arose a word for spout or nozzle or water trough, *gutiere* or *goutiere*, modern French *gouttière.* Middle English borrowed the French word as *goter* or *gotere*, which became modern English *gutter.*

The common modern English meanings are:

1. A channel beside a street to bear away rain or surface water
2. A metal trough under the eaves of a roof to carry off rain
3. A channel for carrying something off; such as the gutter on the side of a bowling lane, to bring balls back to the bowler
4. The gutter on a page of print is white space formed by the inner margins of two facing pages, as of a book, even this book. Generous gutters mean the reader does not have to "crack the spine" of a book's binding (usually glue).
5. Squalid class of human beings or their existential state; the lowest sewer of humanity. From this last meaning arose –

Guttersnipe

First guttersnipe referred to a bird, the English snipe, which frequents mucky, marshy places, then it named a poor child who haunts street gutters seeking refuse or food scraps, and thence a person of the lowest class.

Guttersnipe was used memorably in one of Winston Churchill's Second World War radio speeches. When Hitler invaded Russia in 1941, Winnie went on BBC Radio and described Hitler as "this blood-thirsty guttersnipe." After the war, "reformed" Nazis who had been in attendance upon the Führer in his comic-opera aerie atop Berchtesgaden reported that Herr Hitler was so furious at Churchill's insults that he actually danced in fury, leaping up and down, at Winnie's exquisite putdowns of the degenerate Nazi gangster.

Gout

Gout is a disease in which too much uric acid gets into the blood stream; razorlike crystals of sodium urate then accrete in the smaller joints, especially that of the great toe causing screamingly painful inflammation. If the inflammation is not treated medically, gout can spread to larger joints and internal organs.

The Theory of Humours

The English language inherited the medical word *gout* from Old French *goute* 'drop.' Its name depends on the now utterly discredited theory of humours that ruled medicine in error for more than 2,000 years. Ancient practitioners of "physick" believed that bad, watery humours (bodily liquids) sank drop-by-drop (*goute par goute*) in a sick body and collected in the gout-plagued foot joints causing pain and swelling.

In a nutshell — O apt metaphor! — humorism taught that the human body was filled with four basic liquids: black bile, yellow bile, phlegm and blood. When this quartet of liquid goodies was in balance, one was healthy. When one liquid predominated, illness ensued. In fact, all diseases and disabilities resulted from an excess or deficit of one or more of these four humors. There are many words that originated in humoralism. I'll mention just one. An excess of black bile was said to make one sadder and depressed. The Greek for this black bile was – melancholia from Greek *melas* 'black' + *kholé* 'bile.'

Too much phlegm made one lethargic, lazy, and slow – hence the now learned adjective *phlegmatic.*

Gutta as Architectural Term

Among my favorite users of arcane gibberish are those who compose architectural dictionaries. Read this snooty definition of a gutta in architecture: "Pendent ornament resembling the frustrum of a truncated cone attached inferiorly triglyphically under the soffits of the mutules and regulae of the architrave in the Greek Doric Order."

Oh, well. Why didn't you just say so? I myself often keep a wee guttule under the soffit of my mutule – at least until I hear the police tapping gently on my chamber door and cooing "Come out, come out, wherever you are, you guttulous reprobate!"

Guttae were supposed to repel rainwater and help rain run off the ancient buildings. Water, it was hoped, would drip over the guttal edges, away from the building. Some analysts of ancient Greek architecture suppose that carved stone guttae represent wooden pegs used in the construction of the wooden edifices that preceded the familiar stone buildings of later Greek history.

Well, that's it, folks. Gutta go now. But, before we effect a nifty exitus, check out this pertinent note from a reader:

"Dear Mr. Casselman,

I enjoy your writings! As an architecture grad, I had to endure many insufferably opaque discussions and definitions such as the one you noted for guttae, so I had a good laugh.

There is an alternative and much more colorful possible origin of guttae, as well as for many of the elements of classical temples, put forward by George Hersey in *The Lost Meaning of Classical Architecture: Speculations on Ornament from Vitruvius to Venturi* (MIT Press, 1988). His general hypothesis is that Greek temples are the stone representations of earlier sacrifice-in-sacred-grove rituals, where the bits of animal that were sacrificed were bound up or strung around to decorate the grove to 'reconstruct' and thus honor the victim. So that dentils really were strings of teeth, bucrania were literal ox-heads, astragalos the knucklebones, eggs and claws really eggs and claws, rostra were beaks, triglyphs the 'thrice-chopped' and bound thighbones, and guttae the drips of blood coming out of the bottom triglyphs. A bit gorier than just the 'frustrum of a truncated cone.'

We may never know whether Hersey's speculation is true, but it's much more fun to think about when considering all the Greek-revival portals attached to all the typical New England churches around me. Wouldn't they all be horrified to know the gory pagan origins of what they thought were just expressions of democracy!

Cheers,
Robin Willcox"

Thanks, R. Willcox. For my fellow squalid squatters in the gutter of time's flow, I offer possibly dubious compensatory solace from Oscar Wilde who once wrote: "We are all in the gutter, but some of us are looking at the stars."

Chapter 80

The Many Names of Egypt Influence Some English Words

Gumhūriyyat Miṣr al-'Arabiyyah
in English: The Arabic Republic of Egypt

The modern Arabic name for Egypt is *Misr*, pronounced in English something like mees'err. In street Arabic, one dialectical and colloquial pronunciation is mas-er.

More fanatic anti-Semitic Islamists are always upset to learn that *Misr* may derive from the biblical Hebrew name for Egypt, Mizraim. In Hebrew, the modern pronunciation is 'mitsRAyim' or Tiberian Hebrew 'misRAyim.' The Hebrew noun suffix *–ayim* indicates nouns that come in pairs or twos or doubles and so are declined with what is called a dual ending. This dual ending in the ancient Hebrew name for Egypt may refer to the two Egypts of antiquity, Upper Egypt and Lower Egypt.

El-Mizrach 'The East'

The root is still kicking around in Hebrew. The brilliant Israeli designer Isaac Mizrahi bears a surname that indicates an ancestor came from a Jewish community east of Israel. *Mizrahim* are 'eastern' Jews descended from Jewish enclaves mostly in the Arab world, from the Middle East, from North Africa, and even the Caucasus. *El-mizrach* means 'the East' in Modern Hebrew.

But this name for the land of the Nile appears to be much older than Hebrew and may have been borrowed into Hebrew. In Assyrian and Babylonian records, Egypt is *Musur* and *Musri*. In the Amarna tablets written in Akkadian cuneiform, a Semitic language, in the 1340s BCE, Egypt is called *Misri*.

Misr 'Egypt' may also derive from an Egyptian hieroglyphic word *md-r*, an ancient local name for the Nile lands.

What is an Endonym?

An endonym or autonym, on the other hand, from the Greek root words *endon* 'within' or *auto-* 'self' + *onoma* 'name,' is given by members of a particular ethnolinguistic group to the group itself, its language or dialect, or its homeland or a specific place within it.

Whence did the Term *Egypt* Arise?

The word *Egypt* arose because Greeks could not pronounce one of the ancient Egyptian phrases signifying Egypt and that phrase was *Hout-ak Ptah* 'house of the Ka of Ptah.' Now that is not as silly as it might sound to modern English ears. The ka was part of ancient Egyptian religion. In the time of the Pharoahs, they believed a human soul was made up of five parts: the Ren, the Ba, the Ka, the Sheut, and the Ib. Mixed together with a little shaved lamb and pepper sauce, they made a zesty shawarma. Okay, I jest. The Ka was one's spiritual essence. It dwelt in a living body. After death, the ka left for a little R&R at a good resort in the desert.

So who was Ptah then? Yes, he sounds like the god of spitting. But Ptah was one of the earliest gods of ancient Egypt. He got in first and he got in big time! One of the names of the country in the Pharoanic era was Hout-ak Ptah, for their priests liked to think that the entire delta was not only the gift of the Nile but also a temple of Ptah.

However, visiting Greeks had a great deal of trouble with some of the gutturals in ancient Egyptian. Evidence? We have in writing stumblebum attempts by ancient Greeks at transliterating Egyptian names. The initial *h* and the final *h* in the name were guttural rough breathings. The Greeks could not pronounce them properly, so they left them out. What the Greeks got out of listening to Egyptians saying Hout-ak Ptah was *Aigu-pta*, first as a name for the River Nile and then as the Greek word for Egypt, with a common Greek noun nominative ending to make it *Aiguptos*. When the Romans showed up a little later in history, checking out winter wheat exports to make bread flour for Rome, they borrowed the Greek term as *Aegyptus*. That eventually produced our word *Egypt*, after a trip through French. Middle English *Egipcian* < from Old French *egipcien* < from *Egipte* Egyptian < from Latin *Aegyptus* < from Greek *Aiguptos*.

More Ancient Dubbings for the Land of the Nile

The ancient Hebrew name *Mizraim* was probably a translation of the earliest hieroglyphic name we know for Egypt, *tawy* 'the two lands.'

Kemet

Early in Egyptian history, during the Old Kingdom, the land was referred to as *Kemet*, from hieroglyphic /*kmt*/ 'black land' presumably referring to the rich soil of the Nile Delta and valley. Another name was *deshret* 'dshrt' 'red land,' referring to the brownish-red of pale desert sand in contrast to the Nile Valley's rich, dark soil. Do not mistake that hieroglyphic word as the source of our English word *desert*. It is tempting but not true.

Plutarch, a Greek historian (46- 120 CE), uses *Cheemia* as a name for Egypt, which may stem from that same Old Kingdom name *Kmt*, probably pronounced *Kemet*.

The Slang Term *Gypsy* Stems from the Word *Egyptian*

English racists thought gypsies were Egyptian. After all they were swarthy wogs, weren't they? As the Oxford English Dictionary succinctly explains it: "The early form *gipcyan* is aphetic for EGYPTIAN…"

Gipsy is common in the singular. Gypsies as a plural spelling, is still seen too. The wandering tribe are actually of Hindu origin and their language, Romany, is a dialect of Hindi massively altered by their travels and with additional words they have picked up from many Indo-European languages. The words for gipsy in other European languages are also variants of Egyptian, for example German *Zigeuner*, French *gitan* (think of mediocre cigarettes) and *tsigane* [think of wonderful French herbal tea), Spanish *gitano*, Russian *tsigan*, *tsiganka*, and Modern Greek 'geeptos.'

Coptic comes from _Egypt_ too.

The Coptic people are Christians of Egypt and Coptic also names the principal Christian church of Ethiopia. Almost as revenge upon the Greeks who mangled the ancient Egyptian word for Egypt in *Aiguptos*, when the Arabs invaded and conquered Egypt, the Arabs could not pronounce easily the then Greek name of the country and they came up with *Copti*. As Muslims took over Egypt, Copti came to be applied by the Arabs to the few remaining Christians.

Now, in the altered words of the pop song, let's blow this pyramid stand and 'walk like an Egyptian' — you know, the duck-wristed Tut two-step.

Chapter 81

Religious Place Names of Canada

comprising some travel tips for Canadian visitors

A sampling of Canadian map names shows how eager we have been to assign place names of good celestial omen to the lands and waters of our Canuck homeland.

As several residents will tell you, Heaven is in Ontario—in the form of Blue Heaven Lake and Little Heaven Island. A Canadian conversation about heaven that I particularly cherish occurs in *Sleeping Island: The Story of One Man's Travels in the Great Barren Lands of the Canadian North,* written by P. G. Downes and published in 1942. I happened upon this passage first while browsing through *Colombo's Canadian Quotations.* It is part of an interchange between a man of the Dogrib people and a Catholic missionary:

"Tell me, Father, what is the white man's Heaven?"

"It is the most beautiful place in the world."

"Tell me, Father, is it like the land of the little trees when the ice has left the lakes? Are the great musk oxen there? Are the hills covered with flowers? There will I see the caribou everywhere I look? Are the lakes blue with the sky of summer? Is every net full of great, fat whitefish? Is there room for me in this land, like our land, the Barrens? Can I camp anywhere and not find that someone else has camped? Can I feel the wind and be like the wind? Father, if your Heaven is not all these, leave me alone in my land, the land of the little sticks."

God Names

The Almighty gets short shrift in our place names, due to a too dainty and fastidious piety, although, God knows, there's plenty of loud piety in Canada. Divine indeed is the love that dare speak its name from every smarmy-voiced, granny-squeezing, religious broadcast that ever wheedled a "love donation" from the puckered purse of a lonely widow. And viewers may rest confident that every penny of such a tele-tithe will go toward that important missionary work in Antarctica—among those heathen penguins.

As far as locative denominations of the deity go, there is the village of God's River on the God's River emptying into God's Lake in Manitoba which may well mean 'straits of the Great Spirit'. Nor is the quality of the Bay of God's Mercie strained, lying as it does at the arctic end of Hudson Bay. That's pretty well all she wrote for the G-word. Nova Scotia has Main-à-Dieu on Cape Breton Island. It looks like 'the hand of God,' but it is Mi'-Kmaq as mangled by French settlers, for the word *manitou* or spirit (evil in this case).

Paradise: Sorry, No Vacancies!

Casselman's Devout Travel Service informs all Christian wayfarers that there are dozens of place-names using the paradisiacal word spread across Canada. Paradise is a few miles east of Bridgetown, Nova Scotia. If it's booked full, try Paradise, Newfoundland, just west of St. John's. Or the Paradise, Newfoundland, that's north of Grand Falls. The more adventurous pilgrim can stop at the community of Paradise River, about 120 miles from Happy Valley, Labrador.

Our modern form of the word is from Anglo-Norman *paradis* < post-classical Latin *paradisus* < ancient Greek *paradeisos*. The Greek historian Xenophon used the word to signify a Persian walled garden or pleasure ground. By the time of the Attic Koine or 'standard Greek' of the New Testament, paradise referred to the Garden of Eden, then abode of the blessed, then heaven. It is a Persian word. In its Avestan form, the Old Iranian roots are *pari* 'around' (compare Greek *peri* 'around') + *daiz* Old Iranian 'to heap up, to build.'

My First Paradise

My own amblings 'midst the ferny dells and leafy boscage of Ma Nature began at Cootes Paradise, a marshy Ontario ramble under the excellent supervision of Hamilton's Royal Botanical Gardens. This paradise is named after Thomas Coote, an ardent hunter of wild fowl who as a British officer was garrisoned nearby in the 1780s.

Gone to the Sand Hills

Sand Hills is literally a bit of heaven in Alberta. To the local Blood Indians, the sandy hill country south of Lethbridge is their happy hunting grounds, where the spirits of their warriors go after death. And in popular speech, some Albertans use "gone to the sand-hills" as a synonym for dead.

Gimli: Next Door to Heaven?

The first Icelanders came to Canada in 1873 after several natural disasters on the island of Iceland, including the eruption of the Hecla volcano. Their main permanent settlement on Lake Winnipeg began in 1875. But Gimli is not the home of the Norse gods, as W.B. Hamilton states in *The MacMillan Book of Canadian Place Names.* The chief Norse deity, Odin, dwelt in Asgard, Old Norse *Asgarðr* 'enclosure of the Æsir' where Odin very kindly set aside certain large mead-halls for selected human drinkers (*all male and all soldiers only please*). These banquet chambers included Valhalla, hall of the slain, where warriors who fell in battle could feast and fight again for all eternity. Among the nearby holy buildings was a great hall with a golden roof called Gimli, and here, after their earthly journey was complete, Odin welcomed men who had been particularly righteous during their lives.

Utopias, Dystopias & Made-Up Heavens

How about artificial heavens? "Aren't they all!" is my humanist reply.

Kosekin is one of the first utopias created by a Canadian fiction writer. James de Mille was a professor at Acadia and Dalhousie universities who wrote Victorian potboilers on the side. Nowadays such enterprise is likely to cost an academic his tenure. But such wanton scribbling did not in 1888 when Professor de Mille penned *A Strange Manuscript Found in a Copper Cylinder.* Kosekin is an imaginary country located under Antarctica where everything is topsy-turvy. Darkness is better than light; poverty beats wealth. Perhaps it is better to call it a dystopia. De Mille is worth reading still, for his adventurous debunking of Christianity, British mannerisms, and, just to balance the satire, he takes a few pot-shots at the evolutionary theories of Darwin too.

Nirvana in Canada

When the Buddhist term *nirvana* became popular in English during the mid-19th century, it almost immediately became a slangy synonym for heaven, and so a verbal candidate for use as a place-name by immigrants looking for a wondrous new home. Thus Canada sports Lac Nirvana in Québec, Mount Nirvana in the Northwest Territories, and Nirvana Pass in British Columbia's Pantheon Range. The word is a past participle in Sanskrit, an ancient language of India, directly related to most of the languages of Europe as a member of the huge Indo-European linguistic family. Nirvana means 'blown out like a candle'. *Nirva-* is a Sanskrit verbal root that signifies 'be extinguished', and its components are *nis* 'out' + *va* 'blow.'

In Buddhism, nirvana is the release from earthly troubles that comes when a knowing Buddhist dies. The state may also be attained by a living person who has succeeded through meditation in achieving enlightenment. In Hinduism and Jainism, nirvana can mean the spiritual bliss of reunion with Brahma after death, after the blowing out of the candle of life, but not of course the flame of being.

My skepticism in the face of the spiritual elegance of nirvana as a concept was shared by European intellectuals like Freud, who understood nirvana but could only equate it with his death-wish. He coined a technical term in psychoanalysis, the nirvana principle—and like all such terms it is metaphorical and poetic, not scientific. Freud's current enemies seem blind to the fact that he was a *poet* of the psyche, and no mere clumsy, electrode-attaching prober. Sigmund's hypothetical constructs are only McLuhanesque probes, prickings of some of the balloons that enclose and obscure the air of our true being.

Freud's nirvana principle described the mind's tendency to keep psychic tension to a minimum. But such a passive state was abhorrent to European thought, and Freud could only equate this yearning for psychic entropy to the action of the death instinct, the pining of living things for a return to the peaceful stasis of inorganic things, a notion that modern biology tells us is pure hooey, flapdoodle and twaddle.

Skeptics dismiss nirvanas in general, often summed up in a one, eight-word sentence. When pilgrims ask "What is the Wisdom of the East?" they reply, "Lie down and let it rain on you." They are not fans of existential passivity. Nor am I.

My Humanist Envoi

Human beings have dreamed more heavens than a sky can hold, and conjured more vindictive hells than a Jerry Falwell could assign us damned to. As architects of the hereafter, most fundamentalist religions build the shabbiest of paradises. Their teeny-weeny cubicles of eternal salvation have room only for themselves. The narrow meanness of many contemporary evangelical religions would, it seems to me, deeply offend their founders. Reading the *New Testament*, how can one imagine Jesus flinging shut the gates of heaven on troubled women who have had abortions, on gay people, on those who pray to gods not stamped with the right-wing Christian seal of approval? Nor are we sucked in by that current excuse for hatred: "Hate the sin, not the sinner." Oh, but they do hate—and kill. For shame, you fundamentalist nitwits! How tawdry your devotion that congratulates and defines itself by the number of human beings it can loathe!

Chapter 82

FLUX Words in English

in which we inspect an influx of borrowings like influence and effluent

Effluxion

Here's a quotation from a Canadian government site that explains parliamentary procedures: "The Constitution states that no House 'shall continue for longer than five years.' Mindful of this deadline, all governments since Confederation have resorted to dissolution. In some cases, the dissolution took place within days of when the House would have expired through effluxion of time."

Etymology

Effluxion is an outflow of any liquid or anything flowable. The effluxion of time is constant. The coined noun was formed from the Latin adjective *effluxus* 'flowing out' from the verb *effluere* 'to flow out' from the prepositional prefix *ex* Latin 'out of' + *fluere* Latin 'to flow.' Latin *fluere* and English *flow* seem to be cognates from the same Proto-Indo-European stem, but some linguists say not.

The Efflux of the Afflux of the Influx

The short noun and verb *efflux* 'to flow out' has always been rare in English. *Afflux* and *influx* mean 'to flow up to' and 'to flow into.' The noun *influx* is common. But more frequently used is a related noun, *influence* 'something that flows into a person or thing and alters it.'

Influenza

The Italian word for influence is *influenza*, source of our disease phrase *the flu*. One meaning of influenza in sixteenth-century Italy was 'mysterious influence,' a disease that flows into many people all at the same time, hence epidemic outbreak of disease. The Italian word was borrowed by many European languages during a severe epidemic in 1743 CE that afflicted all of Europe. The mysterious or astral flowing from the sky of an invisible heavenly fluid that flowed down to earth and "influenced" the destiny of humans was one definition of *influence* in medieval Latin and our English poet Chaucer uses the word *influence* in that sense by 1374 CE.

Effluent

From this verb's present participle comes a noun familiar in English ecological writing, *effluent*, literally 'that which flows out of.' Effluent from industrial processes is often polluted and needs filtering before being allowed to flow into natural streams used by people and animals.

Related Words in Other Languages

Latin *fluere* 'to flow' is cognate with some Greek verbs like *ploein* 'to swim,' *pleein* 'to be full,' *plunein* 'to wash,' and to Latin *plorare* 'weep' and Latin *pluit* 'it is raining.' Compare modern French *la pluie* 'the rain' and something used 'against the rain' *une parapluie* 'an umbrella.' They are all based on various vowel grades of the same stem /pl*v*/ (where the italic *v* represents any vowel), a stem that began perhaps as PIE **ple-* 'fill up, be full.'

Effluvium

Once upon a time 400 years ago, this now obsolete scientific word meant an outflow of minute particles. It is only used today, sometimes humorously, to refer to a foul odour rising from some putrid pool of pollution. But do us old Latin hands a favour and don't say effluviums as the plural form when the correct Latin is also correct in English: effluvia. Mephitic effluvia rose from the tar-sand tailings ponds and poisoned the very air of approaching birds.

Flux

From Latin *fluxus* 'a flowing,' flux is an old name for dysentery. Flux once meant any large flow of liquid from an organ.

I well remember learning to use a flux in high-school industrial shop class during lessons on soldering. In my school even those of us students streamed into academic courses could take electives like Industrial Shop.

Soldering is joining together, for example, two pieces of copper pipe. The solder I learned to use then was an amalgam of tin and lead. A flux in our high-school soldering was painted on the surface of the two copper pipes to be joined. The flux was diluted hydrochloric acid. It prevented oxidation of the base metals and acted too as a wetting agent.

Soldering has been useful to humans for a long time, archeological evidence shows soldering used 5,000 years ago in Mesopotamia. Consider *The Old Testament*, Isaiah 41:7 "So the carpenter encouraged the goldsmith and he that smootheth with the hammer him that smote the anvil saying It is ready for the soldering and he fastened it with nails that it should not be moved."

Conflux

Conflux is a flowing together, for example of streams and rivers. The more modern word is confluence. In his tragedy *Troilus and Cressida* Shakespeare preferred the shorter word: "As knots by the conflux of meeting sap, Infect the sound Pine."

Reflux

Reflux means 'a flowing back or a return. In reference to tidal bodies of water, it is used in the phrase 'the flux and reflux' of rivers, bays and estuaries. In medicine, what is commonly and incorrectly termed 'heart burn' is in fact an esophageal reflux, a flowing back up of gastric contents to the esophagus. The injury to the esophagus from refluxed stomach acids is called reflux esophagitis.

Ah, flux, folks. Thus come we, gentle readers all, to the tristful efflux of this day's omniscience. So said he humbly and withdrew, perchance to contemplate the overuse of the predicate-first mode.

Chapter 83

Onion Words in English & French

Chives, ramp, shallot, leek, ail, garlic, scallion

My notes about the origins of common English and French onion words are prompted by the notion that someday you may go gathering ramps or wild garlic in parts of Europe or Canada's southern Quebec. Every year, in moist woodlands, some Quebeckers illegally gather ramps, an endangered member of the onion family. Its taste is much milder and more sensual than common garlic and *l'ail des bois* fetches a good price at Montréal restaurants. So it is widely poached.

This little onion of the woods is also called *l'ail sauvage* and *l'ail trilobé* and has the botanical name, *Allium tricoccum.* One of the American names, borrowed from England, for this wee wild onion is *ramp*, explained below.

Tricoccum = *tri* Latin 'three' + *coccus* Latin 'seed, berry' from Greek *kokkos* berry, anything shaped like a small berry. *Tricoccum* means "having three seeds" and usually implies "breaking into three, one-seeded parts."

Think of all the generic names of bacteria that use this Greek root *kokkos*: staphylococcus 'shaped like a bunch of grape (berries)' or streptococcus 'shaped like a twisted chain of berries' from Greek *streptos* 'twisted.'

Origin of Name: Ramp

Quoted from the internet: "Wild garlic grows wild in eastern North America, ranging from the rich, moist woodlands of Nova Scotia and southern Quebec, south through New England and the central Appalachian states, down into the cool upland portions of Georgia, and as far west as Iowa and Minnesota."

The word *ramp* comes from the British Isles, where a related plant, *Allium ursinum*, grows wild. The British folk name was *ramsen*, the plural form of an Old English word for wild garlic, *hramsa*. The similarity between *Allium ursinum* and *Allium tricoccum* in taste, appearance, and growth habit led early English settlers of Appalachia to call the latter by the English folk name, which later was shortened to ramp.

Allium

Genus: Allium < *allium* Latin, garlic < *all* Celtic adjective 'hot, pungent, spicy.' From the Latin comes the French word for garlic, *ail* and the Italian for garlic, *aglio*. This large genus contains more than 300 species. It belongs to the plant family Alliaceae, the capacious onion clan, including chives, garlic, leek, shallots, and the ornamental onions like moly and giant allium.

Species

For North American gardeners, the flowering onions fill a niche, blooming after most tulips and early spring bulbs have flowered, but before the midsummer show of lilies. One of our native wildlings that well stands transplanting to the garden is *Allium canadense* or Canada Onion. Its small flowerhead blooms in white, pink, or lilac shades. Showier but shorter is *Allium moly*

(Greek *molu*, name of an ancient, yellow-flowered plant) which gives loose umbels of vibrant yellow in June. This has been a popular flowering onion since Elizabethan times. Shakespeare's contemporaries called these onions "mollies."

The Colossus of ornamental onions is *Allium giganteum* (Botanical Latin, unusually tall or large < *Gigantes* Greek, mythological giants so powerful they once laid siege to heaven. Zeus had to dispatch them with lightning bolts, and Hercules tidied up the surviving stray giants by clubbing them to death. These giant onions reach two metres in my garden and bloom in spectacular, dense umbels of purply-blue. They are giants for the back of the border and need plenty of space. Fertilized liberally, giant onions reproduce with glee. One bulb I left in place for four years had burgeoned into a most plump clump and produced twenty-five fat offsets by the time I dug it up.

Word Lore of Onion

Onion < *oignon* French < *unio, unionis* Late Latin, a unity, a oneness of note < *unus* Latin, the numeral one. This word that gives modern English *union* also was used to name, for example, a single, large pearl. Farmers adapted it to name a big, eating onion, a scrumptious oneness indeed, a delectable unity.

Uses of Onions

There are many reports of early uses of the wild Canada onion. The Blackfoot (Siksika) of Alberta made a tea of wild onion bulbs to soothe throats raw from coughing and to suppress the cough. Sinus congestion was treated on early prairie farms by inhaling smoke from a little bonfire of onion bulbs. All of the First Peoples of America had words to name wild onions. One of note is Cheyenne *kha-a-mot-ot-kewat* 'skunk testicles.' Eaten raw in too great a quantity, wild onion bulbs are toxic enough to cause gastroenteritis in young children.

Onions as Herbs

Common names of Allium species with herbal use are: Chives, Garlic, Leek, Scallion, Shallot, Top Onion.

Shallot

Allium ascalonicum is one horticultural designation for the shallot, the fine little onions of French cookery, mild in flavour and aroma, used in salad dressings, chopped and sprinkled on steak, and with dozens of uses in haute cuisine. The shallot has a compound bulb, with each "clove" wrapped in a papery, purple tunic. The specific (the second part of the name) is Botanical Latin meaning 'of Ashkelon,' which was one of the five cities of the Philistines, a harbourless seaport in the land of Canaan. The other cities were Ashdod, Ekron, Gath, and Gaza. Known as Askalon and Escalone in European languages, it was the site of a victory by the Crusaders over the Egyptians in A.D. 1099. Ashkelon is mentioned in one of the most quoted phrases from the *Old Testament*, in the second book of Samuel 1:19-20, when King David laments the deaths of Saul and Jonathon: "How are the mighty fallen! Tell it not in Gath, publish it not in the streets of Ashkelon; lest the daughters of the Philistines rejoice."

Word Lore of Shallot

Shallot < *chalotte* Early Modern French < *eschalotte, eschalette* Medieval French < *eschaloigne* Old French = *scalogno* Italian <**scalonia* Late Latin < *caepa ascalonia* Latin, onion of Ashkelon.

That Scallywag Scallion

Note that from *escalogne*, an Old Norman French form of this common onion word, Middle English derived *scalyon*, which in turn gives another onion word still used in English, *scallion*.

Adding a Bit of Confusion

The perennial forms of the common onion, *Allium cepa* (*caepa* Latin, onion) are sometimes called shallots. But these have no connection with Ashkelon, nor with the delicate mildness of taste of true shallots. The true botanical name of shallots is partially responsible for the present confusion, because that true name of shallots is *Allium cepa aggregatum* (Latin 'clustered', said of the small bulbs).

Leek & Garlic Word Lore

Allium porrum (Latin, leek) is the biennial onion whose outer surface collects sand and soil grit. Always wash leeks well. The Latin *porrum* is also the source of the French word for leek, *poireau. Porrum* has the basic meaning of sword-poke or spear-poke, in reference to the shape of the leaves. The Latin word for leek is akin to the ancient Greek word for leek, *prason*, and possibly to a group of verbs in Germanic and Scandinavian languages such as *porren* Dutch, 'to poke as with a sword,' and Danish *purre*, 'to prod, to thrust.' A *porr* was once a fire poker in English, and we had a verb too, *to porr* = to poke something with a spear. The habit of growth of members of the onion family has seen them named after their long, sword-like leaves, for example, 'spear-leek' in Old English was *gar-leac*, which has the current spelling *garlic*.

Other Gar (Spear) Words

Compare the fish with the long, spear-like snout, the gar or garfish. Those sturdy bardic souls who have fought their way through the monument of Old English poetry, "Beowulf" will remember its opening line:

Hwaet! we Gar-dena in geardagum theodcyninga...

"Lo! We (have heard) about the might of the Spear-Danes,' kings in the early days…"

Gar is also one of the elements in old compound Teutonic warrior names.

Edgar was composed of the roots *ead* 'rich' + *gar* 'spear.'

The two-part Teutonic names did not have to make sense. They were composed from an agreed-upon stock of words thought suitable to make up male warrior names.

Gerard and Gerhart contain *gar* 'spear' + *hardt* 'hard.'

Gertrude, originally a male name, is made up of *gar* 'spear' + *trud* 'strength.'

In the given male name Oscar, the root is hidden. Its Old English original was *Osgar* made up of OE *os* 'any god' + OE *gar* 'spear.' Before the Norman conquest of England in 1066 CE, even the Viking version of the name was in use, that is, the Old Norse form *Asgeirr*.

There are a number of Portuguese, Spanish and Italian surnames like Berengár and Beranger derived from the Teutonic name *Beringar* 'bear-spear.' King Hrothgar is a character in the poem "Beowulf." His name is composed of the Anglo-Saxon elements *hroth* 'fame' + *gar* 'spear.' Through an old French form introduced into England after the Norman Conquest in 1066, this evolved into our familiar modern given name, Roger and its derived surname, Rogers.

Taking a Peek at A Welsh Leek

The leek is the plant symbol of Wales, and an essential of French cookery. The somewhat soft bulb and the lower leaves of leeks are used to flavour soups, stews, most versions of vichyssoise, and served by themselves cooked with lemon butter. Leeks are also boiled, chilled, and presented *en vinaigrette.*

Legend says the Welsh symbol arose during a battle in which Cadwaladr, King of Wales, ordered his soldiers to stick sprigs of leek in their caps, so that during the tumult of battle Welsh troops could be distinguished from those of their enemy, led by King Edwin of Northumbria. The Welsh did so and won the engagement, and the symbolic leek recalls this victory.

Word Lore of Leek

Leek < *leac* Old English, leek, akin to *locc* Old English 'a lock of hair,' itself related to *lokkr* Old Scandinavian 'hank of hair,' and to *lugos* Greek 'a pliant twig, a bendable stick of wood.'

Garlic

Allium sativum (*sativus* Latin 'cultivated,' literally 'able to be sown or planted' < *serere* Latin, to sow) is common garlic.

Garlic Uses

One of the earliest mentions of the curative properties of garlic is in the Ebers papyrus from about 1500 B.C. where cancer is described and one of the early pharoanic treatments for hardened skin cancers is the external application of garlic paste. Hippocrates prescribed eating garlic as a treatment for uterine cancers. Some modern cancer research, still inconclusive, does involve garlic and other members of the onion family. And yes, your Polish grandmother was correct, garlic really is good for you. Among the chemical goodies in those little cloves are antibiotics like allicin, a powerful bactericide, and allistatin, a broad-spectrum fungicide. My Scottish grandmother's rule was one raw slice of onion every day "to keep colds at bay and the meddlesome doctor away."

Chives

Allium schoenoprasum (Botanical Latin < *schoinos* Greek, rush, reed + *prason* Greek, leek) is chives, one of the smaller onions, whose fresh leaves have been chopped and added to various foods for more than five thousand years. As one of the *fines herbes* of French cuisine, chives give a modest hint of onion to many a sauce or main dish. Chives perk up sour cream, cottage cheese, cream cheese, and a moderate sprinkle will brighten an omelette.

The word *chive* entered English from an Old French dialectal variant of Old French *cive*, itself from *caepa* or *cepa* Latin 'onion.' Compare *chivot*, the word for green onion in the northern French dialect of Picardy.

Scallions

Green onions or spring onions, scallions are really just immature seedling onions, plucked before they mature, to preserve the tender hint of onion they deliver to chopped salads, herb butters and dozens of other dishes. Scallion derives from the same Latin word as shallot.

There now, wash the cutting board. We've peeled all our onions.

Chapter 84

Open Some Window Words

But, soft! what etymon through yonder window breaks? It is Old Norse, with English just begun.

I ought not to mangle sweet sentences put upon Romeo's lips by the bard Shakespeare. But, low-born varlet that I am, I succumbed to punny alteration. With what I write below, I beg your forgiveness and your attention for this essay, my little fenestral boogie.

Thurl?

The earliest word in Old English for a hole in a wall that let in air, wind and light was *eyethurl* or, as Anglo-Saxon scribes wrote it, éagþyrel = éag 'eye' + Old English noun *þyrel thyrel, thurl, thyrl* 'perforated hole, pierced opening, aperture' < thorough a noun use of an adverbial form 'orifice, made hole' + *-el* English suffix chiefly diminutive, so that the compound thyrel means 'small cut hole in some object.'

Getting Nosy

Has the word *thurl* totally disappeared from contemporary English speech? Not quite. One of the two external holes in your nose to speakers of older English was *nosþir*l, later *nosðyrl,* later still in Middle English *noistrell,* and by 1677 in *Paradise Lost* John Milton spelled it *nostril* 'nose-thurl, nose-hole.'

"Fling Wide the Window Shutters, Ragnar; Slaughter is near"

Between the late eighth century and the eleventh century Viking raiders invaded England, bringing new words as well as old death. Then it was that, into eyethurl's Anglo-Saxon territory, came an Old Norse word destined to wipe out eyethurl. The Vikings were pagan plunderers, bloodthirsty piratical marauders from Denmark, Norway and Sweden who spoke Old Norse, also called Old Scandinavian, the mother-tongue of modern Norse, Danish and Swedish.

That word in Old Norse that replaced eyethurl was *vindauga* made up of *vindr* 'wind' + *auga* 'eye.' Think of its cognate in German *Augen* 'eyes' and the German word for a moment, *ein Augenblick* 'the blink of an eye.' Thus a window was a wind-eye — quite an apt name. It withstood divers orthographical metamorphoses to arrive at the modern spelling: window; these included Middle English forms like *wyndouge, wondowe, wyndew* and finally *window*. The Viking word drove *eyethurl* completely out of the English vocabulary, replacing it in every instance.

Good Fensters Make Good Neighbours

At the onset of modern English early in the seventeenth century there was a synonym for window, though one not in frequent use, and that was *fenester*, brought into English through French, modern French *fenêtre*. French inherited it from Latin *fenestra* 'window.' German imported it as *das Fenster* '*the* window.' The Latin *fenestra* was cognate with the Greek verb *phainein* 'to show, to let light in, to make an appearance,' whose passive present participle, *phainomenos*, gives us our now common word *phenomenon* literally 'thing which appears.'

Please Check Your Czech at the Window

From the Latin *fenestra* arose a pleasingly obscure word known principally to devotees of European history: the Defenestrations of Prague. Defenestration names the act of tossing someone or something out of a window, the Latin radical *fenestra* clearly visible within the window word. States Wikipedia: "The First Defenestration of Prague involved the killing of seven members of the city council by a crowd of radical Czech Husssites on 30 July 1419." The second and more important but less fatal Defenestration of Prague occurred on May 23, 1618 when "three figures fluttered down from a high window of the Castle Hradshin in the heart of Prague. Landing in a convenient heap of rubbish, they escaped with their lives. Thus began the Thirty Years War (1618–48) in Bohemia (now part of the Czech Republic)."

John Ruskin, English aesthete, art critic and writer of that masterly travelogue *The Stones of Venice,* 1851 CE, coined a neat modifier which — alas — has proved of no use whatsoever to any other writer. But I liked it: "A northern apse is a southern one with its interfenestral piers set edgeways." It is meet for the engaging plenitude of English that we possess a learned adjective that signifies 'between windows.' I am shocked that architectural journals have seen no reason to take up *interfenestral*, a hill-and-dale word, delicious to utter with its metrical feet comprised of a troche (inter ¯ ˘) and an amphibrach (fenestral = ˘ ¯ ˘).

The German noun for defenestration is perhaps choicer than the English one: *der Fenstersturz.* It is taut with Teutonic efficacy. One can almost hear in the word the sound of an insufferable lout plunging to a pavement below while impaled by spicules of shattered glass.

Open Window as Metaphor

Manifold are the metaphorical uses of the word *window.* Here shall I content myself by reporting but one. There is a use I appreciate in the King James version of the *Book of Genesis*, in 7:11, where the Bible makes bold to attach a precise date to Noah's flood. "In the six hundredth year of Noah's life, in the second month, the seventeenth day of the month, the same day were all the fountains of the great deep broken up, and the windows of heaven were opened." Dude, that's a rainstorm.

Earlier English versions of the Bible had snappier translations. The early Wycliffe Bible calls them "the goteris of heuene" 'the gutters of heaven' and the Douay Bible speaks of 'the floodgates of heaven, which is a literal translation of the Hebrew of the Torah *ărubbōth hashshāmayim* 'and the floodgates of the sky.' The Koine Greek is crisp too: *katarraktai tou ouranou* 'the gushing waterfalls of heaven.' The timidly alliterative, copycat Latin of Saint Jerome's *Vulgate* is less powerful, *cataractæ cæli*, although those hard Roman c-sounds clack loudly.

But enough of roaring waters. Let us lift the latch and close the lattice-work of the window. Then for a refreshing lunch shall we dart to my humble refectory table — nothing fancy you understand — a russet mahogany credenza with contre-partie marquetry inlaid with Macassar ebony, steamed pearwood, lignum vitae and wenge. Upon the spalted beech wine-tray rests a stoppered flask of azurn cordial, fermented from summer's bounty of plump blueberries.

Chapter 85

Giclée

A French word used in English as a photographic & printing term

Here's a commercial word from the fine arts, a newish term now common in English. The quick spread and breadth of this word's English usage in less than twenty years astonishes. Giclée is everywhere on the internet at sites where posters and art reproductions are on sale. It names a digital printing process delivering high-quality prints.

Artists who depend on their work being reproduced for sale know it and use it daily. Print collectors bandy it about. Giclée appears in the technical manuals of printers. From lips to lips of art-gallery browsers around the world, the word goes awinging.

A giclée (zhee-**KLAY**) print is a superb-quality copy of an artwork or photograph made using high-end 8-to-12 color inkjet printing techniques coupled with the use of pigment inks, archival inks that maintain image stability and color permanence better than all other known inks.

Note that, like many newcomers to English, the French pronunciation of an initial /gi/ is retained. This /gi/ sound is similar to the /s/ in the word *pleasure.*

Giclées typically are printed on large-format special printers from a high-resolution digital scan of the original artwork or photograph. They are printed onto the best media substrates including canvas, fine art papers, and photo-base papers. The color accuracy of the best giclée printing is not exceeded.

Giclée prints adorn collections in most large museums of the world, including the Metropolitan Museum of Art and the Museum of Modern Art in New York City. At recent auctions giclée prints have fetched $10,800 for an Annie Leibovitz photograph, $9,600 for Chuck Close, and $22,800 for a Wolfgang Tillmans.

Its French & Latin Etymology

Before being applied to the spritz of ink from a computer printer's inkjet, *la giclée* was a French noun (in print by 1852 CE) with bountiful explosive meanings.

Une giclée could be: a spurt of blood, a burst of machine-gun fire, a splashing with mud — all from the old French verb *gicler* 'to spout, to squirt.' In French computer lingo, one term for the nozzle of an inkjet printer is *gicleur*.

In modern French slang, *giclée* means 'cum shot' or 'spurt of ejaculate,' not surprisingly, considering that the noun *giclée* originated as the feminine past participle of the French verb *gicler* 'to squirt' or 'to spurt.'

All those related words hark back to a French verb which arose apparently from Gallo-Roman roots that meant 'to jiggle.' The French etymologist Pierre Guiraud supposed that some Late Latin verb like *citare* 'to shake' had a frequentative form like **cicitare* where partial reduplication of the root supplies the added meaning of frequency. Guiraud suggests this eventually degraded in spoken Proto-Romance to a form like **cicare* 'to shake repeatedly.' Such a verb could have produced the known

Franco-Provençal ancestors of *gicler*, namely *jicler* < *gigler* < *ciscler* < *cisclar* < *gisclar.*

Precise Origin of its English Use

The pre-existing French word was borrowed and applied to such prints by Jack Duganne, a California artist and photographer during the 1990s. Thus he did not "coin" the word, as some of the more artsy-fartsy but illiterate websites insist. How could he have, my little know-no-word experts, when the French word has existed in print since 1852?

As we have come to expect with any term that might earn a grifter a few dishonest dollars, giclée has a proper meaning and a sleazy, fly-by-night, con-artist meaning too. Thus, on certain websites selling copies of posters and famous paintings, what is sold as a giclée print may be smeary, visual garbage spewed from the meretricious nozzle of some one-hundred-dollar inkjet printer by a crack addict in a New Jersey warehouse who finishes the copied work by sneezing on it.

Apt here are the most under-regarded two words of sales advice ever uttered, the Latin warning: *caveat emptor* 'let the buyer beware.'

Is *Sincere Sid's Online House of Photographical Masterworks* going to sell you a genuine giclée print of Lewis Hine's "Powerhouse Mechanic" for six bucks? Certainly not! So, brain up and don't get taken to the photographic cleaners like a clueless ninny.

Chapter 86

Common and Immune were once Opposites

The English adjective *common* meant originally the exact opposite of *immune*. But, in what manner was the word *common* the opposite of the adjective *immune*? Common, as an antonym of immune, is a nifty tale involving ancient Roman legal duties and taxation. Antonym is a word with an opposite meaning. The antonym of *hot* is *cold*. The antonym of *young* is *old*.

Common

Modern English *common*, like French *commun*, Spanish *común*, Italian *commune* and Portuguese *comum* all descend from the Latin adjective *communis* whose literal meaning is 'not under any legal obligation, exempt from public duty or taxes. The compound *communis* = Latin *cum, con-, com-* 'together, with' + Early Latin *munis* 'bound, under obligation either legal or perhaps, in earlier Latin, tribal.' Compare the third-declension Latin noun *munus, muneris* with its earliest meaning of 'burden, duty performed, a service done' and its later meanings of 'public office, favour, public gladiatorial spectacle.'

Two Related Words

From Latin *munus* 'service, exchange of gifts' derive English words like *munificent* (generous) and *remuneration* (payment).

Immune

In its prime and sensuous meaning, *immune* did not refer to health or disease. It meant 'free of tribal obligation, free not to perform any public duty.' The compound was made up of the Latin prefix *in-, im-* not, as many suppose, meaning 'in' but instead a Latin negative prefix meaning 'not,' thus *immunis* = *im* 'not' + *munis* 'obliged.'

Note that the negative Latin prefix *in-* often assimilated to the first letter of the root word to which it was frontally attached, especially if the first letter of the root word was *l, m, p* or *r*, as, for example, in words like *illogical, impatient, irreversible.*

When immune first entered English it meant free of anything regarded as burdensome or damaging. During the 1860s, *immune* began to appear in the pages of *The Lancet*, a prestigious British medical journal, with modern meanings like 'impervious to a specific malady, disease-resistant, not susceptible to individual pathogens, antigens or other disease agents.'

The Difference between Derivative and Cognate

This pair of once-upon-a-time antonyms (common/ immune) presents an apt moment to show the difference between derivative and cognate. A derivative word is borrowed, inherited or descended from another language, as English *common* is a derivative from Latin *communis*. As it happens, we also have in English a word that is cognate with Latin *communis*.

A cognate word is related in origin to another word, but by way of an older language source from which both languages inherit similar basic root-forms. For example, English *brother* and German *Bruder* are not derivatives. Both words are cognate; both stem from a more ancient language, in this case, from common Germanic where the form may have been *brôthar, itself related to Old Aryan *brather with its cognates Greek *phrater*, Latin *frater,* Old Slavonic *bratu,* Old Celtic *brater (Irish and Gaelic *brathair* and Welsh *brawd*).

The English cognate of *common* is our adjective *mean*. In Old English *gemæne,* in Old High German *gimeini* and in modern German *gemein*, an adjective that means 'common, ordinary, vulgar.'

Our adjective *mean*, upon its entrance into English, first meant 'held in common,' then — a logical semantic development — 'ordinary, plain, inferior.' Modern English evolved uses of 'mean' in a moral sense like 'nasty, unpleasant, and hurtful.'

A semantic course similar to the English adjective *mean* occurred with Dutch *gemeen* and German *gemein*:

Das ist beiden gemein 'It is common to both of them.'

Gemeines Recht 'common law'

Das war sehr gemein von dir! 'That was really nasty of you.'

Was für ein gemeiner Streich! 'What a dirty, rotten trick!'

The German word for municipality or community, *die Gemeinde*, is related to *gemein*'s earliest meaning.

Last word I give to the French wit, writer and philosopher, Voltaire, who expressed what may sound like a cliché but is not: "Common sense is not so common."

Chapter 87

Hydroponics, Geopony and Lithopone

& their common Greek root

The word is in daily headlines: "Local Cops Raid Hydroponic Grow-Op." "Arrested Hydroponicist Claims To Suffer 53 Diseases Requiring Strains of Medical Marijuana from Separate Plants."

Hydroponics is growing plants without standard soil, sometimes in nutrient-rich water alone, sometimes with plants embedded in plastic holding trays or standing upright in beds of sand, gravel, peat, or inert media like perlite or coconut husks perfused with water-dissolved fertilizers. Hydroponics is part of hydroculture.

Acquainted with terms like hydroelectric, most of us catch *hydro*, both a bound and a free morpheme, meaning 'water,' but what is that *ponic* root?

The word *hydroponics* was coined as recently as 1937, the year when the learned journal *Science* in its February number reported " 'Hydroponics', which was suggested by Dr. W. A. Setchell, of the University of California, appears to convey the desired meaning better than any of a number of words considered."

Hydroponics < Greek *hudor, hudatos* 'water' and its common combing form of – *hudro* or *hydro* + Greek *ponos* 'work, labour, bodily exertion, exercise.'

Geopony

In their infancy, new-born sciences are paranoid and nervous and wish to appear vastly learned. Often, new sciences flood their earliest publications, their breathless initial *pronunciamientos*, with a protective and obscuring shellac of high-falutin' technical verbiage. Sociology's birth is an exemplary instance of this use of big words to disguise little thoughts. In a similar manner, geopony began as a very fancy wordlet revived from Hellenistic Greek by snobbish French agronomists late in the eighteenth century. They did not want to admit they were studying farm management or rural land use or — Gaia forbid! — common farming practices. *Mais non!* They were sober geoponists intent upon the deeper delvings of geopony. *Mais oui!*

The old Greek etymon just sitting there awaiting their pompousness was Greek *geoponia* 'farming techniques' < Greek combining form geo- 'earth' + Greek *ponos* 'labour, work' + Greek *-ia* common noun suffix often indicating an abstract noun. Note that the Greek word is down-to-earth literally, since it means earth-work. But borrowing it into another language as a slimy blob of grandiloquence betrays in its user — anxiety, professional fear and shoddy taste in words.

But is geopony still on stern and solemn word duty as euphemistic balderdash? You betcha! As recently as 1981, we read of a "scientific" farmer referred to as pursuing "the geoponic profession." What a load of horse manure!

Lithopone

Still widely used is this pigment mix of zinc sulphide and barium sulphate. Industrial uses include cheap white pigment in paint, linoleum and printing ink. Lithopone as filler is added to pulp slurry in the making of thick paper.

lithopone = Greek *lithos* 'stone' + Greek *ponos* 'work, product of labour'

Ponerology

This word means a theory of evil. It is chiefly a technical term in theology, made up of Greek *poneros* 'evil, doing injury' + Greek suffix *–logia* giving the hundreds of science names ending in-*ology* 'study of, body of knowledge of the subject named in the first morpheme of the compound, e.g. geology, mineralogy. Why is it always –ology, except in a few words like *genealogy, mineralogy* and *tetralogy*? Because /o/ is the combining vowel of all declensions of Greek nouns, and the Romance languages, English, and most European languages borrowing or confecting compound Greek words for science, follow the Greek rule.

The extended form of *ponos* to make the adjective *poneros* is an example of that adjectival Greek suffix *–eros* often being in Greek of augmentative force. In other words, *poneros* meant 'really laboring mightily' so that the outcome of your work became too heavy, too onerous, and too negative in force, hence: evil.

While I might wish to utter a trendy exit speech about tiptoeing off to check on my geoponical, hydroponical grow-op out in the barn, I must confess that, as a control freak, I **never** permit myself to ingest the miasmic, cannabinol-sodden effluvium of a *sinsemilla* doobie. I have no need of anything psychoactive. I am already psycho.

Chapter 88

Potty-Mouth

Clean thoughts on a "dirty" synonym & remarks about obscenity as satire

"Burn in Hell, Casselman!"

Today's interest in the featured word began a few years ago when some of my writing was banned on several servers in a nearby county. A coven of brain-dead, born-again female morons actually wrote that I was "a potty-mouth atheist" and that little minds should be protected from my idolatrous seethings.

Now this happened in the county where I was born, in which I have written 13 books about words and been termed in a university text book published by Oxford University Press "one of Canada's best etymologists." It is an industry-poor county trying to attract sophisticated factories to its small towns. Would you want your children living next door to book burners and censorious evangelical nutbars? Are they neighbours you would prefer to encounter, should you ever contemplate moving a business there?

What about intellectual freedom in a place where everything you might want to express publicly must be vetted by fundamentalist thought police who dropped out of school after Grade Three? We'll leave their insult for another time and for a lawyer to consider whether or not "potty-mouth atheist" *et alia impressa et dicta* constitute criminal libel under law. I'd love to sue them white, bleed them of every penny they have! In the meanwhile, I loll in sybaritic degeneracy here in the gold-lamé litter that I use as a hammock on the summer porch, all the while contemplating the small truth that potty-mouth is a fascinating term of abuse, well worth etymologizing.

Legal Bulletin!

A lawyer acquaintance informs me that, because I am indeed an atheist and a potty-mouth, and because truth is an absolute defense of libel, no libel or even slander has been committed by the Ladies' Afternoon Tea Society for the Furtherance of the Punishment of Men (*meeting out behind the Firehall, Wed. & Sat. 2 pm. Members may arrive by automobile or broomstick*). Nor can I prove damages to my reputation. Darn! As the lawyer said, "What reputation?" As for the malice that must be proven in a libel case? Those dear ladies malicious? Since when is a knitting needle driven through a beggar's eyeball *malicious*?

When Dirty Talk is Satire

Obscenity can be satirical; it can even aid and abet self-satire — give it a leg up, so to speak. As an example, take one sentence written by one of the most influential American novelists Henry Miller, a writer who has, among pre-literate brain-stems, the reputation of being a "dirty old man." Henry Miller was no such thing. He was a breathlessly funny, original writer who thought deeply and humorously about zesty questions. But nowadays Miller is unjustly neglected, chiefly because he gloried in full use of the taboo words of the English language. Sour, man-hating women of the Fascist persuasion who now control so many English departments in Canadian and American colleges and universities have ruled that Miller may no longer reside in the accepted canon of the modern American novel. What do I say to that? Why that is base female revenge speaking, not reason.

Henry Miller was independent of all women and so has been branded a male chauvinist pig. In his delightful, achingly funny memoir of Paris before World War Two, *Quiet Days in Clichy*, Miller writes this wonderful line, making fun of his male bulldog reputation, "I'm going to fuck you, Wanda, and when I fuck you, you're going to stay fucked." That is rare, vivid, American, masculine self-satire, impossible without its barking obscenity. *Quiet Days in Clichy* was first published in Paris in 1956 but was banned for sale in the United States until 1965, thanks mainly to the born-again evangelical nitwits who still control so much of the American agenda, for whom even the mildest expletive deserves thumb screws or the cat-o'-nine-tails whipped across naked sinning shoulders. Think I'm being paranoid? Consider this statistic: 36% of all Americans reject evolution (2015 CE survey).

Potty-Mouth

Take the noun and adjective *potty-mouth* meaning 'uses dirty words.' It is a putdown beloved by female do-gooders and by males who have dwindled into pussy-whipped dweebs, timid little tit-sucks who imagine they are more virtuous than persons who do not employ coarse language.

Potty-mouth always refers to words the speaker defines as dirty. Potty-mouth suggests an infant uttering the words poo-poo, kaka or doo-doo for the first time and then being chastised by his born-again mommy, perhaps just a gentle verbal rebuke, perhaps a smite on the side of his little head with a heavy family bible. Hopefully followed by a witness calling 911.

Potty is a nursery evasion for the word *toilet.* Thus the intent of referring to an adult male's cursing as being potty-mouth is to infantilize the curser, as if to say "That's a baaad word and only naughty little boys use it."

Some women wish to impugn the power of all vivid speech. It is yet another way to diminish male power. Don't just cut off men's balls and have them bronzed for the mantelpiece. Castrate male language too whenever possible. Well, guess what, Salomé? There's one hunk of salami you ain't getting' near.

Vulgar words signal that a male's speech has **not** been deballed by the ladies, that he is not the kind of hubbie who pees sitting down because the wifelet says that peeing standing-up causes urinous splatter to collect on and to spot the pristine ceramic rim of the toilet bowl. So what? If piss collects, clean it off. By the way, my little guardian mommies of the pissoir, men urinate standing up. Ugly, isn't it? The position has something to do with evolution, with fight or flight. The primordial *Homo defecans* who squatted to go wee-wee in the tall grass often got eaten by the hyenas. Standing while pissing was defensive. The urinator could take his whizz while keeping both eyes peeled for predators lurking in the tall grasses. Nowadays the predators wear Laura Ashley gingham frocks and drive Lexus SUVs.

The power of verbal vulgarity is incontestable. Obscenity is a vital ploy of vivid argument and I want it at my disposal as a writer, always. Startling language permits one to express with all due contempt everything about current social habits and modern familial culture that is *dégoûtant.* In a world whose ethos bores and appals me, I have at least in my quiver the steel arrows of tabooed obscenity to shoot into this world's shabby, treacle-for-blood heart and watch it die, flopping and gasping like a hooked carp on the dock of reason.

Etymology of Potty-Mouth

Potty is a fairly recent American coinage, recorded first in print as potty-chair (1941) in a California newspaper advertisement flogging plastic chamber pots for wee kiddies.

Then came potty chair to name a toddler's toilet chair with a hole for a chamber pot in the seat. Soon afterward, ever seeking to evade anything natural about the human body and to disguise its functions in a rich syrup of weasel words and unctuous circumlocution, North American mommies discovered that *go potty* could be yet another antibacterial euphemism for "to take a shit, to have a dump." Thus unnumbered generations of children attempting to learn how to speak their language had to look upward into the glazed eyes of Giant American Mom as she whispered, "Lulu go potty?"

I prefer the BBC TV documentary that shows the freely brought-up five-year-old British public school boy who from his sandbox runs across a summer lawn to his mother, stands beside her chaise-lounge and states plainly, "I need most desperately, Mama, to defecate and to defecate at once." Ha! Now that child is learning English, not some edited, censored mishmash of euphemism, some effete dancing class of decorous tippy-toed words that are of no use whatsoever to an adult speaker seeking clear, precise communication. When many Americans see this remarkably articulate boy, they can't believe his early verbal aptitude, can't believe that by speaking adult English to children — wonder of wonders! — kids will actually learn adult English. *Goo-goo oogie-woogie to you, Mom.*

The only use of the word *potty* of which I approve occurs in the American phrase *potty parity*, a growing demand that in public buildings the comfortable number of toilets needed for women begins to equal the number of toilets for men. Lineups in front of women's toilets show the contempt and stupidity of male architects.

Chapter 89

Lobate Scarps on the Moon! Is Nothing Sacred?

Why is the moon sad? Poor blue moon! Our moon is shrinking. Yes, our Luna, beloved of lovers, is on the dimensional wane! It waxeth no longer in moony girth. The heavenly satellite of earth now ebbs in circumference. Yes, shrinking, contracting! The night's own chandlier is but a dwindling sphere, the very moon under whose ghost-pale beams sportive humans have scampered through millennia of sublunary frolic. To offer evidence of this moon swoon, the much pocked face of the lunar surface displays lengthy lobate scarps, multikilometer-long moon wrinkles. Some scarps are much shorter.

Lobate Scarps?

Lobate scarps are thrust-up fault lines that appear as long curved cliffs. Like our earth, the moon began as a fireball and is still cooling, still shrinking. The surface marks of its shrinkage are escarpments or scarps.

Stated no less an authority than Thomas Watters of the Center for Earth and Planetary Studies at the National Air and Space Museum of the United States and lead author of a recent paper revealing the details, "Relatively young, globally distributed thrust faults show recent contraction of the whole moon, likely due to cooling of the lunar interior. The amount of contraction is estimated to be about 100 meters in the recent past."

The news staff at www.Science20.com explained, "As the moon contracted, the mantle and surface crust were forced to respond, forming thrust faults where a section of the crust cracks and juts out over another. Many of the resulting cliffs, or scarps, have a semi-circular or lobe-shaped appearance, giving rise to the term 'lobate scarps.' " Scientists aren't sure why they look this way; perhaps it's the way the lunar soil (regolith) expresses thrust faults, according to Watters."

Regolith

This somewhat obscure but delightful astronomical term refers to rock debris, meteorite dust and sundry interstellar flotsam that has collected on the surface of the moon and may be said loosely to constitute lunar soil. The Greek roots of the word are *rhegos* 'rug, blanket' and *lithos* 'stone, pebble.' An apt word indeed, the regolith is the rug of rock upon the floor of the moon. *Lithos* is a very productive root in modern English scientific coinages like lithograph, lithotomy ('cutting for the stone,' that is, surgical removal of a renal calculus or kidney stone), cryolite, monolith, and Neolithic 'of the New Stone Age.'

Lobate

The basic meaning is patent. Lobate means 'having lobes' or 'lobe-shaped.' In reference to cliffs and fissures and clefts of a planet's crust, lobate means lobe-shaped or quasi-circular.

Scarp

Scarp is the interesting word in this newsy phrase. A scarp is land or rock cut away steeply, sticking out or up sharply, pointedly. *Scarp* is an aphetic form of an earlier word *escarp*, familiar to many in the word *escarpment*. If you cut a sound off the start of a word, the correct linguistic name for the process is *aphesis*, an example being *squire*, an aphetic form of *esquire*.

Cognate Affinities

A basic metaphor buried in the oldest relative of the word *scarp* gives rise to these Indo-European words:

(1) Gothic (an Old Germanic language) *skarpô* 'ending in a point'

(2) German *scharf* 'pointed, sharp'
The Germanic root was very early borrowed into the Romance languages, appearing in Italian as *scarpa* 'shoe' that is, leather footwear with a *pointed* toe.

(3) Consider the Provençal verb *escarpi* 'to rip into pointed pieces, to stick out pointedly.'

(4) Even the English word *sharp* is cognate with German *scharf*, featuring the common change of terminal High Germanic /f/ to Low Germanic /p/ visible in other words like Dutch *dorp*, Frisian *terp* and Old Scandinavian (Viking) / English *thorp*, all meaning 'very small village' compared to German *Dorf* 'village, hamlet.' Consider also Swedish *torp* 'cottage, little farm.' It may be derived from a Proto-Indo-European root whose Latin reflex is *turba* 'group of people, crowd, noisy tumult,' with derived adjective *turbulentus*

and its Greek cognate *turbe* 'crowd.' After the Scandinavian invasions of northern Britain that began late in the eighth century CE, this Viking word *thorp* for 'secondary little hamlet' gave rise to hundreds of English town names, little places like Althorp, where Princess Diana was buried. Add examples like Cowthorpe, East Herringthorpe, Nunsthorpe, Owlthorpe and Theddlethorpe All Saints.

(5) In Gothic and Old High German the root *skarp* undergoes metathesis, with the transposing of the /r/ and the /a/ to give a Gothic form like *skrapa* 'structural support, underlying rock' and an older German form like *Schroff* 'sheer rock' or 'precipice,' eventually leaving the form solely in modern German as an adjective *schroff* 'sheer,' while *Abgrund* became the common modern German noun for precipice.

(6) In sixteenth-century Italian *scarpa* named also the talus of a rampart, that is, the slope of an earthwork, which gradually increases in thickness as it descends, just as in geology the talus is the sloping pile of rock debris that lies at the base of a cliff made up of rocky material that has fallen from the face of the cliff.

I happen to have been born in southern Ontario, Canada, a few miles away from the Niagara Escarpment, a well-known structure formed in the bedrock of the Great Lakes, a long eroded cliff, a sheer-faced ridge that extends hundreds of kilometers through Ontario, Michigan and ends in Illinois near Chicago. One may saunter on and beside the Niagara Escarpment while hiking Ontario's beautiful Bruce Trail. If you are a visiting hiker, do check out an online guide to the Bruce Trail. The trail's vista is best seen in daylight however, not moonlight.

Chapter 90

Ubicity & Bibliothetic

Words rare but useful

Have you ever visited the many-shelved library of a fretful lector whom you find constantly rearranging her books? You might think her pathetic, when correctly she is merely bibliothetic.

The word is chiefly used as a technical term in Library Science, where bibliothetic means 'relating to the placing and arrangement of books on the shelves of a library.'

Of course a mild bibliothetic wont is common to any *personne qui dévore les livres*, as the French say. If you returned a borrowed volume to some stern German, such a *Bücherfreund* would scamper to reshelve the book in its ordained slot.

Biblio- & the Bible

Bibliothetic appears to be a twentieth-century coinage from the ancient Greek word for book *biblos*. Originally *biblos* named the inner bark of the Nile-fringing papyrus plant from which primordial Nilotic sedge an early paper was made, by pounding dry what were laid-flat, transverse strips of its moist pith. Then the word came to mean paper, scroll, roll and book.

Our English word *bible* descends in fact from a diminutive plural form of biblos namely Greek *ta biblia*, (singular *biblion* 'little book'*). Ta biblia* meant literally 'the books,' in later Christian writers it referred only to the Christian Holy Scriptures.

A Thesis

The suffix of this compound adjective *bibliothetic* is *–thetic* from ancient Greek *thetikos* = the Greek verbal stem *the-* 'placed, able to be placed or put,' stem of the common Greek verb *tithenai* 'to place' + *-tikos*, a suffix forming thousands of Greek and later English adjectives. Compare ancient Greek which gives doctoral students their *thesis*, the 'placing' they 'put' before senior scholars as prose or speech in hopes of earning their degrees.

Ubicity

You may have remarked upon the insuppressible ubicity of wordlore websites. Not mine, of course, but the sites of other, lesser verbivores and scruffy logophiles. They are everywhere online, ubiquitous, pullulant. They do stain and besmirch monitorial pixels with the guano of their ignorance, both etymological and syntactical.

James Joyce used the word in playful, satirical mode in the Oxen of the Sun chapter of his 1922 novel *Ulysses*: "No man knows the ubicity of his tumulus." Indeed, except for those born to wealth and destined to moulder in stately mode amidst the echoic marbles of mausolea, most mortals know not the whereabouts of their burial.

Tumble into a Tumulus

Latin *tumulus* named an ancient burial mound and is related to the Latin verb *tumere* 'to swell, to mound up' itself cognate perhaps with the Greek noun *tumbos* 'burial mound,' borrowed into late Latin as *tumba* and still resident in English as *tomb*.

The classical Latin adverb *ubi* 'where' has had playfully tacked on to it a common, abstract-noun-making suffix seen in words like rusticity, simplicity, felicity, and even in concrete nouns like electricity and publicity.

And now, research completed, as devout and tidy bibliothetes, we must place back on their proper shelves our Latin-abounding tomes.

Chapter 91

Abacus

The abacus (**A***bacus*, to rhyme with "**have** a cuss") is a counting device but had earlier meanings and the most significant one was in Hellenistic Greek, or Koine, the common dialect of the Greek language spoken throughout postclassical antiquity, approximately from 300 BCE to 300 CE. It was chiefly Attic Greek with a few nuggets of Ionic (Island) Greek tossed into the mix.

In that feisty Koine street speech, *abax, abakos* named a flat board covered with sand or dust so that one could draw letters and designs in the sand and then "clean" the board by wiping the sand off the board. Thousands of children learned their Greek alphabet on an *abacus*, the form the Greek word *abax* assumed when borrowed into Latin by the Romans. If drawing letters and shapes in sand with a stick or metal stylus sounds complicated, it was not, in a world without cheap paper. Certainly papyrus and parchment existed, but they were expensive media fit only for important scrolls and documents, too dear by far to waste on a mere child's acquisition of literacy and numeracy.

Etymon of Ancient Provenance

The Greeks likely encountered the word in their trade dealings with a Semitic people. Gleaming and winking provocatively from the Semitic word hoard is the Biblical Hebrew masculine noun *'abaq* 'dust, sand, grit, powder.' In Post-biblical Hebrew *'abaq* could mean 'sand used as a writing surface.' Who better to have introduced Greek traders to an abacus than those ancient merchant sailors of the Mediterranean, the Semitic-language-speaking Phoenicians? Remember, ancient Greeks were deft borrowers — not so modern Greeks. What else did the Phoenicians give the Greeks? Their alphabet! Thence stems the Roman version with which alphabet the words of this very page are formed. Then what is the ultimate provenance of the root word? Unknown. But it may have a reflex in two of the languages of ancient Babylonia, in both Sumerian and Akkadian, making the root easily 3,000 years old.

In Greek *abax* had other meanings like wooden plank, hence side-board, sometimes a cupboard placed near a dining table as a place to set wine bowls, flasks, and culinary impedimenta not immediately needed at table. Abacus also named a wooden board on which to play certain "board" games. Much later, as a technical term in ancient architecture, abacus referred to the upper part of the capital of a Greek column.

Beware! A Horrid Plural Form!

In English there are two plural forms: the clumsy American *abacuses* (a hideous, swamp-born sound — like a toad attempting to recite verse by Shelley) or, always preferable, the neat, Latinate British plural, *abaci*. Hard *c*, please, and the stress remains on the first syllable.

Even by Roman times, the abacus had mutated into a counting device. The Romans began to incise grooves and marks along the board, as well as shallow holes into which little counting pins fit, in order to make calculating sums quicker. Later appeared early

Chinese abaci, called *soan pan*, with movable beads which slide, the perforated beads strung on wires to speed calculation. By the way, our English word *calculate* comes from *calculus*, Latin 'small stone, pebble.' The Latin verb *calculare* meant 'to compute quantities using pebbles.' By the middle of the Middle Ages, such large, wired, beaded abaci were in use from China to Britain.

Poets like the word *abacus.* Here's a snippet from "Colophon" by Aleister Crowley, a rather odd, wizard-like gentleman who was, in the apt phrase of British psychiatry's rubber stamp, "A suitable case for treatment." My own personal assessment of Crowley is that he was as crazy as an outhouse rat. There was clutter in his befogged noggin sufficient to occupy an entire convention of psychiatrists for years. But he was an entertaining fellow and a deft little phrase-maker, whatever his faults.

"Be thou mine as I am thine,
As the vine's ensigns entwine
At the sacring of the sun,
Thou the even and I the odd
Being and becoming one
On the abacus of God!"

But no more addenda now, for I calculate that we have attained the summit of our abacus treatment.

Chapter 92

Kiln: A Fiery Word

A kiln is an oven, furnace or heated place designed to fire pottery or to burn or to dry certain substances. In medieval villages kilns were used to make charcoal. Where I was born in southern Ontario, kilns bordered tobacco fields where the long, toxic yellow leaves were hung to dry, awaiting their shipment to innocent human lungs. Kilns help remove moisture from wood to obtain kiln-dried lumber. There are brick kilns, lime kilns and, in beer manufacture, malt kilns.

Kiln derives from the Latin word *culina* meaning 'a place for cooking food, a kitchen, little stove, cooking-stove, a site for burnt offerings at Roman funerals.' Today the most common British pronunciation drops the final *n* and is said as "kil." North American pronunciation appears to be equally divided between persons who say "kil" and those who say "kiln." Most NA potters and ceramicists whom I have met retain the terminal *n* and say "kiln."

But How, Exactly, did *Culina* become *Kiln*?

In these columns I often discuss words being borrowed from one language into another with subsequent alteration of form. It is not always possible to detail the precise mechanisms of such change. But with the word *kiln*, I can make a sound guess.

In the ancient Roman received pronunciation, that is, in the manner that educated upper-class Romans spoke *culina,* the word was probably stressed on the second syllable using a long continental *i,* hence sounding like koo-LEEN-a. But in the slangy street Latin of the Roman soldiers posted to northern Gallia (France) and Britannia (England) the stress accent of *culina* moved to the first syllable with several pronunciatory consequences.

Slangy speech in general seeks to speak words more quickly than any literary language, so unstressed syllables tend to get severely abbreviated, squeezed, and then dropped. In the word *culina*, the length of the second syllable shortened. The vowel *i* shortened so drastically that it became a schwa. It disappeared. Suddenly culina once said as koo-LEEN-a became KUH-luh-nuh. *Culina* was first heard in England when the Romans arrived in 55 BCE and it persisted through the Anglo-Saxon invasions to survive into Old English forms *cylene* or *cyline*, meaning 'large oven,' said with a hard *c* and stressed on the first syllable.

The next change in the word was assimilation in a consonant cluster. In other words, *l* and *n* meet together in a word. Now /ln/ is a consonant cluster we don't like in English because it is too difficult to say quickly. Thus the letter *n* after the letter *l* is sometimes lost or assimilated. Kiln becomes "kil." Much easier to say. The same thing happened in English with our common word *mill* 'a place for grinding corn or wheat to make flour.' Mill began life as the Latin word *molina*. The dislike of uttering /ln/ together appears in our usual pronunciation of the surname of the most famous American president, Abraham Lincoln. We usually say 'Linkin;' the second

/l/ is assimilated and never pronounced and the /o/ is shortened to a schwa.

Verbal Shards

Our English adjective *culinary* began as the ancient Roman name of a kitchen slave, *culinarius*.

When small local kilns disappeared from village life in the nineteenth century, so too did a useful metaphorical verbal phrase disappear from colloquial English. Once upon a gossipy chat, you could have said, "He's a troublemaker. No sooner shows up but he's set the kiln afire." To set the kiln on fire was to stir up a fuss, to engender general turmoil.

Lest I get fired up about any further kiln trivia, I think it's time to douse this topic.

Chapter 93

A Casquet of Verbal Gems

Agomphious, attercop, rusk, quinion et alia, words necessary to be known by all literate persons

What is the Proper Word for an Otter's Den?

English is one of the few languages on earth that has a specific word to name the den of an otter, namely a holt. This lutrine lair can name — rarely — a place of refuge, an abode of safety for humans too. Lutrine is a somewhat esoteric zoological adjective meaning 'pertaining to the otter family.' Holt is a form of the noun *hold* which we use most frequently in English as a verb. But it has multiple uses as a substantive too. Consider only the hold of a ship, a hold on your emotions, a wrestler's neck-hold, put a hold on the contest, to lay hold of someone, to take hold of the company's leadership.

Rusk: Twice-Baked Bounty

Rusk is bread baked twice to render it more easily preserved, for example on a ship's long voyage. Thus it is similar to a German term used in English, zwieback, said of biscuits baked once then sliced and toasted until a dry crispness is obtained.

Rusk harks all the way back to thirteenth-century Spanish *rosca de pan* 'bread twist.' Zwieback is a compound of German *zwei* 'two' + German *backen* 'to bake,' influenced by a now lost English past-participial form, *backen* 'baked.'

Rusk from other roots has other meanings. Rusks are small pieces of coal in certain English dialects. A rusk is a stab wound in obsolete Scottish dialects. To rusk may mean 'to shake violently.'

Agomphious

Literally *agomphious* means 'toothless.' Agomphious is a Victorian British coinage, possibly by a dentist acquainted with ancient Greek. The compound is made up of alpha privative, the initial negatizing Greek prefix *a-* + *gomphios* molar tooth, tooth shaped like a bolt, hence any tooth, hence literally 'not with any teeth.'

As an adjective meaning gutless or chick-hearted, agomphious has a most fitting, creepy, slithery, yellow-streaked sound. For example, to freshen an abusive apostrophe shouted to some base-born fart-catcher, one might vociferate in this wise: "Aroint thee, thou cringing, lickspittle agomphious toady!" Then again one might choose to **not** say such a sentence aloud, for fear of nearby villagers tying you to a burning cart.

Splendeurs et Misères

From French a literal translation is 'splendours and miseries.' It is indeed a splendid phrase coined by the great French novelist Honoré de Balzac (1799–1850 CE), one of the pioneers of the realistic modern novel. The phrase was the title of one of his novel sequences, *Splendeurs et Misères des Courtisanes* (1839–47) in which he depicted the moments of exaltation (few) and the tedious degradation in the lives of Parisian prostitutes.

I recently read a reporter's callid insight into the daily grubwork of a Washington politician's office, in which the reporter spoke of the *splendeurs et misères* of performing paltry and servile string-pulling for the politician's not-very-deserving constituents.

Quinion

It's a set of five things, for example, a quinion of digits is five fingers or toes. Yes, it is mildly obscure but it saves one the use of much clumsier words such as observing that one's mistress has five moles on her nose. A quinion of moles is easier said that "Verna is nasally quinquepunctate."

Quinion derives from a term that appears in the work of the third-century Christian apologist Tertullian, namely *quinio, quinionis* 'a group of five.' Compare the classical Latin number *quinque* 'five.'

Attercop

This is a British dialect word for spider. It may also be used to name a bitchy person. The word has old English roots *atter* 'poison' + *cop* 'spider.' But attercop may have been left in its English cobweb by Vikings, for we find in modern Danish *edderkop* for 'spider.' Of course *cop* meaning spider is still spinning in our word *cobweb.*

I shall close this casquet of verbal gems with a short quotation not entirely relevant, but apposite nonetheless. Oliver Wendell Holmes once said, "Speak clearly, if you speak at all; carve every word before you let it fall."

Chapter 94

Darwin

On the origin of his species of surname

We are well past the 200th anniversary of the birth of one the best scientific enquirers who ever lived, Charles Darwin. To those who dismiss this scientist, I say this: Darwin's scientific discovery of evolution through natural selection is the foundation of all modern biology. It is a unifying logical explanation for the diversity of life. There is no cogent other. Darwin and his theory will be alive through all of human history, long after you doubters and your sullen, born-again, scienceless spawn have dwindled away into scoffers' nonentity within the hollow cave of oblivion you so richly merit as your grave. You will have been yokel clowns blowing farting noises outside the entrance gate at the carnival of knowledge. You are pallid commas of history; Darwin is one of its exclamation marks.

Darwin: Meaning of the Surname

There are two possible sources of the great scientist's last name. The Darwin family name was first recorded in a surviving document dated during the tenth century CE. In Old English it appears as *Deorwine* 'dear-friend,' quite obviously a byname arising from an affectionate nickname, perhaps to describe a loving man who was the founding ancestor of the family. Until rather late in the millennium the name appeared most frequently as Derwen, Derewin and Derwin.

Old English *Wine* Means 'Friend.'

The Anglo-Saxon word for friend '*wine*' was a common element in Old English given names, all of which preceded surnames by centuries. Godwin and Goodwin both mean 'god-friend' or 'good-friend.' The English surname Winger began as a first name Wingar, an Anglo-Saxon warrior name compounded of Old English *wine* 'friend' + Old English *gar* 'spear.' Winston is 'friend's settlement' from Old English *wine* 'friend' + *tun* 'farms, settlement.' The modern spelling of *tun* is, of course, town.

Welsh word for 'Oak Tree' = *Derwen*

Derwen is the Welsh singular of *derw* 'oak trees.' It is common in Welsh for tree names to be plural in meaning, with the singular (which is always feminine) formed by adding the suffix *-en*. In other Brythonic languages of the Celtic family, the oak tree words are similar, e.g. —

Breton: *dero* (oaks), *dervenn* (an oak)

Cornish: *derwo* (oaks), *derowen* (an oak tree), *derowennow* (individual oak trees).

Other Origins of Darwin as a Surname

Darwen or Darwent or Derwent or Darwin are English surnames that may have arisen from an ancestor dwelling on the banks of the English river Derwent. Derwent is a very ancient Celtic river name that means 'oak-river,' named because its banks, at one time in pre-English history, were lined with oak trees. The same

Celtic root for 'oak tree,' **–der*, is found in the word *druid* (possible earlier form **der-uid)* which means 'oak-knower.' There are four Derwent rivers in England. The Derwent River and its lake, Derwent Water, in Cumbria are mentioned in the writings of Keats and Coleridge and another poet, William Wordsworth, wrote of the river with deep affection:

"For this, didst Thou,
O Derwent! travelling over the green Plains
Near my 'sweet Birthplace,' didst thou, beauteous Stream
Make ceaseless music through the night and day
Which with its steady cadence, tempering
Our human waywardness, compos'd my thoughts
To more than infant softness, giving me,
Among the fretful dwellings of mankind,
A knowledge, a dim earnest, of the calm
That Nature breathes among the hills and groves."
William Wordsworth, *The Prelude*, Book I

There is also a Darwen River in Lancashire which flows past a town called Darwen.

Final Advisory Note

Some sloppy readers think Charles Darwin wrote a book entitled "The Origin of the Species." No such book exists. Darwin's short title was "The Origin of Species." He did not discuss only the origin of *Homo sapiens* but how evolution produces many different species. Darwin discusses speciation.

How Best to Remember Darwin

If you would remember for a few moments today this Englishman of agile mind who asked some of history's most pertinent questions, I urge you to read some of Darwin's own words, not those of his enemies or of his supporters.

Almost everything Darwin published is now free online at http://darwin-online.org.uk/.

It's a fascinating site on which you can eavesdrop upon one of the best scientific imaginations ever to inhabit a human brain. The theory of evolution by natural selection has now been proven at the molecular level of a cell! It's that simple, that pervading, that complex.

Here is one sentence from the conclusion of *On the Origin of Species*:

"There is grandeur in this view of life, with its several powers, having been originally breathed into a few forms or into one; and that, whilst this planet has gone cycling on according to the fixed law of gravity, from so simple a beginning endless forms most beautiful and most wonderful have been, and are being, evolved."

I'll wind up my Darwinoscopy by quoting the Greek dramatist Sophocles who enunciated the first great human cry of freedom from superstition, of freedom from man-made gods, of freedom from quaking in fear and ignorance in the face of life and death. The passage is sometimes referred to as the "*polla ta deina*" from its first three words in Attic Greek: *polla ta deina kouden anthrôpou deinoteron pelei.* The passage is found in the second choral song of the Greek tragedy *Antigone* written by Sophocles in the fifth century BCE.

The full passage is well worth the perusal. But the opening line is a great bell that summons men and women to the centre stage of their own lives and orders the swindling gods and sticky-fingered godlets to stumble offstage where an overdue oblivion awaits them. Wrote Sophocles: 'Many are the wonders but nothing is more wonderful than one human being.'

Chapter 95

A Mallet, a Molotov Cocktail & Charlemagne's Grandfather

Here is a motley toolbox of terms derived from the classical Latin word for hammer, *malleus.*

Perhaps the most familiar English derivative is *mallet*, a percussive implement which one might wish to apply every now and then to the forehead of any religious TV pastor. Alas, such a restorative fillip has been deemed by our judicial betters to be a tort, to wit, a wrongful act, however conducive to that pastor's mental correction said mallet might prove. Of course, none of us want to be low tortfeasors. Let us therefore settle for sending the good reverend a few eye-drops, mayhap a wet teabag, to assuage the twin shiners which a just fate has in store for him when, at the Pearly Gates, Saint Peter peruses over his curriculum vitae.

However Focus, that stern goddess, now bids us, for the purpose of this wee divertissement, to press onward. A more pertinent exigency summons us mallet-wielders into the spark-dense smithy of etymology, where the acetylene torch of history noisily breaks words asunder. And then our gained knowledge of a verbal origin lets us weld words together, their prime meanings refreshed, their definitions restated and conjoined in a pristine and tidy newness.

Mallet

A mallet is often a wooden hammer made for pounding down on a chisel, driving a wedge or a gouge.

Mallet or *maillet* is clearly a diminutive of Old French *mail* from Latin *malleus* 'hammer,' so that the common French diminutive suffix *-et, -ette* when added to the *malleus* root produces several forms of semantic verification. One is the very early meaning of *maillet* as 'door-knocker,' in Old French in a document dated 1190 CE. What else are many door-knockers but 'little hammers'?

The Proto-Indo-European root is *mal-, a vowel-gradation and semantic extension of *mel- 'grind, make soft, pound into softness.' PIE cognates signifying tools for pounding and grinding and things ground up for food are widespread. Consider the Russian word for hammer, *molotok,* Latin *molere* 'to grind,' Latin *mola* 'millstone,' Latin *milium* 'millet,' but literally 'that which is ground up,' Greek *mylos* 'millstone, grindstone,' Old English *melu* 'meal, flour,' Middle English *malle*, Modern English *maul* 'hammer, maul' and Hittite *mallanzi* 'they grind.'

A classical Greek tag always adds proverbial spice, so here's a famous one containing the nominative plural of *mylos* 'grinding mill,' namely *myloi* in the original Greek. We shall be content with an English translation: "The mills of the gods grind slowly but they grind exceeding fine." Meaning: Divine vengeance or retribution will catch up with you, however long it takes.

Malleus

The Latin word itself found a home in international anatomical nomenclature, where malleus names the outermost of the three little bones of the human ear:

malleus, incus and stapes, called the three auditory ossicles, where ossicle = *ossiculum* Latin 'little bone,' diminutive of Latin *os* 'bone.' The malleus is the hammer that beats upon the incus thus transmitting exterior noises that vibrate the eardrum to the inner ear for eventual processing in the brain as discrete and possibly meaningful sounds.

Malleolus

Another anatomical relative of *malleus* Latin 'hammer' is *malleolus* Latin 'little hammer' which names either of those bony bumps on each side of the human ankle. The lateral (outside) malleolus is a bump on the fibula bone. The inside ankle bump (internal or medial malleolus) is a bump on the tibia bone. The diminutive form *malleolus* began in early classical Latin as the name of a kind of war-time firecracker, a fire-dart, a type of incendiary small missile thrown at an enemy. It must have had a shape that reminded ancient Roman soldiers of a hammer.

Malleable

A person who is malleable is one whose opinions are easily 'hammered' into a shape pleasing to the person doing the shaping. One amenable to any outside influence whatsoever may dwindle into a malleable chump, a pushover, a pliant gull, a patsy, a low dupe.

A malleable metal is one which is ductile, easily hammered into a wanted shape. *Malleabilis* is the post-classical Latin 'able to be hammered' from the Latin verb *malleare* 'to hammer' + *-abilis,* the common Latin adjectival suffix of capability.

Molotov Cocktail

In Russian transliteration: *koktyil Molotova*

Vyacheslav Molotov (1890-1986) was born, the son of a poor shopkeeper, as Vyacheslav Mikhailovich Skryabin. He was not related, not by one tiny chromosome, to the great and talented Russian composer, Alexander Scriabin.

Molotov was a politician and diplomat, a soulless old Bolshevik who became a leading, lickspittle, partisan Commie toady in the Russian Soviet government from the 1920s, when he rose to power as Stalin's bumboy and proud doer of foul deeds.

Knowing he was a mousy-looking little proto-fascist pipsqueak (like so many human monsters) he changed his name to make it more frightening and more manly. Molotov as a Russian surname means 'descendant of an ancestor named 'The Hammer,' Russian *molotok*. He also liked his new surname's vaguely industrial sound, to give the illusion of his solidarity with the common Russian worker. Ha!

But he did not give his name to the famous quickly-made bomb. The Wikipedia explanation of the name's origin is terse and apt, and so I quote it (also because it is free to reproduce): "The name 'Molotov cocktail' was coined by the Finns during the Winter War. The name is an insulting reference to Soviet foreign minister Vyacheslav Molotov, who was responsible for the setting of spheres of interest in Eastern Europe under the Molotov-Ribbentrop Pact in August 1939. The pact with the Nazis bearing Molotov's name, which secretly stated the Soviet intention to invade Finland in November 1939, was widely mocked by the Finns, as well as much of the propaganda Molotov produced to accompany it, including his declaration on Soviet state radio that bombing missions over Finland were actually airborne humanitarian food deliveries for their starving neighbours.

The Finns, far from starving and engaged in a bitter war for national survival with the Soviet forces, sarcastically dubbed the Soviet cluster bombs 'Molotov bread baskets' in reference to Molotov's propaganda broadcasts. When the hand-held bottle firebomb was developed to attack Soviet tanks, the Finns called it the 'Molotov cocktail,' as 'a drink to go with the food.' Molotov himself despised the name, particularly as the term became ubiquitous and generalized as Soviets faced increasing numbers of cocktail-throwing protesters in the Eastern Bloc in the years after World War II."

Charles Martel

Charles *Martel* (688–741 CE) was the bastard son of Pepin and grandfather of Charlemagne in early French history. Charles earned the moniker because of the fury and bloodthirsty might he employed in slaughtering the Saracens at the battle of Poitiers in 732. The surname spread widely in France and England and sometimes named a founding ancestor of a family lineage who was a blacksmith, from a common Old French word for a blacksmith's hammer, *martel* from classical Latin *martulus* 'little hammer,' itself a variant or more easily spoken remodelling of earlier Latin *malleus* or one of its diminutives like *malleolus*. Note that the modern French word for hammer stems from a Middle French form, *marteau*. *Martel* had a brief life as an English word for two hundred years as the name of a weapon, the *martel de fer* or iron war-hammer or mace.

Now I bring down my adjudicator's gavel, my magisterial mallet, to declare this session of wordlore closed until the opening of my penultimate chapter.

Chapter 96

A Potpourri of Popery

Papal regalia & insignia words

A Papal *Odd*-ience

All genuflecting toward one side, folks, even atheist onlookers must admit that the pope is one sporty-lookin' dude when caparisoned in full Vatican drag, regalia resplendent, swathed in silken ensembles, richly attired in embroidered habiliments, gowned in silver-threaded raiment that would abash a pasha. Kitted out in his Sunday best, that geezer is old but bold. In this chapter I examine the names and origins of papal frocks and insignia. But remember, no peeking under a papal mantle to see if there's a crouching altar-boy. If you do peek, the punishment is Six Hail-Bruces.

Zucchetto

It's his little skullcap, much like a pious Jew's yarmulke. Cardinals and the Pope wear it most often but lesser clergy may don it at times. Zucchetto is a diminutive form of Italian *zucca* 'gourd' which very early became a slang synonym for the human head, and hence *zucchetto* is something 'little' that fits on the head. English has similar popular terms for head like *coconut, the old bean,* and *the conk.* The ancient Romans did too. The fancy Latin word for head was *caput.* But in street Latin the human head was *testa* 'the old jar'. It was Latin *testa* which gave French its word for head, *tête.* Interestingly the word *zucchetto* wore its way into English bearing the wrong grammatical gender. In Italian, it is most widely used as a feminine noun, *la zucchetta*.

The Mantum

What is it? A large, body-covering ornamental, often embroidered cloak or cope which began, humbly enough, as a rain cloak. The *mantum* has a hood and is open at the front. It's fastened in front by a usually ornate golden clasp called a morse, inset with rare gems of Ind and Araby, sparkling with purple amethysts, moss opals, choice chrysoberyls, sards, sphenes, spinels, and rubies red as a starving parishioner's eyes. The word *morse* has the same source as our word *morsel* ('little bite'). In classical Latin *morsus* meant literally 'the bite,' but it also meant the buckle or catch that "bit" two pieces of clothing and held them together.

The mantum is a liturgical vestment that once played a central part in the investiture ceremonial of a new pope. As he donned the papal mantum, the investing bishop said "*Investio te de papatu romano ut praesis urbi et orbi"* — 'I invest thee with the Roman papacy, that thou mayest rule over the city and the world.' The last three words became important in papal history. One of the papal encyclicals, wherein the pope pronounced now and then upon various religious matters was called "*Urbi et orbi*." Here too the church plays fast and loose with Latin. Nowadays the pope gives an "*urbi et orbi* once a year and the Vatican always tells journalists that the Latin means [an address] "to the city [Rome] and to the world." But that meaning would mean the Latin words would have to be in the accusative case. They are in fact in the regnant dative, because their original meaning is "this papal address rules over the city and the world." Thank some deity that such pontifical fascism no longer applies.

Mantum is a Fake Word

The source of mantum as a word is evidence of a certain ecclesiastical hocus-pocus. Whenever the church could not find the Latin root of a word, they snuck into the vestry and simply made up a source. The etymology-assigned monklets and nunlets in the Vatican scriptorium had trouble finding *mantum* in classical Latin, for a very good reason: it didn't exist. The Romans had *mantellum*, an uncommon word for cloak and *mantica* 'a bag to hold a folded cloak, a knapsack.' The pontifical serviles saw *mantellum* in a Latin word list. It looked like a diminutive. They didn't want the glorious pope clad in anything so second-rate as a diminutive. So, probably sometime in the seventh century appears what is called a back formation. They stripped off the diminutive suffix *–ellum* and made up a stark root word *mantum*, a form which appears nowhere in 1,500 years of legitmate Latin text.

Mozzetta

This is a short cape with a hood and buttons down the front, worn over an all-white cassock by the Pope, cardinals, and certain other high-ranking ecclesiastical bigwigs. The capelet is said to symbolize papal authority. Its root is probably as a nounal diminutive of the Italian adjective *mozzo* 'cut, shortened.'

Pallium

A papal pallium is an often white, embroidered band of cloth thrown around the Pope's neck and shoulders. In classical Latin, it was the large cloak worn by Roman soldiers to keep warm. Earlier, it was the preferred 'modest' garb of wandering philosophers, Roman and Greek. Later, early Christians wore a pallium instead of the pagan Roman toga. The word looks like a deliberate neutering of what was a feminine word. *Palla* in classical Latin was an outdoor robe for ladies, a rectangular mantle, worn especially as a garment by women. Making the feminine Latin noun neuter probably added a macho mode to the word and removed its femininity.

Cappello Romano

A *cappello romano* (Italian 'Roman hat') is a red hat with a wide brim and a rounded rim worn by Catholic clergy. Its other name is *saturno*, a playful synonym, so dubbed by some wag who thought its brim resembled the rings of Saturn. The *cappello* has no ceremonial purpose. It's a hat for private life. The papal noggin is clad in a red *cappello* with gold cords. Cardinals' *cappelli* are black like all other clerics.

Falda

This white-silk vestment, whose wearing is restricted to the pope is a long skirt-like cloth extending from under the alb. The alb (Latin *album* 'white thing') is the simple white linen tunic of the ancient Romans, the garment of daily choice for Roman men. It touches the ankles and is often belted with a cincture. Its use is confined to a Pontifical High Mass. Upon the death of a pope, it is draped over the Pope's body during the funeral.

Falda is an Italian word whose basic meaning is 'layer,' borrowed into Italian from some Germanic term directly related to English 'fold.' In Spanish, *falda* is the common word for 'skirt,' something with folds.

The Piscatory Ring

Proclaiming that he is the mystical successor of Saint Peter, the Fisherman's Ring is newly cast in gold for each papal investiture. When a pope dies, this signatory ring is removed and crushed in front of all the cardinals, so that, during *sede vacante* (Italian 'the empty papal chair'), the interregnum before the new pope has been chosen, no impostor may forge papal documents by sealing them with the old pope's signet. The Fisherman's ring shows St. Peter in a boat, fishing, with the name of the new or reigning pope circling the scene.

Now, gentle pilgrims, I think it best that we tiptoe from the Pope's *stanza di armadio* (or *camerino*) and let that frail cardinal finish ironing the pope's delicate lace collar.

Chapter 97

Mortal Nouns

A sombre yet humorous and mercifully brief introductory note about my death, but only as the most modest of prolegomena to the etymology of the Latin noun mors, mortis

Many years from now, when Fate has had the very bad taste to press my final delete button, I hold no hope of everlasting survival crouched at the feet of a Jewish carpenter while I perform some menial, lickspittle, toady function such as eternal toe-jam inspector. I am writing these mortal ponderings at the age of 74 while in robust health.

Likewise I toss the damp blanket of disbelief over the death-evaders, those cheery etherized brethren who rise from hospital gurneys having been pronounced doornail-dead. As they merrily yank catheters from lower orifices, they yammer on and on about the moment of death when they were being pleasingly pulled toward a warm white light. For me, the light at the end of the tunnel has always been the oncoming train.

In any philosophical pondering about my demise, I follow my late hero and scholar of religion, Joseph Campbell, who appeared on PBS TV with Bill Moyers after having been given a fatal prognosis, a ticket to the land "from whose bourne no traveler returns." They were old friends and so Moyers could say, "Joe, you're going to die. You've spent your entire life studying all the known religions of the world. What's the answer to death?" Campbell, in his late seventies, raised a palsied hand to the TV camera and to Moyers. With his other hand Campbell pointed to his upraised arm and said, "Today, Joe Campbell's arm." Then he snapped his fingers. "Tomorrow, star dust." He went on to explain that, for him, what we need to do as death approaches is to find a way "**to contemplate with equanimity our utter dissolution**."

Has mental preparation for one's own death ever been stated better? Granted, it is no facile task. Death is the ultimate insult to our ego, but for me expecting a black, velvety void is nobler and wiser than a life spent as a sinning Uriah Heep, a crawling wretch slobbering over tall tales from the ancient Near East and murmuring to oneself, "There must be an afterlife. How could a creation as wonderful as me just disappear?" To which question Fate for eons untold has always answered, "Just watch how easy it is, pal!"

Onward Now to Life-Positive Etymology!

Lest my petty thanatopsis stretch out and bury our word topic, let us tidy the gravesite and sweep rude bones into the lime pit, all the better to proceed with our notes and queries, today chiefly about the Latin word for death, *mors mortis*.

Mors of course abounds with Indo-European cognates. There is Old English *morth*, English *murder*, Old Irish *marb*, Welsh *marw* 'he died,' Lithuanian *mirtis* 'death' and Sanskrit *mṛtyu*. The ancient Greek cognate hides slightly in *brotos* 'mortal,' from an earlier *mrotos, itself perhaps a metathetic form of *mortos* 'mortal.'

That Greek root is still kicking around in our English derivative *ambrosia* 'the food of the gods,' that is, the sustenance which made the gods immortal, not subject to death. The Greek adjective *ambrosios* 'pertaining to the immortals' derives from an earlier adjective *ambrotos* 'immortal,' made up of alpha privative /a/ 'not' + *mbrotos* > *mrotos* > *mortos* 'mortal.'

In Mexico, I learned a neat Spanish phrase equivalent to English "Drop dead!" *Se pusa muerte* means literally 'become yourself dead.' I caution against use of this phrase in any low-class cantina.

Mortiferous Apophthegms

The Latin words for the dead and for death appear memorably in many sayings. But first here's an explanation of my playful, gobbledygook subhead: Mortiferous Apophthegms. Mortiferous means 'bearing or concerning death' = Latin *mortalis* 'pertaining to death' + apophthegm or apothegm 'a short, meaningful saying, a pithy maxim' from classical Greek *apophthegma* 'something spoken aloud, a terse saying = *apo* 'forth' + *phthengesthai* 'to speak.' The Greek verbal component may look exotic but it resides inside our common English word *diphthong* literally 'word with two sounds, two syllables.'

De mortuis nil nisi bonum

'Concerning the dead, say nothing but good things.'

Really? But why encourage such post-mortem reticence? If the guy is a stiff, rigor mortis 'the stiffness of death' having already set it, and you have a beef against the corpse, then why not criticize the defunct bastard. As a lawyer tells me, "You can't libel the dead."

In one of my failed novels, there is an emaciated English vegan pest named Pallida Morse. Pallida Mors is a phrase from the Latin poet Horace who in his first book of Odes wrote memorably:

pallida mors aequo pulsat pede pauperum tabernas regumque turris

Speak those lines aloud. What stark, resonant, alliterative Latin! It means: 'Pale death comes kicking with the same heavy foot at the hovels of beggars and at the castle door of kings' (my translation). Ancient Greeks and Romans did not hand-knock at doors; they kicked at them. In all poetries, death is pale not because the Grim Reaper has neglected his Nivea but because corpses are pale.

In articulo mortis

This chiefly Roman Catholic phrase means 'at the point of death' or 'just before death.' It appears in antique testamentary dispositions and wills to which codicils and revisions have been attached. For example, a criminal patient *in articulo mortis* may make an important death-bed confession. Or, at the quiet suggestion of an attendant priest, a final act of contrition may grease the holy gates of eternity as a dying person expires, with the hope that St. Peter's portals shall swing open easily and permit a pious soul to scamper over to crouch at the Lord's tootsies.

Mortgage

To break any dead silence, I'll now offer two final mortiferous words. Today a mortgage is money lent to a borrower who gives some of his property as security for the loan. But the historical meaning of the word tells the real story, as detailed neatly in this web explanation: ". . . when the oldest son of a nobleman needed large sums of money which his father refused to give him, he often turned to borrowing."

In arranging the loan, he would gage or "pledge" to repay the debt when his father died (at which time the son expected to receive his inheritance). So it is that mortgage originally meant 'death-pledge,' a promise (gage) to repay debt upon the death (mort) of one's father.

Neomort

This is quite new medical jargon (1974) naming a person, literally a 'new-dead,' who is brain-dead but whose body functions are being maintained artificially by machines. There is some resistance to the word in current clinical literature.

Thanks for reading my book. Until we all take the gurney-journey up to Bye-bye-land covered with a white sheet, I wish my readers a free pass through the Pearly Gates or through whatsoever portals to Paradise are offered by your particular religious convictions.

About the Author

"Bill Casselman is one of Canada's leading etymologists." So says Professor Jennifer MacLennan in her book *Readings for Technical Communication*, Oxford University Press, 2008.

Bill Casselman has published 14 books about English words and one medical dictionary, including his first Trafford volume, "At the Wording Desk" (2016). His books include the bestselling Canadian Sayings in three volumes, As the Canoe Tips: Comic Scenes from Canadian Life, Casselman's Canadian Words, and in 2010 Where a Dobdob Meets a Dikdik: A word lover's guide to the weirdest, wackiest and wonkiest lexical gems. All their titles and availabilities appear in the front matter of this volume.

Casselman was a columnist for Maclean's magazine and wrote monthly for Canadian Geographic in a column entitled "Our Home & Native Tongue." As a free-lance producer at CBC Radio and CBC TV for twenty-seven years, Bill was one of the founding lights of "This Country in the Morning," a seminal program that introduced Peter Gzowski to Canadian radio audiences. Casselman's work has taken him to many states, to Europe, to Africa and to every province and territory of Canada, where he has pursued his chief delight, the study of words.

Bill's newest word writings continue on his website: https://www.wordingroom.com

Readers may contact Bill with e-mail questions and comments at lutrine@rogers.com.

Printed in the United States
By Bookmasters